SURVIVING SURVIVAL

Also by Laurence Gonzales

The Still Point

The Hero's Apprentice

One Zero Charlie

Deep Survival

Everyday Survival

Lucy

SURVIVING SURVIVAL

THE ART
AND SCIENCE
OF RESILIENCE

Laurence Gonzales

W. W. NORTON & COMPANY

NEW YORK   LONDON

Printed in the United States of America
First Edition

For information about permission to reproduce selections from this book,
write to Permissions, W. W. Norton & Company, Inc.,
500 Fifth Avenue, New York, NY 10110

For information about special discounts for bulk purchases, please contact
W. W. Norton Special Sales at specialsales@wwnorton.com or 800-233-4830

Manufacturing by RR Donnelley, Harrisonburg
Production manager: Devon Zahn

Library of Congress Cataloging-in-Publication Data

Gonzales, Laurence, 1947–
Surviving survival : the art and science of resilience / Laurence Gonzales.
p. cm.
Includes bibliographical references and index.
ISBN 978-0-393-08318-7 (hardcover)
1. Resilience (Personality trait) 2. Resourcefulness. 3. Disasters—
Psychological aspects. I. Title.
BF698.35.R47G66 2012
155.9'35—dc23

2012015592

W. W. Norton & Company, Inc.
500 Fifth Avenue, New York, N.Y. 10110
www.wwnorton.com

W. W. Norton & Company Ltd.
Castle House, 75/76 Wells Street, London W1T 3QT

1 2 3 4 5 6 7 8 9 0

For my wife, Debbie

CONTENTS

Thine hands have made me and fashioned me
together round about; yet thou dost destroy me.

—Job, 10:8

The drama's done. Why then here does any one step
forth?—

Because one did survive the wreck.

—*Moby-Dick*

SURVIVING SURVIVAL

NO WAY HOME

DEBBIE KILEY WAS a sailor in her twenties when her ship went down in a hurricane. The captain's girlfriend, Meg Mooney, tried to make her way across the listing deck so that she could swim away. A towering wave swept Meg's sweatpants off and she fell naked into the rigging, which cut through her thigh down to the bone. Debbie had already leapt into the water, which now filled with Meg's blood. As Debbie watched, Meg screamed and another wave collapsed upon her, again sending her into the wires. Debbie swam back to the boat to help Meg into the water.

The first mate, Mark Adams, panicked. He inflated the life raft before tethering it to the ship. It blossomed into a perfect kite, and the gale-force winds whipped it away, carrying Mark with it until he was able to let go. Another crew member, Brad Cavanagh, managed to get an 11-foot Zodiac into the water. The five crew members swam for that boat. All the supplies for survival had been lost with the raft. They had nothing to sustain them. They were as good as dead.

Deep inside the brain, the hypothalamus monitors your bloodstream, its pressure and volume as well as how much salt is in it. When you become dehydrated and the hypothalamus sends its command to drink, it is nearly irresistible. Debbie described it this way: "Thirst begins as an urge, a need, a want, but after a while, it becomes an all-consuming passion, then an incandescent pain that begins in the nose and mouth and eyes and spreads to consume the whole body." Debbie and Brad were able to resist this torture. Mark and the captain, John Lippoth, were not; they drank seawater on the third day. Within 24 hours they both went mad. They began hallucinating and became convinced that they were a short distance from shore. John began talking to Meg in a calm and seemingly rational way, saying, "I'm just going to get the car. We're just off Falmouth." He went over the side. Debbie screamed at him to stop, but he calmly said, "I'll be back in a few." Brad joined Debbie in trying to talk John out of going, but he replied, "I can't take this anymore. I'm going to get the car." And he pushed off into the sea.

The sun was setting. Thin decks of cloud lay upon the horizon like crimson smoke. In a few moments, they heard John's shrieking as he was eaten alive by the sharks that had been circling the Zodiac. Meg lay in the bottom of the boat, covered in saltwater and seaweed, naked from the waist down. Debbie could see how severe her injuries were, her leg and torso deeply lacerated by the ship's rigging. Later that night, when Mark climbed on top of her in his delirium, all Meg could do was whimper. Then Mark flew into a rage, screaming, "I'm tired of playing games. I'm going back to the 7-Eleven to get some cigarettes." He, too, slipped over the side. Everything was quiet for a time. Then the Zodiac was hammered from underneath and flung into the air. A second concussion spun the boat around, lifting the bow and slamming it back onto the surface of the water. Debbie and Brad lay in the bottom of the boat, holding each other in terror, as they realized that sharks were in a feeding frenzy over Mark, just below the hull.

Full night descended, and above the moonless ocean the Milky Way emerged like a faint galactic mist in the sky. All was quiet once more. New stars drifted along their upward trajectory. Debbie and Brad fell asleep together. She woke to the sound of Meg speaking incoherently as if in tongues and waving her hands in the air. Meg seemed at peace, her voice without inflection. Soon the muttering ceased and Meg closed her eyes and stopped breathing. Brad and Debbie committed her body to the sea. They then made a pact to look out for each other, to take turns sleeping, not to drink seawater. To survive.

The next day, their fifth without water, they were picked up by a Russian freighter 290 miles off Cape Hatteras. When I told that story in my book *Deep Survival*, that's where it ended: with the rescue. But the rescue marked the beginning of an entirely new story for Debbie, because a relentless system for making memories had been hard at work throughout her ordeal. She endured excruciating pain over the course of the five days she spent adrift at sea. In addition to the pain of thirst, the terror, the physical brutality of the sea, she witnessed the horrifying deaths of three friends. Much of what the brain does is unconscious. It works behind the scenes to forge memories of what is dangerous and what is beneficial so that in the future we can respond correctly and automatically. During her crisis, Debbie's brain was working overtime to map out those memories in preparation for the next assault. In the brain, the cardinal rule is: future equals past; what has happened before will happen again. In response to trauma, the brain encodes protective memories that force you to behave in the future the way you behaved in the past. Any sight, sound, or smell, any fragment of the scene in which you were threatened, can set off that automatic behavior. The trouble was that in all likelihood, Debbie would never again face a similar hazard. It is rare to be shipwrecked. The chances of its happening twice to the same person are vanishingly small (though, as we'll see, that can happen sometimes). In other words, Debbie's natural and normally useful systems for forming important memories were working on a job that had no practical value. Indeed, those systems were working to make her miserable.

AFTER THEIR rescue, when they were out of the hospital, Debbie and Brad, the sole survivors, went to lunch with their families. It was a celebration. They had survived. They were going home. But after the meal, Debbie and Brad walked away from the group and down to the harbor to look out and say good-bye. "Somehow," Debbie later said, "we couldn't fit in with those people, we couldn't yet return to the world." That clearly echoed what Viktor Frankl wrote about being liberated from a Nazi death camp at the end of World War II: "We did not yet belong to this world." That is one of the most common sentiments people express after an experience of extreme survival. Frankl said that when he and his fellow inmates were freed from the horror of the Nazi death camp, they experienced no joy. Their first steps into the world were timid and tentative, and they were not yet able to trust their own freedom. Although they passed through fields of flowers, they were unable to form an emotional reaction to them. The men came together that evening to examine their feelings about liberation and discovered that they had literally forgotten how to feel anything at all. The experience in the camp had inscribed a set of memories that obscured the old. The memories of survival had to be slowly overwritten by a newer layer of experience. Only then could freedom be trusted.

Dougal Robertson drifted in a life raft for 37 days, trying to keep his young family alive after their sailboat, the *Lucette*, sank. The parents and four children were picked up at last by a fishing boat. Safe on deck, Robertson said he felt "like a merman suddenly abstracted from an environment which has become his own and returned to a forgotten way of life among strangers." Those feelings of alienation and displacement represent one of the most common responses to trauma. Just ask Jessica Goodell, a Marine who served in Iraq. Her job with Mortuary Affairs was to reassemble human bodies that had been blown apart by roadside bombs so that they could be sent home. After eight months of that horror, she tried to go home but realized that she, too, felt that there was no place for her in the world. After being trapped underground for 69 days in 2010, a Chilean miner expressed this same sentiment. "Part of me stayed down there," he said.

Survival is one triumph, but living through that ordeal delivers us into the next stage of the journey. Adaptation means adjusting the self to a particular environment. If the environment changes, as it does through the experience of trauma, you are lost and must adapt once more. The bigger the trauma, the more dramatic the requirement for change. In many cases, the necessary adaptation is so extreme that an entirely new self emerges from the experience. In those cases, there is no easy return to the old environment. Sometimes you can't go home at all.

It is nearly impossible to live a full life without trauma. It may not be a shipwreck or war. It might be a husband who tries to kill you. It could be a bear that tears off half of your face. It might be cancer. But all such events share a dramatic quality that seems irresistible to the storyteller within us. The stories always end like this: Just when Debbie and Brad seem doomed, the Russian freighter heaves into view and they are rushed to the hospital. Music up. Roll credits. Then they all live happily ever after. Offstage, of course. But let's put the players back on stage and see what happens next.

DEBBIE KILEY flew to New Orleans to recover at her mother's home. While still on the plane, she began reliving the moments when the captain, John Lippoth, mad from drinking seawater, began talking about going to get the car. She could see him climbing over the side and slipping into the water. She watched him appear and disappear in the swells as he swam away. Merely closing her eyes brought the saturated images before her. She could still hear his horrifying screams like outraged metal as he was eaten alive by sharks. Each time the plane hit a bump, she said, "It felt as if someone was standing on my chest." During her five days adrift, she had used pleasant daydreams as a way to distract herself and to cope with the pain and terror. Now she couldn't rid herself of the powerful illusion that she was still at sea. The airplane ride was just another dream. Echoing Robertson, she later said, "It was as if some part of me still lived, could only live, on the raft, adrift at sea." That made perfect sense in terms of the parts of the brain concerned with survival: It would store away as much information as possible for future use. Debbie just wanted it all to go away. Her system for forming protective memories had done its job too well and had split her in two. Now her job was to knit herself together again.

She managed to get through the plane ride without going mad, but once she reached her mother's house, she lay in bed for days. She carried glass after glass of water back to the bedroom. An inner compulsion made her drink half of each glass and leave the rest to reassure herself that there would be more. After a week in bed, Debbie forced herself to go outside. This is the self divided by trauma: The rational part of her brain knew that her behavior was odd.

Out on the street, all the sights and sounds and people were too bright, too loud, overwhelming her senses. "I felt like I was not really there," she said, "or didn't belong there. I felt like I was on the verge of insanity." She went to St. Louis Cathedral and sat in a pew and released herself at last to uncontrollable sobbing. Debbie wondered how she would ever get back to her own life. But as she was to learn, you cannot return from a journey such as hers. Your only choice is to go forward.

DEBBIE SPENT most of that first month weeping in the cathedral. Angry and frustrated with herself, she decided to head back out to sea and confront her fears directly. She signed onto a boat that serviced other vessels during races. A storm broke over the race, sinking a number of boats and killing several sailors. Debbie returned worse off than before. She spent almost all her time hiding in church, praying and weeping. She tried getting a job and going back to school. She would be all right for a time, "white knuckling it," as she put it. But almost any adverse event would send her into panic. She would exhaust herself, fall into depression, and then lock herself in her apartment and cry for days on end. Over the coming years, she attempted many strategies. She tried getting married. She tried pregnancy and childbirth. And she still stood in the shower sobbing each morning. The constant stress began making her physically ill.

As Debbie told me about the nightmare in which she'd become trapped, I began to wonder what determined who did well after survival and why. I wanted to know what natural systems in our brains could make us respond the way Debbie had and what we could do to get on with our lives. Some people are innately more resilient than others in the wake of catastrophe. But we can also take steps to help ourselves. It turns out that many of the beliefs about this subject that psychotherapists have long held sacred are simply not true. For example, when the World Trade Center was attacked, the Federal Emergency Management Agency spent $155 million to make psychological counseling available to anyone who wanted it. The experts thought that a quarter of a million people would seek help for unmanageable grief over lost loved ones or for debilitating anxiety as a reaction to the horror they had witnessed. Just 300 people showed up. Of course, more people may have been in need of therapy, but new research suggests that if the bad news is that most people will experience trauma, the good news is that the majority are able to go on with their lives. Richard Tedeschi, a professor of psychology at the University of North Carolina, says that most people return to normal within two years after trauma. James Pennebaker, a social psychologist at the University of Texas, called this fact "one of the best-kept secrets in the mental health world." But the quality of life during those two years can be drastically different if you employ sound strategies for moving forward. After major trauma, few people find an exact fit into the old way of life. And this means that you face the task of building a new life and, in some cases, as we'll see, even a new sense of who you are.

Your experience of life in the aftermath may be even more dramatic, sometimes more painful, than the experience of survival itself. But it can be beautiful and fulfilling, too, and a more lasting achievement than the survival that began it all. What comes after survival is, after all, the rest of your life.

ONE

BE HERE NOW: FROM VICTIM TO RESCUER

THE PREMONITIONS went way back. More than three decades, in fact, to the time when they didn't really know each other. They simply worked in the same office. The annual Christmas party was under way. Lisette duPré Brieger had seen Marshall Johnson sharpening an ax. Sharpening and sharpening and sharpening. She thought it odd, but perhaps it wasn't as odd as it seemed. They worked for an oil company and the company owned a 400-acre farm in the Virginia countryside. Various employees went out to the farm, so maybe the ax was for chopping firewood out there. Or maybe it wasn't.

Lisette liked Marshall the first time she saw him. There was an instant electricity. A friend had driven Lisette to the party, and now, as the crowd began to thin out, she realized that she had no way to get home. So, when Marshall offered her a ride, Lisette accepted. As they drove through that dark and snowy night, Marshall asked if she'd ever been out to the farm. She had not. He turned off the highway and drove away from the lights of town and out into the countryside. It was a pleasant enough ride and they made small talk. By and by, they arrived at the farm. There was a long rutted lane, now snow-blown and wintry, and the car bounced along in the frozen ruts, sweeping its beams of light across the house, then the cottage; the hilly ground and dried weeds sticking up through the snow were colorless in the night. Beyond the cottage was a coppice of trees and bushes and beyond that the plowed fields wreathed in darkness. Marshall drove down by the barn and parked the car. Then he reached into the backseat for the ax. Without having to think about it, Lisette threw open the door and began running across the snow-covered ground in her high heels, her party dress, escaping what she was sure would be the end of her. She was making her way up the hill, struggling toward the farmhouse, when she glanced back and saw him standing in the illumination from the headlights, holding a small box and looking out at her with a puzzled expression on his face. Lisette slowed and turned, then stopped altogether.

"What are you doing?" he called out.

She still hesitated. What was that in his hands? Not the ax. He held it up. A little box. Lisette's breathing began to slow. She took a tentative step toward him, reading the subtle cues of his body language. No threat there. Where had she gotten the idea? What subconscious signal had she picked up? What sixth sense had read the awful truth? Her logical mind dismissed it. Suddenly unsteady on her heels, Lisette wobbled her way awkwardly back down the hill, now conscious of how wet her feet were, how ruined her shoes and stockings, how silly her notion, how terrified she had been, and how sure that he had meant her harm.

"What's going on?" he called as she approached. He was smiling. He handed her the box.

"What's this?" she asked.

"Open it," he said. "What were you doing?"

"I thought you might be about to murder me with that ax."

"I'm hardly an ax murderer," he said with a chuckle. All at once, it was a joke. And the flicker of something sinister that she had seen in the car subsided beneath the surface once again.

She opened the box. It contained a necklace. She was the administrative assistant at the company, and he was technically one of her bosses, so this was in keeping with the Christmas tradition. Even so, Lisette was touched. How silly of me, she thought. And: What an odd thing to think, that he wanted to kill me. Where had such a notion come from? Lisette was split in two. Years later, looking back at the contours of her life, it was sharply evident that something sleek and bony had been racing along, tracking her at every turn, invisible beneath the surface. As she stood there holding the necklace, she had no idea that 30 years later she would stand on the same spot in an icy scene much like this one and that same man would be ashes and she would scatter them into just such a wintry wind as this.

HERE'S HOW it happens: It's October 4, 2009. You've just returned from church. A fresh breeze sighs through the sliding glass doors that open from your bedroom onto the patio. A kaleidoscope of falling leaves, yellow and tan and orange, drifts through autumn light. You can hear the feet of children rustling through them. You've hung up your dress and you now sit on a chair in a corner, wearing bra and panties, reading e-mails on your laptop. You no longer sleep together, you and your husband, not since the children were born. Graham just turned ten, Natalie eleven. The psychological and verbal abuse have become too extreme. It's time that you all stopped living in this haze of emotional terrorism. You've told him that you're leaving.

He enters the room now. From deep within the unconscious layers of memory, something rises to the surface. Your whole body goes on alert, though you don't know why. You set the laptop on the floor, to be unencumbered. Your first conscious thought is that the towel covers nothing more than his hand, held like a child's hand in the shape of a pistol. It's pretend. It's not real. But beneath the surface, in the memories that your brain has been silently writing all along, you know something else to be true, something terribly important for your survival. Your body is now preparing for what it must do. It has no time to ask your permission. It must sweep all your thoughts out of the way and simply act.

He's very calm as he says, "I love you too much to live without you." Then, even before he lifts the towel, the subterranean memory bursts into action. You had just seen it in that book you were reading the night before: Be here now. It's real. You don't have to think. You see the revolver in his hand, rising. Time expands to encompass the whole world.

LISETTE JOHNSON had felt a strange sense of foreboding the night before. Darkness came slowly as the autumn shadows gradually absorbed her world for what, she felt, would be the last time. The moon rose full and tremendous as she lay in bed reading. Earlier that day, she had celebrated her son Graham's tenth birthday with eight of his friends: *Toy Story* at the cinema and birthday cake at home. And then the quiet of a suburban night, the breathing of the house, and Marshall acting strangely. He had been threatening her, first saying that he'd never see the children again if she left and then that she'd never get custody, because she was crazy. Only later would Lisette remember the ax and the scene at the farm, when she had run from the car. Thirty years. Thirty years of her emotional system working secretly beneath the surface, gathering information, waiting to protect her in the fullness of time.

The next morning was Sunday. She went to church, leaving the children at home with Marshall. She returned at one o'clock. She had plans to meet her friend Gretchen and take a walk on the James River. But she found her husband sitting on the bed in the guest room. He asked her to lie down with him, but again that foreboding soured within her. Her sixth sense. She knew that something wasn't right. She couldn't say what, but she refused his request. Whatever he had in mind, she didn't want any part of it. He had been strange enough over the years and all the more so since she'd announced that she was divorcing him.

Lisette turned and went to her bedroom. Marshall rose and followed her, asking that she please come and lie down with him or at the very least give him a hug. She refused again, sensing the danger there. He lashed out angrily, saying, "I want to know how you are going to live when you leave here. What are you going to live on?" He stormed out of the room and Lisette sighed with relief. She undressed and sat to check her e-mail. She was due to meet Gretchen in less than an hour. Then Marshall returned with the towel over his hand.

Lisette stood immediately, suddenly knowing what she knew in that deep place of knowing that required no conscious thought: Be here now. She stood at the exact moment that he pulled the trigger, firing point-blank at her head. And because she stood instead of sitting there in disbelief, the bullet struck her not in the head but halfway between her collarbone and her right breast. She bolted for the open door and he fired a second time, hitting her in the abdomen. As she ran across the yard, she screamed for the children. He fired again, hitting her in the back. She could hear her daughter screaming, "What's wrong? What's happened?"

Lisette managed to call out, "Daddy shot me!" All the time running, running. The woods. The grass. The rustling of the yellow leaves. The neighbor's house, all brightly lit with luminous colors, festive with ghouls for Halloween. She heard another shot but felt nothing. Then, all at once, she knew what he had done. That last shot had been for him. She put it from her mind. She had a single purpose now: Survive. For the children. She was heading for the neighbor's house, where someone could call an ambulance. She collapsed in a pile of leaves, for it was autumn and everyone was raking leaves in that quiet woodsy suburb. The smell of leaves. Smoke. Natalie kneeling over her, crying, "Mommy, mommy, wake up!"

"Like a dream," Lisette would later say, "where you can't run. Your feet are anchored to the ground and your mouth opens to scream, but no sound comes out."

They lived in an upper-middle-class suburb. They'd been married for 21 years. He was well liked, successful, and had many lifelong friends. Lisette later learned that he had taken the phone off the hook so that the children couldn't call the police.

LISETTE WAS given 10 units of blood in the emergency room. Both of her lungs had collapsed. She still has one of the bullets in her liver. But she got up by herself in the first week. Her physical recovery went well. She returned to work, took care of the children. She functioned. But the deep systems of memory had done their work too well. Driving her son, Graham, to therapy, the sound of an ambulance set off the emotional cascade and she found herself driving through a veil of tears, her heart hammering wildly in her chest.

On her first Christmas without her husband, she was up at two in the morning, struggling with the paradox of missing him, loving and hating him. She knew the children would feel the loss. She wrote in her diary: *All I want to do is fall apart. Just be in the sadness and not fight it.* She lay in bed and longed to be held.

Lisette took the children to visit her family for New Year's Day and, like Debbie Kiley, she began to feel how such extreme survival sets you apart. "I was surrounded by love," she said, "but I had this odd sense of isolation. Difference. Like I knew something they didn't." At midnight on New Year's Eve, she simply burst into uncontrollable sobbing.

The children experienced hysterical crying jags. Lisette had to stand in the middle of it, the rock, trying to calm them when she, too, felt like curling up in a ball and falling apart. Back at home during the first week of 2010, she went through the motions of pretending to be normal. She took Graham and Natalie to school, practiced *tai chi* for a while, took a shower, checked her e-mail, visited her attorney to sign some papers. Made a business call. Then hung up and burst into tears. *It is there. Just like standing in front of the mirror and touching the scars, it is part of me now. Part of who I am. I am beginning to accept the scars as a completion of my uniqueness.* Lisette resolved to do whatever was necessary for the children. She recognized that ultimately her responsibility to be happy was the same as making sure that her children survived. And she wrote in her diary something that is true of all of us: *My scars are my victory.*

She was not alone. She had a generous network of friends and family who hugged her and made food and conversation. It was comforting but also a bit eerie. Lisette began to feel as though she were attending her own funeral. And she was beset by the clash of feelings. At one time she had cherished the intimate physical relationship with her husband. But that was so far behind her now. Lisette began to turn her feelings of fear and loneliness into anger. In her diary, she wrote: *Fuck you! I hate you! What a fucked up pair we were. Well, guess what? I'm not going back there. I'm done. Thank you for facilitating that. For bringing me to the point where I had to choose survival over death. I had to make a conscious decision. And I did it and I can do this, without you, without anyone. It's in me and always has been. The truth is, I feel more alive than I have felt in years.*

In mid-January, she began cleaning out his closet. She felt at last that she was saying good-bye, cutting him out of her life, deleting him and any evidence that they had existed as a couple. Driving the car full of his clothing to donate it to charity, she felt on the point of emotional collapse.

Spring came. The woods that surrounded the house were exploding with life. The leaves spread out in fans of green. Lisette was cleaning out the linen closet, moving sheets and blankets, when she discovered the bullet hole in the wall. The workmen had patched the hole in the bedroom where he had shot her and then himself. But they hadn't seen the exit hole inside the linen closet. She stared at it now, marveling at how the bullet could have passed through her husband's brain and then through the bedroom wall and through this wall as well. She felt a sense of peace and detachment. A new kind of strength filled her.

Even so, the dreams still came. Fewer as time went on, with more space in between, but sometimes they were overwhelmingly vivid and would leave her feeling haunted through the next day, as though she moved in a world of living ghosts. She dreamed that she was with him in the guest room, where she had once found him loading his revolver. She approached him and he looked up at her, put the pistol to his temple, and shot himself. In her dream, she passed out. She awoke so disturbed that at first she couldn't even cry. She just lay there paralyzed. Then she broke down, alone in her bed in the middle of the night.

At times she could not remember the dreams themselves and

was left with just the feeling of them, the tremendous aching melancholy underneath everything she did that day, as if she moved under water. The tumult of her emotions embodied mourning and rage and terror and longing in endless combinations. Before Marshall shot her, Lisette used to dream about the river flooding, about being trapped on one side when she needed to get to the other. But the James was too wide, too violent. She never had that dream again after he shot her. One memory, more powerful, overwrote the other. That is how experience revises us.

LISETTE BEGAN giving talks for the police at the domestic-violence task force. For them Lisette provided a rare glimpse inside a world that they usually viewed as a grouping of corpses. She had been there and had survived. They wanted to mine her for clues to future cases. Talking, helping others, gave Lisette strength, but the trauma had filled her world with emotional land mines.

She went to a friend's wedding and "Jesu, Joy of Man's Desiring" by Bach was played as the bride walked down the aisle. It was the same song that had been played at Lisette's wedding. She fled to the bathroom and cried. *Cried for the dream lost, the anger of a promise broken, the betrayal. How raw my emotions were just below the surface.* But she gradually began to feel grateful for having any feelings at all. She began to realize how long she had been completely numb in her marriage, and how deeply she had denied all the warning signs, beginning with the ax three decades earlier.

One day in early May, the weather turned cool and she had the windows open just as she had on the night before he shot her. That eerie sense, the same foreboding, descended on her once again. She got up and went into the bathroom. Marshall was standing by the bathtub. Lisette was so excited that she ran to him, embraced him, and told him that she was glad he wasn't dead. She reassured him that they could work it out. Then she began to hear the sirens approaching, one, then three, then five, then choirs of sirens wailing. She asked Marshall not to let them take her, because she wanted to be with him now. Then she realized that the bathroom was actually an operating room.

She woke to silence. It was morning. But it was as if every bird had died. Lisette rose weeping and walked through the day in a trance, upset with herself but not knowing why. Perhaps for begging him. For loving him. Even as he stood there and simply ignored her as he had done in life. Her feelings were doubly confusing because her trauma was also bereavement for a loved one, and that loved one was also her murderer. Moving through spring, she began to recognize some of the other paradoxes of her marriage. She used to feel lonely all the time. Now that she was really alone, she rarely felt true loneliness.

As the season wore on, Natalie turned thirteen. She made dinner for her mother one evening. Afterward, they walked along the river, and Lisette saw how beautiful the sunlight was on the water, the lawny clouds, the luminous mist in the distance. She felt the serenity of the water in the failing light and watched the grace of a paddler gliding along in a kayak, the whisper of his strokes. She felt alive, excited.

Then something remarkable happened. Lisette was sitting in the waiting room while Graham was in therapy. An eleven-year-old girl named Betty struck up a conversation. Betty told Lisette that she had been shot in the neck and that the bullet was still there and it hurt all the time. Lisette told her that she, too, had a bullet and pointed to her abdomen. Betty tried to reassure Lisette. She said that her mother had been shot twice and her brother was shot four times. Her father had done the shooting. Her brother, aged ten, was in the hospital on a ventilator.

A few weeks later, Lisette and Betty again found themselves together in the waiting room. Betty was sitting with her sister, Ruth, a girl like Lisette's daughter, Natalie, who had just turned thirteen. Betty was happy to see Lisette and told her sister the story. She said that Lisette's children were lucky because they hadn't been shot. Then Betty told Lisette that on the day that it happened, she had been playing outside with her little brother and had a premonition that something bad would happen. A gut feeling. A sixth sense. Betty wanted to stay away from home, but her brother was cold and wanted to go inside. When they went in, their father was telling their mother that if he couldn't have her, no one could. Then he shot her. He tried to shoot her in the head but missed and shot her in the side of the face. As he shot each of the children, he told them that it was their mother's fault that he had to do this.

Lisette was trying to hold it together as she listened to this tale told by the beautiful child before her. She tried not to burst into tears and fall sobbing to the floor. She tried to view herself as someone who had come a bit farther down this road, who could perhaps help these girls along the way. Then the thirteen-year-old sister, Ruth, spoke up. She said that people think she's lucky because she wasn't shot. Lisette asked if she was out of the house that day and escaped because of her absence. But Ruth said no, she was right there the whole time. She said that she wished that her father had shot her. Shot her dead. But instead, he made her watch him shoot the other children and then he forced her into the bedroom, where he raped her. Then he made her watch him shoot himself. But before he pulled the trigger, he told her to take the gun and shoot him once more when he fell down, to make sure that he was dead.

Lisette could hear the screaming noise in her head, like metal on metal, and see the room cloud over as if the walls had caught fire. She could feel the world move beneath her feet as if the very edifice of reality was faltering upon its pilings. Yet she forced herself to hold on for the sake of these girls before her and she managed to make her mouth move, to make her breath come forth so that she could tell them, promise them, that while what they experienced will never go away, they will learn to live again. She promised them that they would be happy one day, because she was happy. They exchanged phone numbers, and Lisette promised to be there for those girls. And since their mother couldn't drive a car yet, she promised to take them to their appointments. Lisette had found something apart from herself to care about more than herself. Of course, she had her children to care about. But now, in light of what Betty and Ruth had told her, she could see that there were people who were even worse off than they were. If Ruth could survive, then so would Natalie and Graham.

In achieving her success in the aftermath of extreme survival, Lisette was exhibiting several important traits. And in many ways, both surviving and the aftermath of survival require similar traits. If "be here now" saved her life, it also allowed her to go on with it, because she focused on what had to be done. She paid attention. But she also got out of herself, struggling both for the sake of her children and for Betty and Ruth. In that way, Lisette became a rescuer and she left behind the persona of the victim.

Helping others is one of the most therapeutic steps you can take. Lisette frequently tells her story to groups, especially to women who are the victims of verbal and psychological abuse and also don't realize that it is a precursor to violence, perhaps even murder. Her talks are electrifying. After each one, she told me, "People always want to touch me, hug me. I'm not sure if it is to comfort me or to comfort them." It is both. An area of the brain called the anterior cingulate cortex interprets pain, including social pain, such as grieving. It can also send signals of pleasure from sensing skin-to-skin contact. When emotional pain occurs, our first impulse is to put out the fire with skin-to-skin contact. When the unspeakable happens, people hug one another.

After I had known her for some months, I asked Lisette how she was doing. "I have some very dark times," she said. But she referred to her progress as "amazing" and said that she was reconciled to the new facts of her life. "I'm never going to leave this behind. I have a very fulfilling, very happy life. I've always been a very optimistic person. Even on my worst day I'm so much happier than I was."

TWO

THE CROCODILE WITHIN: THE BURDEN OF INVISIBLE MEMORY

EILEEN BERLIN SENT me a photograph of herself and her husband, Scott, relaxing in the pool at the hotel. They were on vacation in Mexico. Buff and beautiful. Grinning. Scott was laid out in his red trunks with a drink in his hand. Eileen was seated next to him, knees ricked up, wearing an athletic visor as if she'd just gone running. White plastic chaise lounges were arranged around the quarry-tile deck. Blue water. A tan and happy couple. Eileen's sister Beverly took the photo. It was Beverly's first anniversary with her husband, Charles. They felt like kids playing hooky.

After relaxing by the pool and taking a ride on the Jet Skis, the foursome dressed and went to dinner. They had a few drinks and watched as sunset leached all color from the scene. They decided to go for a swim. The surf was up on the ocean side, so they chose the peaceful bay behind the hotel. Full moon. Glassy smooth water. No worries.

The dock behind the hotel was deserted. The quiet warmth of the night seemed too good to be true. They stripped down and left their clothes and slid into the bay. The water was deep and warm, caressing. They drifted around, treading water, talking in whispers, giggling, in awe of the beauty beneath the full moon. Eileen let herself float away from the dock, moonlight sweeping across her long tan body. Indigo shadows lay all around, sparkling with the million daggers of moonlight that reflected from the water, the brightness of her naked skin seeming impossible against the smoky ripples. The tarry smell of the sea and of cut grass and pine mingled with the feel of the water to complete the impression of dreamy peace and contentment.

As she glided away from the others, she heard a hissing, roaring noise. Instantly, she knew what it was. Some ancient system in her brain had kicked in: a dragon, a reptile, a demon of old. The eight-foot crocodile took her head in its jaws with such force that it broke her cheekbone and severed her ear. The blinding pain, the riptide of adrenaline,* an explosion of light behind her eyes. The crocodile pulled her under. She knew what was coming. Somewhere in her past she must have heard: They roll with you until you drown. As they roll, their teeth tear off parts of you that they then swallow whole.

Beneath the surface of the water, Eileen managed to struggle out of the jaws. The crocodile thrashed around and attacked again, savage, relentless. It took her torso in its jaws and slashed her right breast, slicing through the muscles of her back. Eileen struggled free once more and instinctively dove, sensing that the crocodile would be looking for her on the surface. From her vantage on the bottom, she could see the tremendous black shape above, slithering along in search of her, silhouetted by moonlight that fell in silty spokes through the water. She surged to the surface behind its tail. Scott and Beverly got hold of her arm to try to pull her to safety. The crocodile shot forward yet again, this time nearly ripping off Eileen's thumb. Her brother-in-law Charles fought furiously against the attack, beating the crocodile back, while Scott and Beverly moved Eileen to the dock. The animal snapped its tail one final time and then the black water sucked it down. With the crocodile gone at last, Eileen lay naked on the boards in a welter of

---

*The chemicals that are released are actually epinephrine and norepinephrine, but for better or worse, everyone says "adrenaline."

blood, her back muscles ripped to shreds, her thumb hanging by a bit of skin, her breast half gone. It was June 6, 1998.

It took the ambulance forever, she later scrawled in a spiral notebook. *Trying not to pass out—so much blood loss. Will I make it? Scott close to hysteria in the hospital, pain medicine not working, is it Demerol? I throw a fit—crying. Wake up all night—blood coming out of my left ear. This really scares me. I need rabies shots.*

Even before birth, we begin adapting to the environment in which we find ourselves. We learn its rules. We unconsciously take actions that help us avoid danger. But a catastrophic experience can undermine all that learning. Once we're safely beyond the shipwreck, the husband, the crocodile, we try to return to normal life. But there is no normal anymore. Yes, Eileen was rescued. And yes, she had surgery that saved her life. She returned home with Scott and Beverly and Charles and found a loving family around her. And then strange things began to happen. She had not escaped the crocodile. It had taken up residence inside her.

I will cry at anything. Tears for almost an hour. I had a bad nightmare. I was standing on the dock and a huge crocodile was creeping toward me. Water on one side, crocodile on the other. I woke up with my heart beating wildly, terrified. It was 3:20 A.M. I didn't sleep much after that. I feel exhausted and sad today.

Eileen was struggling to get back to normal, not yet fully aware that she would have to reinvent what normal meant to her. She was going to have to come up with a new set of adaptations, because the person who went into the water behind that hotel was not the same person who came out.

Undergoing surgery after surgery was bad enough. She was in constant pain. Her two-year-old daughter was afraid of her. *She won't come near me,* Eileen wrote. Her jaw wouldn't open. *I am soo tired of eating mush. My teeth are loose. All I eat is soup, pudding, oatmeal.* She took her daughter to school and came home in tears. *Awful, everyone stares—it exhausts me. I always feel dirty. Lots of bites on my head.* July, August, September, she was beginning to despair of ever being normal. In early October, she went back to work for the first time.

I had to present myself to my supervisor for inspection (this meeting was disguised as concern), I guess to make sure that my appearance wouldn't frighten any of the [customers]. All this made me feel like some freak show. I am fighting the urge to yell, "Just go ahead and look!"

In the midst of the attack, as Eileen looked up at the crocodile from the seafloor, she became sharply aware that she might die down there. All that she loved—her daughter, her husband, her sister, this life—snatched away from her in the single appalling act of a mindless creature. As she hid there, a secret swimmer beneath the sea, that thought made her angry. She found inside herself an unfamiliar determination, a new kind of resolve, as fear turned to anger and anger turned to action. She would fight, she told herself. She would never give up. She would live. And she did that. She was a success, a real survivor. Once she was out of the water, bleeding on the dock, she felt the certainty that she would live. She had met the new Eileen, this fighter, this determined winner. Eileen completed one journey of survival only to be plunged into a new and unexpected one: how to live the rest of her life. Ben Shaw, a journalist and a veteran of the war in Iraq, wrote an essay to describe to soldiers how they would feel coming home after the trauma of combat. Home would not feel like home, he wrote. Everyone you loved before would now appear as a stranger. It was a good description of Eileen's experience.

Scott and I are going to counseling. We are not getting along very well lately. I am so miserable and I never sleep through the night. I feel crazy and can't concentrate or get along with anyone. I feel alone, separate, different. I wish I could make it go away.

IN ADDITION to healing her body, Eileen faced a more difficult journey. Her experience with the crocodile had physically changed her brain. A large amount of new information about herself and her environment had been dumped into that miraculous vessel of learning. This information was about survival. Certainly, the brain and the body would want to remember it. But the very system that evolved to save her became her worst enemy. She just wanted to forget the whole thing. But the system simply doesn't work that way.

Most people are familiar with what psychologists call conditioned responses. The most famous one was demonstrated by Ivan Pavlov, who conditioned a dog to salivate at the sound of a bell.* This happens because when two nerve cells fire together, even if by accident, they will fire together in the future. The saying is: When they fire together, they wire together. The cells become physically linked into what a Canadian psychologist named Donald Hebb called cell assemblies. When one fires, they all fire. And if, in the beginning of their assembly, they fire together because of an event that comes with high emotions, then it becomes difficult to keep them from firing together in the future, even if that firing represents the pairing of two completely unrelated events. Bells have nothing to do with food. They have no value for the dog's survival. But the sound became what's known as a retrieval cue, also called a trigger: It called up a memory and initiated an action. After the relationship between bell and food had been established, the sound alone was enough to make the dog salivate. This effect is often manipulated by the people who make movies. In the movie *E.T.: The Extra-Terrestrial*, the tinkling of keys on Peter Coyote's belt was paired with the threat of the bad guys' capturing E.T. Despite the fact that keys have no meaning in the movie and present no threat, the tinkling sound was so crucial to the emotional progress of the drama that the character played by Coyote was identified in the credits only as "Keys."

When an experience is highly charged with pain or pleasure, the learning can take place instantly. For Eileen, this meant that any stimulus that was present during the attack had become inextricably linked at a cellular level with all the mad fear and frantic struggle that she experienced in the water. The retrieval cue might be moonlight, water, the tarry smell of the sea, darkness. Moreover, because of continuing pain and fear, many more things in her

---

* Pavlov used other signals as well, including a metronome.

environment could become incorporated into those hair-trigger cell assemblies that could send her into a full-blown panic.

Joseph LeDoux, a neuroscientist at New York University, uses the example of a car wreck to illustrate this effect. If you're injured in an auto accident and the horn is blaring, in the future, the sound of a horn alone may cause anxiety. LeDoux calls this emotional learning. When the accident happened, the brain laid down an important trace of unconscious memory to mark what was dangerous in the environment. The trace was essentially a message that said: Next time you encounter something that looks, smells, sounds, or feels like this, prepare to survive. So pain and panic were paired with car horns. They fired together, so they were wired together. As Eric Kandel, a neuroscientist at Columbia University pointed out, this effect may be permanent. LeDoux told me, "Meaningless stimuli that occur in connection with trauma . . . can later trigger fear and stress themselves. Evolutionarily speaking, these kinds of associations help us anticipate harm. But sometimes, they also end up tying us up in knots." Antonio Damasio, a neurologist at the University of Southern California, compared these activities of the emotional system to a flashlight beam cast into a dark room. It illuminates the thing you wish to see, but the light falls on everything else around it as well. Then, when any of those extraneous objects is perceived again, the emotional system rebroadcasts everything that was associated with the trauma. When something elicits a powerful feeling, it's almost impossible to resist the automatic response. That's why we can't get back to normal life after trauma.

When the crocodile attacked, Eileen's emotional system responded first to the hissing roar. That set her body in motion to fight back. Her fight began within milliseconds, before her conscious mind could even form thoughts about the attack. Earlier, I said that she instantly knew what it was. I might have said that her amygdala instantly knew what it was. The amygdala* is the cen-

---

* Two of these small structures exist in the brain, one in each hemisphere, but it's conventional to use the singular.

terpiece of the emotional system and helps create instant reminders of what the danger looks like (or sounds like or smells like).
It writes down indelible memories of everything in the scene and
turns whatever you did into a reflex for the next time. In reaction to
Eileen's severe trauma, her amygdala helped create an entirely new
emotional landscape. Some of what the amygdala knows is inherited from our ancient ancestors (fear of loud noises, for example,
especially the hissing or roaring of an animal). But most of what it
knows is written by experience. And when bad things happen, this
system can be the source of much sorrow.

An emotional system much like our own has served mammals
well through millions of years of evolution. It relies on two important
features. It initiates automatic behavior that requires no thought.
And it creates long-lasting memories so that we can instantly do the
same thing in the future. It interprets any fragment of the situation
as representing the whole. So you don't have to crash another car to
get the reaction you had during the first crash. A honking car horn
does the trick. For Eileen, the attack forged strong memories of what
to look out for: sights, sounds, smells, pain. Once she was back at
home, each time she was exposed anew to any one of those triggers,
her emotional system told her that another crocodile was attacking.
Most of Eileen's emotional memories remained hidden. As a result,
many of her reactions seemed to come out of nowhere. She couldn't
say what was setting her off. I've heard more than one New Yorker
report having an anxious feeling on clear autumn mornings. That's
what the weather was like when two airliners burst through the
World Trade Center. During that traumatic event, for some people,
the amygdala irrationally labeled the weather as a sign of danger. A
new trigger was created to bring on an attack of anxiety. This same
system of emotional memory caused Lisette to feel fearful and to
have bad dreams on cool autumn nights like the one when her husband shot her. The brain can seem at times like a confounding
bureaucracy with different departments arguing with one another.
The amygdala is not in the Rational Department. It doesn't care
that, at times, its responses might make no sense. The emotional
system can't allow you to think about your reactions. That takes

too much time. If you stop to think, you'll be eaten. So it's tuned for instant reaction. And remember, too, that if Eileen had lived 50,000 years ago, that complex of memories would have served her well to avoid crocodiles. The system is driven by natural selection. If it gets you to survive long enough to reproduce, it gets passed on. It doesn't care that it might make you miserable in certain circumstances.

Kathy Russell Rich, who survived stage-four metastatic breast cancer, said that even a decade after her treatment, the mere memory of chemotherapy could induce nausea and "a horrible, druggy stomach burn." She said those intrusive memories could literally cut off her ability to think. That's because under extreme stress, the emotional part of the brain shuts down the frontal lobes, the area of the brain that we use for logic and reason. The frontal lobes have the calm and sensible voice that Eileen tried to use: My husband brought me home. I've been treated by competent doctors. I'm in my own bedroom now. The doors are locked. There are no crocodiles where I live. But to get its work done, the amygdala vetoes those distracting, if reasonable, thoughts. To the people around her, it must have seemed that the tremendous anxiety and terror that Eileen was experiencing weren't really real. It was all in her mind.

PEOPLE ONCE thought that the mind was some kind of spirit with no physical reality, a soul consisting of insubstantial ethereal force or energy. In 1861, a French neurologist named Paul Broca introduced the concept that the mind is simply an expression of physical processes in the brain. Mind, in other words, is meat. The brain and body are so intimately connected that there is little point in talking about one without the other. Sensory and motor nerves exist everywhere in the body. And the circulatory system carries hormones and neurotransmitters everywhere to directly influence the brain and body. Damasio calls it "the brain–body partnership" and says that neither brain nor body does anything alone.

It is common to see the brain characterized as a splendid invention that has to drag around behind it a primitive throwback bag, the gross and sluggish body. That conception misses the point. In fact, it misses two points by a rather wide margin. The brain is not an elegantly functioning jewel, as it is often said to be. As my father used to say of certain aircraft that had been distressed by long over-use, the brain is a collection of spare parts flying in close formation. David J. Linden, a neuroscientist at Johns Hopkins, calls the brain "a kludge (pronounced 'klooj'), a design that is inefficient, inelegant, and unfathomable, but that nevertheless works."

In addition, with all the attention the brain has been getting in recent years, we tend to forget that the brain is the body. It is of and in the body. The body directs behavior through its control of the brain, which is there to serve its needs and whims. The brain itself cannot reproduce, so it had better pay attention to the body or it will go extinct in a hurry. In fact, during the body's attempts at reproduction, it generally tells the brain to go sit in a corner and pay no mind. That's why Damasio calls the brain "the body's captive audience." All feelings are generated in and by the body and they are all about the body. And feelings, conscious or occult, direct behavior. Unfortunately, we do not yet have a word in English that can unify the brain and body, the thing that gives rise to motion, thought, consciousness, feeling, and to the self that we perceive as whole. Maybe classical Chinese can help in the meantime. Lu Chi's ancient text, *Wen Fu* (*The Art of Writing*), says, "Emotion and Reason are not two," and suggests the word *hsin* to unify heart (body) and mind (brain). So when I say "mind," I mean *hsin*, the mind that includes a heart (and a hand for doing and a gut for feeling). And when I say "brain," I also mean *hsin*, the body that includes a brain. The body is an organ of experience. Through its captive audience, the brain, the body is constantly recording what happens and what those events mean (bad or good, pain or pleasure). As it records, it looks into the past and tries to predict the future. The body's best guess is that they will look the same. The body is the instrument for these recordings and the brain is the tablet on which that instrument writes. This work is daunting and mysterious. It sometimes seems almost magical. For it always tells us, eventually, what it has learned. But it may do so when we're not looking.

So, if Eileen's trouble was all in her mind, then her fear and anxiety, her tears and anguish, were all being expressed as feelings in the material stuff of her body. Certainly, clusters of cells were all communicating furiously with one another through electrical and chemical signals in her brain. But you cannot feel your brain. It has no sensory nerves. What was troubling Eileen was what she felt in her body, the racing heart, quaking muscles, churning gut, dry mouth, and pouring tears. It was her body that experienced the sweating, the hyperventilation, and an inability to sleep or eat properly. All in her mind, *indeed*. It was entirely in her body, and her body played out those feelings over and over again for the audience, the brain, which allowed Eileen to perceive, consciously, what a mess she was. If she was to feel better, she had to do something with her body.

Emotion and reason work like a seesaw. (Daniel Kahneman, a psychologist at Princeton and winner of the Nobel Prize in economics calls these System One and System Two.) The higher the emotion, the harder it is to think straight. But it can also work the other way around. If you can just get yourself started thinking straight, you can sometimes override emotion. In fact, that's what makes us different from the other great apes. One of the most important functions of the frontal lobes, the part of your brain behind your forehead, is restraint, the thoughtful and deliberate domination of reason over emotion. So, if you can manage to think clearly enough, you can start to tone down the fear. Easier said than done for a variety of reasons. One obvious reason was that Eileen was severely injured. An injured body makes recovering the mind that much more difficult. Physical injury produces stress, which involves a host of changes in your muscles, your digestion, even your immune system. Stress dumps special chemicals into your bloodstream. And while those chemicals were necessary for the burst of energy that Eileen needed to survive the attack, if they continued to circulate over a long period of time, they could do real damage.

One of the chemicals of stress is cortisol, a steroid. A little bit of stress, a small rise in cortisol, makes you more alert and puts you in a better mood. It improves your ability to concentrate and helps you form explicit (conscious) memories. A little bit of stress improves performance in sports and intellectual activities. A little cortisol improves your appetite. But that same chemical in large and prolonged doses has the opposite effect. It can disrupt the machinery of explicit memory. It can cause malfunctions in the frontal lobes so that you can't think straight. Making matters worse, too much cortisol stimulates the fight-or-flight reaction. So it becomes a feedback loop.

Many kinds of memory are formed in the brain and body. Explicit memory tells you such things as what you intend to buy at the grocery store. Another kind of memory, called episodic, allows you to tell someone everything that happened at that awful party last Saturday night. Implicit memory includes things such as learning to tense your muscles when the dentist brings the shrieking drill toward your mouth. It's an emotional memory, so you don't have to think about it. It just happens. Implicit memory also includes procedural memory, which allows you to learn, for example, to ride a bicycle or to tie your shoes. Automatic behaviors, such as your golf or tennis swing, are part of implicit memory.

The same cortisol that makes it difficult to create new explicit memories makes implicit memories stronger and faster, strengthening your response even when you can't remember why you're responding in the first place. While too much cortisol interferes with the work of the hippocampus (for making conscious memories), it improves the working of the amygdala (for producing fear and unconscious memories). When that steroid disrupts the formation of conscious memories while enhancing the formation of unconscious ones, you feel anxiety without ever knowing where it came from.

When Eileen wrote in her diary that she was miserable, never slept through the night, felt crazy and unable to get along with anyone, it was because she was experiencing the effects of those chemical changes I've been discussing. What Eileen needed, then, was to find some way to get at the cell assemblies in her brain that were setting off her alarms. She needed a way to readjust the chemistry that was causing her such disruptive anxiety. And if Eileen's trouble was all in her mind and her mind was a manifestation of her body, then it would be through her body that she would ultimately ease her mind.

EILEEN HAD gone to college and earned a master's degree in psychology, so she knew the fancy name for what was troubling her: post-traumatic stress disorder, or at least some of its symptoms. But Eileen's response to trauma is not a disorder. It is, in fact, the inviolable command of memory: Learn this to save your life. It is a perfectly reasonable response, given the way our brains are organized. An injury leaves scars. Let's call it post-traumatic stress. It sounds as if Eileen should have seen a psychiatrist, but psychiatrists like to talk, and in many cases, talking therapy won't work for severe anxiety disorders. Moreover, talking therapy can backfire. Jonathan Shay, in his book *Achilles in Vietnam*, wrote that in the early days of the war, psychologists encouraged veterans to tell their stories, to get it all out, in the belief that this would help them release themselves from mental anguish. He called the results of this misguided effort "catastrophic." This technique of forcing people to talk after they experience trauma is known as Critical Incident Stress Debriefing and it's been shown to be ineffective and even harmful. In fact, a lot of the patients committed suicide. This does not mean that keeping trauma secret is the best approach. It means that writing about your experience or talking with friends and family only when you're ready are often better than being forced to unburden yourself in a formal, professional setting.

From the press and popular culture, we may get the impression that you have to go to war to experience post-traumatic stress. But injury can affect us along a broad spectrum, ranging from very mild symptoms to completely debilitating ones. If you're chopping onions and cut off the tip of your finger, you may find that your mind involuntarily replays the accident at times, causing you to flinch inwardly each time you remember the adrenaline-soaked sensation of knowing that sharp metal just slid through your own flesh to contact bone. That's one end of the spectrum. You'll get over it. Or not. It won't disrupt your life. At the other end, in the realm of extreme trauma, lies the abyss. Some people are able to go on. Others are not. But in dealing with the aftermath of trauma, it's important to realize that we don't get over it. We get on with it.

Eileen took off running. She had always been an enthusiastic runner. And she knew that exercise produces profound chemical changes in the body that could improve her mood. For example, it activates a system in the brain that produces dopamine, a chemical that provides motivation to do something and a commitment to a particular course of action. Cortisol and dopamine work together to improve mood and relieve pain. People who are depressed are usually low on dopamine. Without sufficient dopamine, you wind up with Parkinson's disease.

Several months after the attack, still struggling with her nightmares, Eileen set a goal. "I began to approach my recovery as an athletic event," she told me. "Here's my future, let's get on with it." She got angry and made a decision to take action and do something. George Vaillant, a psychiatrist at Brigham and Women's Hospital in Boston and a professor at Harvard Medical School, is the director of the Harvard Study of Adult Development, the longest-running study of adaptation in humans ever undertaken. He found that one of the most effective responses to adversity is to fight back. He called it "creative aggression." In baboon societies, if someone hits you, you turn around and hit someone lower in the hierarchy. In human societies, that's not okay, so instead, you hit the track, hit the gym, hit the books, or even hit the road as we'll see.

Taking it slowly, then, Eileen returned to running. Making the decision to employ creative aggression was an important turning point. It meant taking action. But following through with that decision was excruciating at first. *I try to run*, she wrote. *My thumb throbs in a sickening way and my whole face—all the bones, cheeks, jaw—feel like they are going to crumble. This is depressing, makes me wonder if I will ever be normal. Will I lose all the strength that I've worked so hard to build?*

On and on she ran through the pain. Slow and steady. She did one of the key things that survivors do in the aftermath: Trust the process. Let go of the outcome. Whatever happens, happens. Walk the walk. Pretend. Imagine. She gradually grew stronger. The chemical changes brought on by exercise began to have their salutary effect. As her body healed, her shocked nervous system slowly began to calm down and stop tormenting her. The excursions into panic became less pronounced, the nightmares less frequent. The storming waves settled into smaller swells. Having an explicit goal gave Eileen's thinking brain something to hold on to, that slight edge of the frontal lobes over the amygdala. And significantly, being engaged in directed action, carrying out a deliberate plan, gave her a new sense of control that she had been forced to abandon when she was an invalid. Her feelings became more predictable. The rational began to dominate as the peaks of high emotion moved into the background.

It is well known that what you do with the body deeply influences the way you think and feel. If you act strong, you feel stronger. If you act happy, you feel happier. If you move your facial muscles into an imitation of a smile for a time (say, by biting on a pencil), you gradually start to feel better. Just as a car horn can become paired with a feeling of panic, cell assemblies exist that connect feeling good with the position that the muscles of your face assume when you're smiling. If something is funny or makes you happy, you smile. Nerves throughout your face let you feel which of those muscles are contracted. And an implicit memory of that pattern is then connected through a network of neurons to your feelings of mirth or joy. Once that connection is made, a smile alone can give rise to those feelings in the same way that the sound of a bell could make Pavlov's dog salivate. These conditioned responses can run in either direction. Feeling good can make you smile and smiling can make you feel good. Feeling good is the retrieval cue for smiling and smiling is the retrieval cue for feeling good.

Before the attack, Eileen had spent years creating cell assemblies that connected running with all sorts of good feelings, such as power, strength, health, self-sufficiency, control, well-being, predictability. So even though it was painful at first, just getting out and acting like her old self made her feel better. She was replacing the cues for panic with the cues for feeling well. She was working to overwrite those traces of memory that had been left by the crocodile.

Then something marvelous happened. Marvelous and terrifying. The penmanship in her diary was visibly shaky as she wrote: *Found out I am pregnant. Excited and scared. I really can't believe that my body is capable of sustaining a baby after all that it has been through.* For three years, Scott and Eileen had been trying unsuccessfully to have another child. Perhaps even more remarkable than the fortunate timing was the fact that she managed to get pregnant when there was scarcely a spot on her anatomy that didn't hurt.

But the pregnancy had a number of important effects. It radically changed the chemistry of her brain and body, imposing a new kind of order on her emotions. It also gave her a clear point to aim for. The new Eileen would be a new mother. She would face an entirely new set of adaptations. The focus of her concern would shift from her own troubles to her baby's well-being. Like Lisette, she would be doing something for someone else. Even before the baby was born, he began pushing the crocodile into the background. Then there was noise, laughter, and even a good reason for a bit of sleeplessness. The house that had been littered with emotional cues for danger became littered with cues for the joy and happiness of a new baby. Eileen had a new concern, freighted with emotion and much larger than herself. Given the way our brains have evolved, it's difficult to have too many overwhelming emotions at the same time. We simply don't have the processing power. So a high dose of joy is a great antidote to debilitating anxiety. This is one reason that so many victims of Nazi concentration camps threw themselves headlong into raising children. Paula Gris, who was in the death camps as a child, expressed another reason. She gave birth to her five children, she said, to replace the children killed in the Holocaust.

How well a person does after a crisis has a lot to do with the attitude and personality she has developed over a lifetime. Eileen was lucky. Her focus, optimism, and capacity for hard work combined with her inborn tendencies and created a person who could take something really bad and turn it to her advantage. Several years later, looking back at the events of her life, Eileen reflected on how the experience had helped her reinvent herself.

"I feel different from others and different from who I was before," she told me. "I have had that second chance, yes. But I have also been tested mentally and physically to the point that other people never experience, and I have passed. That's a weird sensation. People always want to know: What am I made of? Well, I know. Instead of feeling like a freak show, I'm proud of myself. I'm just fine. And I have such incredible empathy when I look at people who suffer, like someone who loses a child: What's the big deal about me?"

As time went by, Eileen told me, "I feel strong. I feel like whatever life hands me, I can deal with it." Rather than letting her experience define her life, she came to regard it as "a platform for growth."

THREE

THE WAY OF SURVIVAL: RAGE IN THE REALM OF THE SPIRITS

"PEOPLE DIE HERE," the ranger had told me. An immense red wall cut a jagged line against the sky. As I hiked, more and more ranks of walls appeared, with great snowy peaks beyond. Each wall, more thrilling than the last, seemed to present itself forcefully, like a whale rising from the sea. Wildflower, cactus, grass, all gave off an aroma that was nearly sexual. Sunlight cooked an exotic perfume off the stunted cedar trees, the tamarack and greasewood, in the cool and heady air. I sat on a rock and took off my shoes to feel the red sand in my toes as if I walked on some remote island beach. And I felt myself being swallowed by that kingdom. There was something cunning in the patterns that had been fashioned by slow catastrophe. The evidence was all there: Those walls were falling. All day. All night. Right now. Here huge slabs had cleaved away, then turned somehow to the red dust beneath my feet, the constant grinding of stone on stone like a ruminating beast. Most of us never realize that we're seeing it. It looks so solid, like our own flesh: We can't imagine its not being there. But each of the boulders I saw before me fell from somewhere. And high above, the ruined battlements of a fort bespoke the furious fighting. Where were its warriors? When did it happen? It's happening all the time, somewhere.

The place was alive, dancing, dissolving. If you could set up a camera so that it took a single frame of movie film once a century, you could watch a million years go by in half a day. Then maybe you'd start to see the true and lively nature of this adversary. No wonder it excites a strange lust in us. You go simple in the head, like a mad lover. You sneak off, telling no one where you're going. And there you do dangerous and stirring things.

AS ARON RALSTON scrambled through Blue John Canyon on April 26, 2003, it was like entering the womb of the world, red and dark and too narrow even to extend his arms from side to side. The slim crack in the earth was in the Maze District of Canyonlands National Park near Moab, Utah. Aron slithered on his back beneath boulders that had fallen from somewhere above and now hung wedged between the walls. The slot just got tighter and tighter. It was as if he were being unborn. "It was a rather serpentine canyon," he said later. "Very narrow walls, somewhat technical, and very giving of its solitude. I was quite alone there." When I heard him say those words, it was 12 days after the event that drew hundreds of reporters from all over the world. We were crowded into a conference room at St. Mary's Hospital in Grand Junction, Colorado.

Aron had clambered under and over a series of large boulders wedged between the walls—chockstones, he called them. At last, he came to a boulder hanging over a drop of about 10 feet. Embracing the stone with a hand on either side, he put his weight on it to lower himself, planning to drop to the bottom of the canyon. But the stone began to roll toward him. In a rush of adrenaline, he let go and then tried to push the stone away as it fell. Time shifted into slow motion as he watched the rock crush his left hand against the wall. The stone bounced, and Aron withdrew his hand. But with his attention on his left hand, he was not quick enough with the right, and the rock pinned it. It took but a second. But now the rock gripped his right hand in the hearty handshake of a brute: Welcome to eternity.

The searing arc of pain shot through him, and in a panic, he slammed himself against the rock again and again. The rock held fast. He forced himself to stop, to breathe, to calm down and take stock. It was hard to think in the grip of this thing, but he gulped air and stood still where he'd landed and forced himself to consider it all logically. One of his first thoughts was that no one knew where he was.

Aron had worked on a search-and-rescue team. He knew that you always, always, tell people where you're going. It's common courtesy: That way, when you screw up (and we all screw up), they'll know where to look for you. In fact, Aron had put up an erasable board in his house. He'd write down where he was going and when he'd return, along with the phone number for search and rescue. This time he wrote nothing, told no one, slipped away, pulled by the irresistible force that had drawn him to so many other places where death waits.

He felt a rush of sadness and remorse for the thing he'd done. The people who loved him, cherished him, would never see him again. It wouldn't take much rain to wash his body away. The rain might fall many miles away, but when it passed through this venturi, the force of it would snap trees and sweep away that boulder as if it were so much Styrofoam.

It wasn't the first time Aron had succumbed to impulse. Tim Mutrie, a reporter for *The Aspen Times* who knew Aron and had skied the back country with him, told me, "Aron has had many other close calls." Less than two months earlier, Aron had gotten frostbite on Capitol Peak outside Aspen. He had thrown himself into the Colorado River and nearly drowned while friends watched helplessly from the bank. A few weeks after the Capitol Peak incident, Aron led two friends into an avalanche in the back country on Resolution Mountain near Leadville, Colorado. He made a public apology, calling it the stupidest thing he'd ever done. "It was horrible," he told a local paper. "It should have killed us all. All for a dozen turns. We never should have been there."

Which could be said about Blue John Canyon, the place where he now found himself. Even if by chance someone guessed right and searched the area, the slot was so deep and tight that he'd never be seen from the air. No other hikers would come there, either. One ranger I spoke with called it "the other side of the earth: You can't get there from here. Rangers in every park will tell you they have some of the most remote places there are. The Maze District can honestly say that. Until the seventies, there weren't even contour lines on the topo maps for that area." And when they appeared, it was because of satellites, not because of people on the ground.

When his hand was crushed, Aron's immediate response was reflexive. An ancient pathway in the brain, which scientists call the rage pathway, connects several areas to produce what neuroscientists call "affective attack." *Affective* means "emotional." When you are attacked, you automatically fight, scream, and bite. All mammals are born with this response. You don't have to learn it. The rage pathway begins in the amygdala and sends signals to the hypothalamus, which monitors the state of your body and imparts tremendous powers of persuasion to all sorts of appetites, such as thirst and hunger. The rage pathway ties those structures in with an area called the pariaqueductal gray (PAG). The PAG is one of the places where you represent the physical self, both the outer and the interior body, and is involved in feeling pain and in responding to fear (freezing or fighting). The PAG also sends nerve fibers into the parts of the brain stem that control the jaw and face; biting and baring your teeth are part of the rage response. This response is so powerful that it can be overwhelming. It is, after all, meant to free you from the grip of a predator. It's what helped Eileen get away from the crocodile. To Aron's brain, then, the rock was the predator. So when the rock landed on his hand, Aron at first had no ability to control his rage response. He screamed, grimaced, and attacked the rock, trying to yank his hand free from it and slamming his shoulder against it. He was injuring himself further. But then he did something that is unique in the animal kingdom: He used his frontal lobes. Aron let himself see the rock. It was huge. It wasn't going to move. He let himself see the relationship between rock and hand. The hand was irretrievably stuck. Smashed flat. Dead meat. So Aron employed the first step in the process of survival: Perceive and believe. An animal in the thrall of rage runs that pathway unto death. Only the highest of the apes can do what Aron did: throw cold water on the emotional system and start thinking.

So standing up, unable even to sit, Aron forced himself to calm down. He couldn't say why he'd done this to himself. Maybe this was what he'd been looking for all along. You perceive yourself as a single self. But neuroscience has shown that the unity we feel is mostly an illusion. We are made up of various systems of memory, various motivations and appetites, desires and goals. At times our behavior may appear to represent a seamless cooperation of these parts, as we rationally set about achieving our goals. But in reality, we are constantly suppressing one appetite to satisfy another, dampening one memory system to highlight the one we need at the moment, and refusing one motivation to follow another. You can think of these as many different selves competing for primacy and existing in constant tension with one another. They push and pull in different directions. Because at our core we are divided selves, something in many of us leads us to places of penance and reckoning. A darker self. Aron believed that something inside him had led him there. He believed that he had always been in search of a challenge like this: life or death.

He began using the rational part of his brain. He looked at the tools he had at his disposal and began planning what he might do to save his life. He had a cheap knockoff of a Leatherman tool and tried to use it to chip away at the rock and make enough room to slip his hand out or get the rock to move. It was futile. And he was getting tired of standing. His left hand was slightly injured but functioning. He used it to anchor a rope to a rock above him so that he could tie the rope to his climbing harness and sit down to rest. He had one liter of water. He had a couple of burritos, a few crumbs from a muffin. How long could he last?

THE NIGHTS were cold and sleepless in Blue John Canyon. Standing, sitting, shivering, Aron tried to think through his situation as his emotions now ricocheted from despair to elation. He prayed. He worked out various scenarios for freeing himself, thinking like the engineer he was. He had designed clean rooms for building micro-chips at Intel before he quit to be an outdoorsman full time. He was capable of very precise and controlled reasoning. By the second day in Blue John Canyon, he had begun experimenting with rigging a pulley system to try to lift the rock. He eventually managed to get what he believed to be a 5-to-1 mechanical advantage. The issue was academic. It would eventually take a hydraulic jack to move the rock.

Over the next days of his entrapment, Aron experienced some-thing profound: the voyage of survival. From prisoners in concen-tration camps to sailors adrift at sea, to stranded mountaineers, survivors go through surprisingly similar transformations. Sur-vival is a vision quest. At first your emotions may be all over the place—panic, denial, anger. If you exhaust the rage pathway, you may fall into despair. But if you're going to survive, the rational brain must take over. Yet logic alone won't work: Reason and emo-tion must cooperate for correct decisions to emerge. For emotion is the realm of intuition and inspiration, essential helpmates in surviving. Survival requires entering what might be called a state of grace.

Those who survive waste little time whining. We've all met people who are constantly blaming others or outside forces for their troubles. They do not make good survivors. Survivors recognize, as Epictetus wrote, that all good and all harm come from within us. It is telling that Aron took responsibility for the accident in Blue John Canyon. It is the mark of a survivor to be responsible and truthful.

The survivor also does not stop trying; he always does the next thing. Even resting becomes a task. Aron referred to waiting as "an active option." Sometimes resting, waiting, conserving energy, represents the best strategy.

In a seeming paradox of survival, the very same relentless drive that led him into trouble was instrumental in getting him out. The tenacity that could drive him up five different mountains in 15 hours allowed him to survive more than five days with his hand trapped and mostly without food or water. The survivor faces the requirement of monumental, sometimes superhuman, efforts.

Trying to fathom them could arouse strong emotions that could disrupt thinking. So he breaks those tasks down into manageable steps and completes them one by one. He has the future in mind, but he doesn't think too far ahead. He concentrates his efforts in the moment. In doing the things he must do, he is organized and meticulous. Chipping at the rock, setting up his haul system, and even waiting were logical steps. And although that activity didn't free him, it served the purpose of continuing the struggle to survive. "Get organized or die," say the survival instructors. It is the struggle that is key; those who cease to struggle, die. Lost, injured, under the extreme stress of weather, hunger, exhaustion, fear, it is easy to die without any obvious organic cause. Some people just give up. If you're working on the problem, then by definition, you're still alive. Survival does not mean right or nice or heroic or even pretty. It just means that you're alive.

The survivor takes comfort in memory, mind games, music, poetry, prayer—anything to allow the mind to rest. Joy is a way for the organism to tell itself that it's all right. That's essential information in the ongoing conversation between brain and body, between reason and emotion. Aron prayed and took peace and joy from memories, reviewing his life, the beauty he had seen in the wilderness, the friends he'd had. During the long cold nights, he reviewed the exotic travels he'd enjoyed with friends and family in places as diverse as Peru and Hawaii. He bathed in memories of mountaineering.

Hallucination is common during the experience of survival. Aron said his friends joined him in the canyon. They encouraged him and gave him strength. "We're here when you need us," they told him. Yossi Ghinsberg, lost and wandering in the Bolivian jungle for three weeks, beset by floods and flesh-eating insects, hallucinated a beautiful woman and took care of her for days, wheedling, cajoling to keep her moving, to stop her crying, as he made his way to safety. Such a companion also served the function of giving him someone to help who was worse off than he was, like Lisette with Betty and Ruth, the two girls whose father had shot his family and himself. During his ordeal, Aron remembered Warren MacDonald, whose legs had been trapped when a boulder rolled onto them in the wilderness. MacDonald was trapped for two days before rescuers could get the equipment needed to move the boulder. He lost both legs, learned to use prosthetic ones, and returned to mountaineering. By remembering this, Aron was reinforcing a crucial idea: If he can do it, I can do it.

The true transformation in the journey comes when you see the amazing beauty of the place in which you are trapped. This is the vision of the vision quest. You embrace the pain, discard your concerns about death, and then the world opens up to you. Lauren Elder was in a light plane that crashed at the top of a mountain in the high sierra. She watched the pilot and his girlfriend die up there at nearly 12,000 feet. She was the sole survivor. Wearing a light skirt and high-heeled boots, with one arm broken, she spent 36 hours climbing down and hiking out to civilization. On the way, she was required to descend some sheer faces of rock and ice with neither gear nor training. About three-fourths of the way down, she reported peering over a ridge and seeing a water-filled hollow in a rock shelf. She took off her clothes and slid into the pool. She bathed and drank in the mountain pool. She said that she felt as if she were in paradise. Then she warmed and dried herself in the sun, lying nude on a rock—"emptying my mind . . . resting on the edge of sleep." She had done something every survivor must do. She had accepted her new environment instead of grieving for the one she'd lost. As Dougal Robertson said after being castaway at sea for more than a month, "Rescue will come as a welcome interruption of . . . the survival voyage."

Aron found the beauty in flights of fancy as he soared over land and sea in his imagination. Nevertheless, by Tuesday, he had run out of water and food and knew that no one would come. He'd either get himself out or die. But he was no longer bothered by thoughts of death. This stage of the journey is known as survival by surrender. This is where you let go of the outcome and trust the process.

Once past that stage, you are filled with an ecstatic certainty that you will live. Steve Callahan, who drifted in a raft for 76 days at sea, called it "a view of heaven from a seat in hell." Aron described this paradoxical state: He both accepted death and embraced the belief that he would live.

Survivors are willing to do anything to survive. They take a kind of action that is both bold and cautious. Its audacity shocks normal people. And yet survivors retain a level of precision and control that holds them back, if just barely, from death. Aron's friends all agreed that he had an obsessive will that wouldn't let him turn away from his goal. "He doesn't back down," one friend said. "There was no stopping him." And while that characteristic may have annoyed or endangered others at times, it served him well once he was trapped in Blue John Canyon.

Through countless episodes of survival, it has become clear that people don't become survivors overnight and may not do so through years of training. Survivors live their lives in the Way of Survival. In one sense, when Callahan was shipwrecked at sea, it was trouble of his own making: He was crossing the Atlantic solo. In another sense, it was just bad luck: He was rammed by a whale. Callahan wasn't considered reckless. Lots of people sail alone. But a lifetime of mechanical skills, self-reliance, endurance, perfectionism, precision, self-deprecating humor, optimism, and attention to detail had prepared Callahan for his ordeal. Unlike Aron's, Callahan's preparations for trouble had been meticulous. His emotional makeup allowed him to practice being calm in the face of tremendous danger and to keep reason and emotion in balance while performing extremely difficult tasks, such as hunting fish and repairing his deteriorating life raft. His spiritual nature allowed him to get in touch with the deepest recesses of himself, to find solace and even contentment there. And his attitude of acceptance allowed him to sit quietly in a terrible situation without going mad. Whatever criticism might be floating around about Aron's impulsive exploits, most of that could be said of him, too, in the clinch.

In their transformation, survivors become so self-reliant that their behavior becomes scarcely believable to us ordinary folks. On April 21, 1982, when Callahan was within sight of his goal, a small island in the Caribbean, a group of fishermen in a skiff came out and offered to take him to shore. Callahan shouted joyously, "I can wait. You fish. Fish!"

Lauren Elder reported the same thing. She was filled with a new energy. She felt as if she'd slept and eaten, even though she had done neither. She had no idea where the energy came from, but it gave her the strength to go on.

Aron, too, went onto afterburner near the end. Without the help of that energy, people tend to perish. David Boomhower set out on a 10-day solo hike on the Northville–Lake Placid Trail in New York State in 1990. Although he had made extensive preparations, he ran low on food. So he looked at his map and decided that Sucker Brook Trail would take him to a road, where he could hitchhike to town to stock up. He was not in trouble yet, but he had begun putting together a plan that would end his life. Unlike Aron, he had left a copy of his route with the authorities. But by improvising, he had rendered that information useless. No one would know where to look for him. All he needed now was one or two surprises and he'd be in big trouble.

It began to rain "cats and dogs," as he wrote in his journal. The unfamiliar trail was far more rugged than he'd expected. It crossed a stream 14 times before it petered out. He tried without success to retrace his steps. He was completely out of food by that time and could not start a fire because of the rain. Although he was just three and a half miles from the road he sought, he didn't know it. Even so, he'd done his homework. When he admitted to himself that he was lost, he did it by the book: He made camp and awaited rescue.

The search for Boomhower was begun three days after he was expected to return. Of course, they were looking in the wrong place. As the Fourth of July approached, he expected to hear the fireworks that were set off annually at a nearby lake. He reasoned that he could then walk toward the noise. Another piece of bad luck contributed to his death: Because of the rain, the fireworks show was canceled. Soon he was too weak to hike. *Can't take ten steps now without stopping*, he wrote on the twenty-sixth day. One of the last entries in Boomhower's diary was, *I wonder if anyone has died out here, waiting, believing in that "stay calm and help will arrive bullshit."* David Boomhower set out on June 5, and his body was found accidentally on October 20. According to his journal, he had lasted 55 days.

But those who do survive often go through a dramatic transformation. Many survivors have said the same thing: They suffered horribly, but they wouldn't give up the experience they had for anything in the world. Lauren told me, "It's the biggest gift of my life. I often wish I could be living with that single-mindedness and clarity and focus. It's absolutely unequivocal what has to be done. It was thrilling when it happened and I wish it would happen again." Aron echoed Lauren's words. Things were hard but clear while he was trapped in the canyon. Back in the world, he wrote, "I felt unprepared to adapt to my new circumstances."

DEATH REDUCES us to clichés. We cannot conceive it even when we are faced with it. When Aron saw how close death was, he scratched a message on the rock. He began with "Good luck now," the letters gradually getting more out of control, as if he had slowly backed up in time to become a four-year-old. Then he added something illegible, as if the four-year-old had held on to its language skills for a few scant minutes before the fog of prehistory closed over him.

Drifting in a half-conscious state, Aron saw one of his friends in a white robe before him. He led Aron to a panel that opened into the wall of sandstone. Together they walked through the opening and down a corridor to a living room where all his friends were gathered. Time passed as he moved back and forth between the reality of the canyon and his gentle hallucination. A day or so later, Aron slipped through the wall again, this time on his own. His friends were gone. A small boy about three years old sat playing on the floor. He ran to Aron, who lifted him onto his shoulder. They danced across the gleaming hardwood floor in glorious sunlight. They laughed. And that was the moment when Aron knew that he would live. The little boy was his son, destined to be born at some time in his own future.

Not long after that, Aron had the vision that would save him. He stuck his knife into the thumb of his trapped hand. Gas hissed out and the foul odor of decomposition hit him. Smell is the most powerful of the senses, and it set off Aron's rage pathway once again. He began thrashing against the boulder, and as he did so, he felt his arm bending in a strange way. "An epiphany strikes me," he wrote, and the clarity of it ended his frenzy in a heartbeat. It was so simple. Why hadn't he thought of it before? Simply by jerking his arm against the rock, he could break his own bones. He asked himself if he would be capable of remaining calm, making clear decisions, taking precise actions. He prayed and grew peaceful at last. He packed up his gear to leave and arranged everything neatly in preparation for cutting off his hand. He called it his "surgical table."

When survivors talk about the spiritual elements of survival, I believe that they are really talking about a special state in which we can gain access to those parts of the brain that normally remain unconscious. This is the realm not of actual spirits but of gut feelings and abrupt leaps of the imagination, of sudden inspirations. Those unconscious memories feel like spirits because they make up the multiple selves that we normally perceive as cooperating in a unitary self. Those memories direct our behavior without asking permission. Aron now entered that secret place as he put his inspiration into practice. He referred to it as being on autopilot. "I'm not at the controls anymore," he wrote. Once he broke the bones of his arm, the long job of cutting through the flesh, blood vessels, and tendons with a dull pocket knife lay ahead. Like so many survivors, he managed it by employing patterns, rhythm, counting. Joe Simpson, the British mountaineer who wrote *Touching the Void*, used this technique to get himself off of the snowbound mountain in Peru where he'd broken his leg at 19,000 feet. He fell into a rhythmic pattern of hopping on his good leg and placing his ice axes. He then went into a kind of trance while following that pattern. "I began to feel detached from everything around me," he said.

The pattern became his whole world, and as we'll see, that altered state of consciousness is one of the keystones of both surviving and of surviving survival itself once the main event seems to be over.

Now Aron did the same: "Sort, pinch, rotate, slice" became the repetitive pattern that allowed him to proceed calmly and cut off his hand. "Patterns;" he said, "process." When required to, he altered the pattern to suit the needs of the job: "Grip, squeeze, twist, tear." He was also acutely aware of the need to keep his emotions under control. When he was about to sever the last nerve fibers, he recognized how painful it would be and he avoided touching them until the end. He knew that he shouldn't know the full impact of the pain he was going to experience. It would upset his fragile emotional balance.

Responses to trauma can seem paradoxical at times. Dissociation during trauma often leads to symptoms of post-traumatic stress later on. But a curious transformation takes place under certain circumstances. If you're in control during the trauma, it can strengthen you for dealing with the aftermath. Having a task is paramount. After Steve Callahan's ordeal as a castaway was over, he went straight back out to sea. So did Douglas Robertson, who was just sixteen when his father's boat, the *Lucette*, sank with him and his family on board. (Douglas wrote to me: "I went back to sea as a deck officer and was shipwrecked a second time. Foundered in a force-twelve storm also in the north Pacific after the condenser intake pipe fractured from unknown cause." I asked if it was even worse than the first sinking. "Naah," he said, "the second shipwreck was a cakewalk. We had sent an SOS, had rescue ships standing by. Had to leave her in a lifeboat in heavy seas though.")

As Aron cut the last of his skin and freed himself from the rock, he was filled with intense euphoria. And then he did something truly strange but typical, it seems, of Aron. He didn't rush away to get the medical attention he so desperately needed. Instead, he used his good hand to take a photograph of the rock and the hand that he would leave behind. It was wedged in there beside the blue-and-yellow climbing rope, which he'd tied in a neat bow.

A few days after the accident, 13 park rangers hiked into Blue

John Canyon to retrieve Aron's hand. They carried a winch, heavy nylon webbing, cable, a cable puller, and a hydraulic jack. Only then were they able to move the stone a few inches and reach in for the hand, which by that time looked like an old discarded glove. They put the hand into a bag and hiked back out.

Like so many survivors who do well in the aftermath, Aron was grateful. He called his ordeal "the most beautifully spiritual experience of my life" and went on to say, "I have no regrets." The very qualities and traits that made him such a good survivor, the steps he took to rescue himself, served him well in the coming months and years following the trauma. He already had confidence in his ability to calm himself in the face of calamity, to think clearly and plan, to set small goals and celebrate his successes, to surrender to the process, and to keep on trying.

But there were other influences that propelled Aron in the aftermath and helped him build his new self. For one thing, he was instantly famous throughout the world. He was given a fat contract for a book, and the process of writing that book was part of the process of defining his new self. In building that self he also had all sorts of cool prosthetic limbs custom made to allow him to return to climbing. He appeared on *The Oprah Winfrey Show*. In terms of helping others and finding those who are worse off, Aron was suddenly everyone's role model, giving inspirational talks and getting paid handsomely for it. And what could be better than seeing yourself 40-feet wide on the silver screen as portrayed by James Franco? As I write this, Aron is hard at work on another book of his own. His premonition about his son came true, too. He met Jessica Trusty three years after he cut his hand off. They married and had a son, Leo. Aron hasn't slowed down yet.

FOUR

THE GIFT OF ADVERSITY: A SURVIVOR'S ATTITUDE AND THE PERSONAL SCUM LINE

MICKI GLENN WAS on an expedition to scuba dive and photograph sharks off Caicos Bank. The location was a clifflike formation at the French Cay, which she described as "an underwater Devil's Tower that drops straight down 6,000 feet." The 20 people on the boat had finished their first dive of the day and were relaxing when someone suggested that they snorkel for a while. Micki worked managing her husband's practice as a trauma surgeon. Among the others on the boat were Randy Samberson, a vascular surgeon, and Libba Shaw, a nurse in an intensive-care unit. They all shared an enthusiasm for scuba diving.

Micki drifted beneath the surface, breathing through her snorkel. Looking down, she was not surprised to see a seven-foot-long female shark just beneath her fins. Micki's husband, Mike, was underwater on scuba gear, photographing through the cathedral light that fell into the bright blue water and faded to deep purple and then black, as it dropped away to the benthic deep. It was their fifth day of diving, and Micki and her companions had become accustomed to having sharks nearby. It was one of those unconscious adaptations that we make all the time, and it was not a good one. Her emotional system had labeled sharks not as something to fear. They were just fascinating creatures. "I love animals," Micki told me. A lifelong equestrian, she referred to the sharks as "powerful, graceful, like watching horses."

The female shark stopped beneath Micki's fins and changed direction. Then the animal moved slowly upright, aligning its body with Micki's. The shark brushed its sandpaper skin against Micki's leg and slid all the way up her body until the two were staring at each other. "I was looking right into her eye, just inches away, this beautiful gray eye with a vertical pupil set in gray skin. I saw the slit of her mouth, and the hair was standing up on the back of my neck. I thought I was the luckiest person ever." In that intense moment of eye contact, Micki held her breath, as the shark moved slowly against her, then bent its head to the left, flicked its tail gently, and glided away like a mythical mermaid.

"It was almost like a caress," Micki said, "very deliberate." As she let out her breath, Micki felt a powerful surge of water hit her side as the shark flipped around and took Micki's arm in its mouth. The shark's upper rows of teeth were across Micki's back all the way to the spine. She felt no pain, only pressure, "like I was in a vise." Like many people caught in a life-threatening emergency, Micki described "time slowing down." She "could perceive the most minute details." Like a razor, the lower jaw sliced her breast from the lateral border almost to the nipple. The upper jaw took the entire posterior half of her armpit. Then the shark began thrashing with such force that Micki suffered whiplash. At the same time, she was trying to power her left hand around to strike the shark and drive it away. At last the shark planed away and slid beneath the boat, taking a huge chunk of meat with it. It was about eight in the morning, a beautiful sunny day, on November 14, 2002.

Micki looked around and saw four other sharks. The water all around her was not just red but deep, deep crimson. She saw the ragged flesh and the bare humerus bone of her arm. "The rest of my arm was in the water. I was beyond terror." She knew that there was no chance of making it to the boat. She had heard about sharks' going into a feeding frenzy. From the catastrophic flensing she'd just experienced, she already knew what a shark attack felt like. She'd recorded that memory instantly. Now her brain brought forth vivid images of what was going to happen if the other sharks were to grab her legs and begin ripping her apart. The situation seemed hopeless, but she began kicking as hard as she could toward the boat, paddling with her uninjured left arm. Encumbered by his scuba gear, Mike could do nothing at first but try to struggle free of it.

"I looked behind me," Micki said, "and the water was so red that I couldn't see my arm. Then I saw this thing jerking behind me and I stopped for a second." The thing that followed her was a white and chalky creature in a sea of red. As it moved toward her, she saw that it was her own hand, hanging by a flap of skin. "That scared me more than anything. I thought my severed hand was following me."

Her friend Nancy had been snorkeling nearby and reached Micki when she was nearly to the boat. She grabbed her around the waist and helped propel her toward the dive platform at the stern. From force of habit, Micki began to take off her fins. "The things that you do automatically kick in even when it's ridiculous," she said. "Those were my favorite fins, and it was really important to keep them." Under stress, you don't invent new strategies. You revert to automatic behaviors. She dropped one of the fins and started to go after it. "Then I snapped out of it," and she began screaming Mike's name. "I knew he was the only person who could save me." Moments later, she heard his scuba tank crash onto the platform.

Micki's mind was crystal clear at that point. She knew that she might lose consciousness at any moment. "The blood loss was crazy," she told me. "I don't know how anybody can lose that much blood and live. I was very focused. When I saw how much damage had been done and how much blood was in the water, I acted exactly as I needed to." Micki climbed higher onto the boat so that someone could reach her. Nothing but a thin strip of bicep muscle remained on her arm. Her brain was trying to fire signals to it to move the hand. Each time it fired, "it felt like a strong jolt from a cattle prod and that hand slapped me in the face. It was really painful. The hand wasn't completely severed, and the wrist area was banging me on the side of the head as I was climbing the ladder. Then I made the mistake of looking behind me into the water. It was so thick with blood, I felt pretty hopeless then."

As Micki lay on the stern of the boat in the bright sunshine off French Cay, the chances that she would survive were fading fast. The shark had taken out her armpit and part of her shoulder containing a rich nest of blood vessels, and she was rapidly bleeding to death. Chance always plays a role in survival. It entered Micki's story here. Horrified, terrified, convinced that she would die, she looked up and saw Mike, who had untangled himself from his scuba gear and scrambled onto the boat. Behind him stood Dr. Samberson, the vascular surgeon, and Libba Shaw, the ICU nurse. They had all brought their medical equipment on the trip as a precaution against just such an emergency. Without this team so close at hand, you would not be reading this story, because Micki would have bled out in perhaps another minute. What happened next was crucial.

Mike reached into the flesh of Micki's shoulder and groped for the torn end of her brachial artery, which was ejecting the fountain of blood that she had seen in the water. Samberson ran to get his equipment and moments later handed Mike a hemostat. Blood was still pouring out. Mike worked his way deeper into the wound to clamp the artery higher up.

"That's when the pain hit," Micki said. "It was surgery without anesthesia. I started screaming so loud that I couldn't hear. I stopped to apologize and started right in screaming again." Mike found the artery and pinched it off, while Samberson broke out his instruments and clamped off other blood vessels with hemostats. Meanwhile, Shaw was trying to start an IV. Micki had lost so much blood that her veins had started to collapse. Shaw couldn't get the needle in. Micki encouraged her, saying, "You can do it, Libba." Everyone cheered when she finally got it in.

"I still didn't think that I was going to live through it," Micki said. "You can feel when you've lost so much blood that you're just hanging on a thread. I kept my feet in the air, because I didn't want to pass out. I refused pain meds because I didn't want to relax and lose the ability to fight and stay alive." She was displaying all the characteristics of a true survivor, working every second with what little she had left.

But even good survivors have emotional breakdowns that they have to overcome. At one point, Mike saw Micki crying, and he snapped, "You stop that right now. You can't afford to lose any fluid." She didn't shed another tear. Once the blood vessels were clamped off and gauze was packed into the gaping wound, Mike sat beside her, monitoring her vital signs as the boat sped toward shore. Twice he lost Micki's blood pressure and pulse. Micki looked out of the corner of her eye at one point and saw him crying. "I saw several tears slide down his cheek." Mike had hunkered down around her knees to hide it from her. "That was the most emotional part for me when I saw Mike. We had used humor through the whole ordeal. Despite the gravity of what was happening, one funny thing after another was said just to get through it, but seeing Mike crying just got me."

During the seven-and-a-half-hour trip to Miami, Micki knew that it was important to stay awake and that the pain could help her accomplish that. As so many survivors do, she developed a mantra: Pain is my friend. A mantra can focus the mind on the goal and engage the deliberate and logical part of the brain. Since the response from the rage pathway is so exhausting, this is important in conserving energy, which the body needs for survival. Micki's mantra carried her through the excruciating journey to the hospital, by dinghy, police boat, helicopter, ambulance, and at last a Coast Guard jet.

When they reached the hospital, the surgeon who met them told Micki that he was going to amputate her arm. Mike blew up in his face, saying, "I could save her arm. Unless you let me do it, you need to get off the case and bring somebody here who's willing to try." As the surgeon stormed out, Micki thought: Great. I've come all this way and he just chased away my surgeon. But another surgeon soon arrived and she agreed with Mike's assessment. She took Micki's latissimus dorsi muscles and fashioned new triceps out of them. She took skin grafts from Micki's legs to reconstruct her upper arm and her back. Micki received a dozen or more units of blood. She underwent six surgeries over the next two weeks. She survived the attack that should have killed her. In the TV version, Micki's story would end there.

But the more profound drama, the ordeal of trying to reenter the world, began while she was still in the hospital. "If I didn't focus on something every minute, as soon as I relaxed, it was like the wall in the hospital would turn into the sea again, and I relived the shark attack over and over and over." She would wake up screaming with her mother standing over her, saying, "It's just a nightmare. It's just a nightmare."

She went home the day before Thanksgiving. To take her mind off the shark, she returned to work just 16 days after the attack, still wearing bandages and plaster. "I could do only half days." Her arm would swell and she'd have to lie down every half hour and elevate it.

As with Eileen's experience of the crocodile, Micki found the pieces of her life now dispersed, leaving her with an unfamiliar puzzle. The multiple selves that make up the unity of normal experience were split apart and scattered. One of her first tasks was to admit that even if she could put the pieces back together, the whole would never look quite the same. It was going to be a new Micki in a new world. Making her job harder was the fact that she didn't know anything about the process. No one had given her a road map for this journey. She was going to have to trust her feelings, her intuition, and listen carefully on those secret channels that give us our inspirations.

Micki had become an alien in her own home. "I had the feeling that pieces of me were scattered in the ocean. And they were: Physical pieces of me were missing. They were in the ocean. But it was more than that. I felt so much not like myself. I was such a different person. I felt like I had completely lost who I was." And as we'll see, the secure sense of self that most of us feel and take for granted all the time is completely tied up with how we feel about our bodies. When the body is radically changed, so is the self.

Suddenly, Micki was terrified of sharks and even pictures of sharks. One night she happened to be watching a James Bond movie when a close-up of a shark flashed onto the screen. "I came unglued, blubbering and crying." By now we're familiar with precisely what she was going through. After extreme trauma, memories combine in odd ways to produce flashbacks that are even more vivid than reality. Micki never actually saw the teeth of the shark that attacked her. But in her flashbacks, she saw an open mouth bristling with teeth coming at her.

People who have not experienced them underestimate the power of flashbacks. They aren't just annoying memories. A true flashback is an all-out assault of the emotional system that takes control of your senses and your behavior and can wipe your memory as clean as electroshock therapy does. One veteran of the Vietnam War returned home and was receiving treatment for post-traumatic stress in West Haven, Connecticut. He came out of a flashback in the middle of the night to find himself in a forest in Ohio, wearing battle fatigues. He had no notion of how he had gotten there. Another vet was walking along a street in Boston and came out of a flashback in a motel room in Texas. Micki's experiences were virtually identical. She was sitting in a restaurant, waiting to pick up a pizza, and the next thing she knew she was curled up in the fetal position on the floor of her truck. She had no memory of leaving the restaurant.

This new and fearful self drove Micki absolutely crazy. She hated this wimp. "I never wanted to trade places with anyone," she told me. "The things I did, such as stepping off the Okaloosa Island Pier into an 18-foot crest in hurricane surge, galloping my big Swedish Warmblood, Gent, in the woods around Eglin Air Force Reservation at night and watching the tracers from the gunships that were doing night ops. Those aren't just things I do. That's who I am." But after the shark attacked her, she felt the split as she was cleaved into two identities: the old fearless Micki she remembered and the lame new Micki who seemed to be controlling her life. "The Micki I loved was loud and clear in my head," she said. "But the new fearful, injured, careful, timid person emerged as the dominant me, and to my dismay, she controlled my actions, my body. The old familiar me had a strong voice and sense of who I should be, but she had no control. She was a ghost. I aligned myself with her, and we hated the alien Micki. My voice was mine, and in my mind and sometimes aloud I harshly berated the frightened injured me." Caught in the middle of this infuriating division, she completely lost her sense of self.

One of the things bedeviling her had to do with a certain type of memory that we store. In the past, I've used the term that the neuroscientist Joseph LeDoux uses, originated by Philip Johnson-Laird: "mental models." David Eagleman, a neuroscientist at Baylor College of Medicine in Houston, Texas, calls them "internal models." Murray Gell-Mann, a Nobel laureate, uses the term "schema." Elkhonon Goldberg, a professor of neurology at New York University and the protégé of the famed neurologist Alexandr Luria, favors "categorical perceptions." At the simplest level, mental models are representations of objects that allow you to identify things quickly and to know the rules by which they behave. *That's a bunny. It hops away across the grass when I enter the yard. That's a bird. It flies away.* This system would never allow you to think that the bunny will fly. Neither will it let you think, even for a second, that the bunny is a cat. One kind of mental model we can learn allows you to catch a ball because it is an internal model of how Newtonian physics and gravity influence objects.

The retina sends images to the visual cortex, which makes a prediction about what is being seen and forwards that to the thalamus. The thalamus returns a message telling the difference between the actual visual information and the prediction. The part that's correctly predicted is ignored. Whatever is new then serves to revise the mental model for future use. Eagleman wrote, "When the world is successfully predicted away, awareness is not needed because the brain is doing its job well." This is another way of saying that the brain is tuned to detect novelty. But this system, while fast and generally useful for avoiding predators and finding prey, can make all sorts of mistakes in our modern world.

We also use mental models in searching. If you misplace your phone, one strategy for finding it is to go around the house and examine every single object in every room until you come upon the phone. That might take you a few days. But if you have a target image—a simplified mental model of the phone—then you can rapidly scan a room, and if any portion of the phone is visible, the complete image will instantly jump out at you.*

The emotional system labels our mental models so that you immediately know their value or their danger. When you see something that you've never seen before, you have to spend a bit of time figuring out what it is. But once you've done so, you'll identify it instantly from then on and know its use and its significance. Our fearful reactions to loud noises and big looming shapes are innate mental models. Mental models can represent sight, smell, touch, and sound. They can also swap information. When someone puts a key in your hand, you know what it is without having to look at it. When someone shakes a ring of keys, you know what they are by the tinkling sound. Because of mental models, you don't really see what's in the environment. You take in sensory information and try to match it to what you expect based on previous experience or on some innate model. When you see the popular symbol known as a smiley face, you know what it is, not because it looks like a face but because of an organ in the brain called the hippocampus. Gyorgy Buzsaki, a neuroscientist at Rutgers University, says that if you think of the neocortex as a library, the hippocampus is the librarian. The hippocampus is what's called an autoassociator. "Give the autoassociative network part of the content," says Buzsaki, "and it returns the whole." This system is the basis of mental models. The hippocampus always tries to bring into your conscious mind a pattern it has already stored (and not something new), even when what it sees isn't really a representation of that thing. Caricatures don't look much like the people they portray, but they work because of

* The term "mental model" is shorthand for a process that is extremely complex. In actual fact, the brain stores detailed images, but they are broken into fragments and widely dispersed within the brain. But if you perceive any fragment, your brain will efficiently call up the whole image. I'm using the term "mental models" to refer to the fragments as well as the process that leads you to identify the whole.

the autoassociator. It takes almost no information to make this system work. You have a lot more detailed information in your brain about faces in general and in particular, but the scant marks of a good caricature are enough to call up the appropriate face. The hippocampus is doing this all the time with everything you perceive through the senses. After trauma, the emotional labels carried by mental models can be the source of much pain. Extreme trauma can destroy your trust in your mental models. This condition is known as hypervigilance and it makes sense. One veteran of the Vietnam War said that he had to look at everything twice to be sure of what it was. Since mental models are the heart of all perception, this cuts you off from your world.

This process of storing mental models can help us understand why young children are afraid of things that may seem odd to adults. They haven't yet cataloged much of the world, so a pile of clothes in the corner of a dark bedroom might look like the face of a monster. A shadow might be a terrifying bird. Those are perfectly reasonable interpretations to a brain that has few mental models. Children have less experience creating those models, and at night they are instinctively on the lookout for whatever is dangerous. In that sense, post-traumatic stress can make us behave as if we are children again. Like a child, Micki was now afraid of images of sharks.

Her husband, Mike, had, in fact, managed to photograph the shark just before it attacked Micki. Now he put a close-up image of that very shark on the screen of her computer. Her screen saver became the monster from the deep that stole her life away. "Every time I walked in, I had to look at her again," she said. Her heart would go into overdrive, then she would deliberately calm herself and look at it. "It took a week or two, but I was gradually desensitized to sharks." Micki was systematically writing a new memory over the traumatic one. She was sending a new message to her emotional system concerning the mental model of a shark. It said that seeing a shark did *not* feel like pain and screaming terror. It felt like walking into her office. She was relabeling her mental model of a shark with feelings of gratitude to and love for her husband, who had saved her life and was now saving her emotional system, too. This process is known as extinguishing a conditioned response.

There's some pretty sophisticated work being done on this sort of overwriting of memories and relabeling of mental models to deal with trauma. While researching this book, I was privileged to visit the Center for the Intrepid at Brooke Army Medical Center in San Antonio, Texas. There Colonel Jim Ficke, head of the Department of Orthopaedics and Rehabilitation, put me into a virtual-reality system called the Carren dome. I walked through a completely realistic village in Iraq. Jim said, "It took me two years to be able to pick up trash from the side of the road after Iraq." Because trash makes a good hiding place for an improvised roadside bomb, it had become labeled by his emotional system just as with Micki's shark: Danger. Panic. To extinguish this conditioned response, they put soldiers in the Carren dome. A soldier walks through the village, and at first, the street is completely clean, with nothing on it that might set off a panic attack. Then the technician operating the system gradually starts adding details. As the soldier walks through the village, the technician adds things one by one until the soldier can walk down a busy, chaotic street and pass by a trash can without hitting the dirt. So it was with Micki and her shark.

As we'll see in later chapters, not everyone succeeds at this. Part of Micki's progress involved her own personality. "I don't like weakness in myself," she said. When she had the flashbacks at home in the middle of the night, she went into the closet and curled up in a ball, pressing her back into a corner so that she could see out. I believe that everyone has what I call a Personal Scum Line. For each of us, there is some level below which we must not sink, or else we lose all respect for ourselves. We become, in our own eyes, scum. For some, it's as simple as being unemployed. For others, it might be divorce, obesity, incest, treason, murder. For Micki, this sort of behavior, hiding in the closet and generally blubbering her way through life, represented a descent below her own Personal Scum Line. She was fiercely determined to get out. She went back to her mantra: Pain is my friend. Pain is my friend.

. . .

MICKI HAD grown up in southern Mississippi. Her family life was rich. Her parents loved the outdoors. When she was two, her grandfather gave her a pony named Nico, beginning her lifelong love affair with animals, especially horses. She used to sit on Nico for hours, trying to teach her to talk.

Micki had seen what deliberate rational behavior in an emergency looked like. She had seen discipline and self-control. When she was three, a grease fire erupted in their kitchen. Micki was outside when her father snatched the skillet full of blazing oil from the stove. He burst through the screen door to throw it out. Then he saw his little daughter starting up the steps. To save her, he threw the flaming oil back onto himself. "He suffered terribly," she said. "The skin on his forearms hung to his knees."

She told me, "I have been acutely aware of the fragility of life since I was a little girl." When she was five, her best friend died of cystic fibrosis. When she was eleven, two of her close friends drowned. The next year, her friend Dale died of leukemia. When she was in high school, she was misdiagnosed with leukemia, and for three weeks she and her family thought that she was going to die. "So the shark attack reinforced that life is a precious, fragile gift."

In college, Micki was so poor that she worked two jobs and sold plasma twice a week just to eat. While saddle-breaking horses for $2.35 an hour, she was thrown off and broke her neck. She was twenty-one years old. No one would wish to have experiences like that. But they build character and a solid foundation for the larger emergencies to come. Like staring at the picture of the shark that attacked her, those experiences had helped Micki become familiar with pain and act calmly under exceptional levels of stress. If you look into the background of the best survivors, you almost always find lessons like those. And when you talk to them about rebuilding after disaster, you find that those who have been given the gift of adversity often fare better than those who have lived lives of comfort and ease. One of my survival instructors told me that poor kids from the inner city did better than rich kids from the suburbs.

It seems in keeping with Micki's character that her love of horses led her to ride bigger and bigger ones over the years, what she calls "the big warm-bloods." Eskan is a Friesian that weighed in at 1800 pounds at the time of Micki's accident. (Today she sometimes also rides a Percharone named Dublin that weighs a solid ton.) Two weeks after the attack, she begged Mike to let her sit on Eskan. True survivors, as well as those who survive survival, are willing to take big risks in their own best interest. An old friend of mine named Harry Crews used to put it this way: "If I can't have it all, I don't want any of it." Micki was a lot like that in getting back into life. Despite the grave risk so soon after her accident, Mike agreed to make it happen and four friends helped Micki mount the titanic Eskan. She sat there on high. She held the reins. For her entire life, Micki had built her identity, her core self, around horses. Her nervous system grew out into the horse so that its hooves were her own legs. Her emotional system intimately knew the saddle as a place where she was in control, was safe, and where the world was predictable. "I felt like I was on top of the world," she said. "That did more for me emotionally than anything at that time. I felt like everything was going to be all right." This is another instance of using the body to redirect mind and emotion. She put her body where it had learned to feel good and it obediently felt good.

An experiment done at Pitié-Salpêtrière Hospital in Paris by Yves Agid, a neuroscientist, makes clearer what was happening. Agid placed an electrode in the brain of a woman who had Parkinson's disease. When he turned on the current, the woman stopped talking, lowered her eyes, and her body assumed an attitude of profound grief. She began weeping. Then she began talking about how pointless her life was. "I don't want to live anymore," she said. "Everything is useless." But as soon as Agid turned off the current, the despair vanished. Soon the woman was joking with the doctors. She had no history of depression. How, she asked, could she have said those things and felt that way? How could she have so deeply believed in her own despair?

The answer lay in the placement of the electrode. While the doctors were trying to use it to control her Parkinson's disease, the electrode had accidentally stimulated an area of her brain stem that gave her body a posture characteristic of sadness. Everyone can recognize this: head bent, eyes downcast, body slightly contorted. The electrode also produced the automatic physical reaction of crying, taking control of her diaphragm and larynx and even the glands that produce tears. When her body assumed that position and performed those actions, she experienced the feeling that matched that emotion: despair. And here's the most interesting part: The left hemisphere of the brain is involved in making up stories to explain the things we do and feel. For example, when Lisette's husband went mad and shot her and himself, she adopted a posture of grief and felt despair just as Yves Agid's patient did. Lisette's left brain said: You feel bad because terrible things have happened. In that case, what the left brain said happened to match reality. In the case of Agid's patient, however, there was no apparent cause for the grief. That did not stop her left brain from making up a story.

Steven Pinker, a professor of psychology at Harvard, refers to the left brain as a "baloney-generator" that offers up explanations of our behavior. Often those explanations have nothing to do with reality. They're simply the stories that we tell ourselves to help us get around in the world. "The conscious mind," Pinker said, "is a spin doctor." LeDoux concurs: "People normally do all sorts of things for reasons they are not consciously aware of." And: "One of the main jobs of consciousness is to keep our life tied together into a coherent story." LeDoux and Pinker confirm a long line of thinking going back to William James (and probably beyond, to Plato) concerning how well we can know ourselves consciously and how that knowledge or the lack of it influences the decisions we make. In Agid's patient, the physical movements and posture of sadness (i.e., the emotion) led to the feeling of sadness, which the baloney generator immediately began to try to explain. ("Everything is useless.") But now we see that the system can work either way, thoughts leading to emotions or the physical actions of emotions leading to matching thoughts and feelings.

In a related experiment, Itzhak Fried, a cognitive neuroscientist at UCLA, electrically stimulated a woman's frontal lobes. When they threw the switch, she was seized by uncontrollable laughter. Nothing funny was happening. The poor woman was suffering from epilepsy so severe that she was seated in a surgical theater. And yet, not only did the woman laugh hysterically, she felt all the gay merriment consistent with that laughter. Moreover, the surgeons found her laughter so infectious that they fell into fits of laughter along with her. When they turned off the current and questioned the woman, her left hemisphere had explanations ready: "You guys are just so funny . . . standing around." Again we can see how the physical expression of an emotion without any logical cause behind it can lead to the feelings associated with that emotion, but it can also lead to thoughts that serve to impose a rationale upon it. And although it is a complete confabulation, we can use this mechanism to trick ourselves into feeling better.

AFTER THE ACCIDENT, Micki had told her husband to get rid of her scuba gear. She never wanted to see it again. He kept it anyway. Two years passed. Then, Nancy, who had helped Micki to the boat after the attack, coaxed Micki into taking a trip to Dominica in the Caribbean. For two days, Nancy sat holding Micki's hand at the edge of the water. During that time, Micki practiced putting her face into the water. Just her face. "The first day that I actually went to dive, I threw up my breakfast. Sitting on the bow of the boat on the way out, I could see the shark thrashing on the top of the water with me in its mouth." Two years in and she was still flashing. But she went anyway.

When she was 80 feet down on a wall, a big barracuda surprised her. "All I saw were teeth. I completely came unglued and crashed into the wall and cried into my mask and got all snotty." She had again slipped below the Personal Scum Line. She forced herself to stay in the water and work through it. She told herself: Focus on the beauty underwater. Focus on the beauty.

"After Dominica," she told me, "I felt that I was whole again."

So much of Micki's story represents the quintessential attitudes and actions of the best survivors, from her clear and immediate perception of the gravity of her situation to her focus on taking action on her own behalf and her steady resolve to overcome the long-lasting emotional injuries. But at the heart of all those qualities is an attitude toward life in general that I've encountered over and over again in the survivors who return to life most successfully after trauma. One of the first things she ever said to me reveals a great deal about that attitude: "I'm really lucky." She went on: "I don't regret that this happened to me. What surprises me is how something so horrific has been such a positive experience in my life. I would never wish it on my husband or my parents if I had it to do over, but for me, it was transforming. It's probably the single most positive experience I've ever had." Indeed, research by James Pennebaker at the University of Texas, among others, has shown that "all kinds of upheavals bring people together" and "terrible experiences can bring out the best in us."

We live on. But we also live with.

FIVE

THE TYRANNY OF REASON: BLINDSIGHT, GUT FEELINGS, AND THE SIXTH SENSE

WHEN I FIRST MET Chris Lawrence, I felt a strange dissonance in his appearance. It felt as if my brain were trying to resolve the conflict between my existing mental models and what I saw before me. The parts weren't matching up. Chris was tall, athletic, handsome, and fit, wearing shorts and a T-shirt, sport shoes. As he approached me across the hotel lobby in Milwaukee, he came forward with a jaunty rolling gait. He gave me a firm handshake and a welcoming grin. But his right leg was gone and in its place was one of those high-tech biomechanical prosthetic legs. His left arm looked as if it had been scorched in a fire. The hand was not working right. Something devastating had clearly happened to this young man, and yet there he was, full of life and looking the picture of health. His friends referred to him as a cross between Muhammad Ali and Rambo. You could instantly see how intimidating he might be. But he had a great engaging smile and a booming baritone laugh. He immediately put me at ease, and the conflict detectors in my brain began to assimilate his appearance just as his own brain must have back in 2007, when he got that arm and 2008, when he got that leg.

We went to a small diner to have breakfast and talk. Chris had enlisted in the Marine Corps in 2005 at the age of eighteen. He said it was just like the movie *Jarhead*. For the first month, he was asking himself, "Am I stupid? What the hell did I do?" But he gradually realized that it was a pretty good place to be. From the age of sixteen, Chris had been more or less homeless in a bad neighborhood in Milwaukee. After two years of couch surfing, he had found a bed of his own with the Marines. He said that Iraq compared favorably with his old neighborhood. "And this is the United States."

After three months of boot camp, he was sent to train for combat. He graduated with honors and was given the "Gung Ho Award" for being the most motivated. On the 10-mile hikes, people would fall behind and Chris would pull them up the hill. "I guess that was motivating," he said with a laugh, "because if you see one guy pulling two, well, what's your excuse?" He was already using the tactics that would see him through the crisis that was rumbling down the tracks toward him like a locomotive.

Chris gave me a rundown of everything he had done and every place he had been assigned since joining the Marine Corps. His narrative was precise, orderly, and detailed. Here was a man who was clearly dialed in and squared away. Yet I almost didn't get to meet him that morning after driving up from Chicago. We had made an appointment for ten o'clock. But when Chris woke up, he had only the vaguest sense that he might have agreed to do something with someone, somewhere. He couldn't imagine what it was. We'd talked on the phone just two days earlier, but the memory was gone. "Something told me it was early," he said over omelets and coffee. "So I decided to wait around until ten-thirty and then head on out." The lapse of memory didn't seem to fit with the man I saw before me. There was nothing about him that seemed confused. And the story of his time in Iraq was thoroughly organized. It took me two hours to realize that very little was left of his memory of Iraq. He'd had to hear about it from others and memorize it.

After being trained as a radio technician, Chris was settled with his unit in Iraq, where he earned a reputation as someone who could fix anything. "I don't fix things," he told me. "I just make them work. There's a difference." And throughout his first year, he passed all his training with honors and was promoted in rank right on schedule. He was thinking, "I could do twenty."

Reflecting on the events leading up to his injury, he said, "There were so many signs. Don't do it, don't do it, don't do it. And I did it anyway. But the injury has made me more spiritual and aware of some of the signs the universe puts in front of you. A lot of things had to go just wrong for me to end up in my situation." In *Deep Survival*, I talked about how accidents don't just happen. They have to be assembled, carefully, piece by piece; and if one piece is missing, they simply don't happen. Many times we never know how close we've come. In Chris's case, all the pieces fit together perfectly.

Chris's outfit had been deployed in several troubled areas where they worked efficiently to bring about calm. At that time, one side of the Euphrates River was relatively quiet, while the other had been largely ignored. So his outfit, Second Battalion Fourth Marines, was "tasked with pushing through there again and killing everything all over again," meaning that they were sent to calm the wild side of the Euphrates. There were a lot of battles, a lot of people killed, but they did their job and were moved once again to another neglected area. They gradually earned a reputation for being good at going into a troubled spot and bringing things under control. So each time they did a good job, they were moved yet again.

"Competency is a curse," Chris said. "You're a good fire-team leader, we'll make you a vehicle commander. You're a good vehicle commander, we'll make you *lead* vehicle commander." And being a radio technician, he should not even have been outside the wire. They arrived at a new area to replace some soldiers who were leaving and were doing an exercise they called "left seat, right seat." That meant that the soldiers they were replacing would sit in the right seat and let the replacements drive. They would show the new guys where the dangers were and familiarize them with the area. "And the Iraqis know this, they know: Oh, they're new. And that's usually when stuff happens." As soon as the experienced soldiers left, Chris's platoon began getting shot at and blown up.

But what Chris described as the key ingredient in staying safe was precisely that ineffable sixth sense that told Lisette that her husband was dangerous 30 years before he shot her, that same sense by which someone with complete amnesia can learn new skills and improve day by day without ever remembering the time spent practicing. The sixth sense, which we sometimes call intuition or gut feeling, is real. To understand it, we need to know a little about how the human brain evolved.

PAUL MACLEAN, a senior research scientist at the National Institute of Mental Health, coined the term *triune brain*. David Linden at Johns Hopkins refers to it as a three-scoop ice-cream cone. At the bottom is a small scoop that is essentially the same brain that a reptile has. Evolution added a second scoop that amounts to what mammals such as dogs and cats and rats have. They also get a small amount of the third scoop. Humans get a huge third scoop, the neocortex, the part that gives us language and the ability to think logically and make plans. But as evolution moved along, the additional scoops didn't erase the earlier ones. Those stayed much the same as they had always been. That's why Linden refers to the brain as a kludge. We have, for example, the same midbrain visual system that a frog has. But we don't use it for seeing. We use it only to help orient ourselves in the right direction. People who have gone blind due to damage to the brain (as opposed to the eye itself) are able to point to a light in a darkened room with near-perfect accuracy because of this frog brain, even though they are completely unaware of being able to detect any light through their eyes. That trick is called "blindsight." So here is why we are tormented in the aftermath of trauma: Because we have a frog and a rat in our brain. But that is also one reason we have a sixth sense. The frog and the rat are always watching out for us.

One of the experiences that shapes and teaches the sixth sense is what neuroscientists call trial-and-error feedback. This is similar to conditioned responses such as car horns that make you afraid. Your emotional system records in great detail everything in a traumatic scene but does not necessarily bring everything to conscious attention. The frog and the rat know a great deal that the human can't know. But as we saw with Eileen and Micki, the next time something looks vaguely like that scene, the frog and the rat do give up something: They give you a bad feeling. And you can't quite articulate it because the frog and the rat don't use logic or language. Damasio calls those gut feelings somatic markers because they're feelings in the body that mark something as important.

At Baylor in Houston, David Eagleman has written about this vast area of unconscious knowledge and perception. He uses the example of experts who can tell male and female chickens apart as soon as they hatch. The experts look at the chicks and sort them in one box or the other, and they're mostly right. But no one, including those experts, has any idea how they do it. To teach someone, you have to immerse him in the activity and give him feedback about when he's right and when he's wrong. He gradually learns to do it correctly but never knows what new perceptions he acquires. We all carry out these mysterious perceptual tasks in our daily lives but, for the most part, we go through life unaware of them. For example, in 2004, a team of scientists from the United Kingdom and the Czech Republic published an article in *The Royal Society Biology Letters* that showed that many normal, healthy men can tell when a woman is ovulating just by looking at her face. Most men don't know that they can tell, so they don't go around on the street yelling, "Hey, there's one now!" Like sexing the chicken, they see it, feel it, and react to it. ("Hmm, she's awfully attractive.") In fact, scientists at the University of New Mexico demonstrated that lap dancers in strip clubs earned significantly more in tips when they were ovulating. Richard Feynman could do something similar with equations. Without doing any calculations he could take one look at them and tell if they were right or wrong. He had no idea how he did it.

"Once you've been there long enough," Chris said of the war zone, "you start to know: That ain't right. It's like when you walk down your block. You know your neighborhood. And you know when things are normal." You can't tell people exactly what you see, because the frog is doing the seeing. The frog or the rat. "It's so hard," Chris said. You can feel it, "like there's an energy it's giving off. The energy is wrong. Like: I've seen this guy. I see him all the time. But he's not right today. Or it's schooltime and you go outside and there's no kids. It ain't right. And this gets into how I was injured." Because the one time you ignore that sixth sense, you may be putting your life on the line.

Yet another piece in the puzzle had to be put in place to get Chris injured: With his reputation as a man who could fix anything, the parent unit of his company had asked him to transfer. They needed him. They offered him a Navy Achievement Medal if he'd work with them. "You could have hot chow every night and a good shower," they cajoled. "You'll get Internet if you come with us." But he didn't want to leave his boys. He didn't trust anyone else to take care of them. "The universe was saying: 'Take it, take it, take it! You're stupid!' I could have been out of there." But he stayed. He stayed out of loyalty.

How much more we know than we can ever know we know. How deep the well from which we draw our experience and behavior, our choices, our expressions, and even our salvation. Lisette knew, 30 years before the fact, that her husband was a murderer. She knew in the same way that Chris Lawrence knew.

Here's how it happened.

FRIDAY, AUGUST 17, 2007, early morning. Chris was the only one up. He brushed his teeth and cleaned his weapon, made sure the radios were working, got ready for patrol. He called home to talk to his girlfriend.

"I don't want to be with you anymore," she said.

"Are you serious?" Chris asked.

"Yeah. I don't think I can do it. This is just too much for me."

"All right, whatever. Bye."

He tried to put it out of his mind. He had more important things to worry about. His unit's vehicles had been blown up a few days earlier, so they were going to go out on foot.

As a fire-team leader, he didn't have to carry a radio anymore. The radios, he said, were ridiculous. In an age when a high-definition video camera fits in your shirt pocket, these monsters seemed to weigh 40 pounds. With a full combat load, it sometimes amounted to 100 pounds of gear. So that day, they gave the radio to the fat kid. "He needs some exercise," someone said. But Chris felt sorry for him and said, "Hey, you take a break. I'll carry the radio." He had just put one more piece of the puzzle in place.

Their patrol base was on the banks of the Euphrates and they were going to a small island that had been joined to the land with a pontoon bridge. The spaces between the pontoons were covered with sheets of half-inch steel so that a vehicle could drive over them. Shots had been fired from the island, so Chris's platoon was going to hike over and look around. "We had been in the area only a week, and that's when stupid stuff happens." Chris described "a bunch of Marines" who had died on that bridge the week before. He thought that perhaps their vehicle had flipped. "But it was the radiomen who died," he said, because they fell into the water and sank.

Chris and his staff sergeant and the four other members of the platoon crossed the bridge to the island. "It was the most beautiful day in Iraq," he recalled. "It was eighty-five, and the island was like something in the Caribbean—palm trees, nice people, kids running around and playing. And we're like: Man, did we just go to the Bahamas?"

They spent about four hours exploring the island and then found an abandoned house where they could "go firm," as he put it: sit down, rest, eat, hydrate, check their equipment, and get ready to go back. While they were eating, Chris said to his staff sergeant, "I'm going to buy this island. When this place is civilized, I'm going to buy it."

"What-everrr, Lawrence."

As they were leaving the island, they stopped to play with some goats. People approached the soldiers and gave them bread. When they reached the foot of the bridge, kids were playing soccer there. The staff sergeant peeled off and started kicking the ball with the kids, laughing and joking around. When at last they were ready to cross, they looked up to see a man advancing toward them over the bridge. And that sixth sense kicked in: *This guy ain't right.* They sent two soldiers out to meet him. One trained a gun on the man while the other patted him down and checked his papers. Everything checked out, but Chris still knew: "This guy ain't right. But we can't just hold him." This is where the sixth sense can be derailed by logic. "He didn't have any guns, but it just wasn't right." It was maddening for Chris to have to stand there, knowing what he knew, yet not knowing how to make it count for something when making his decision about what to do next. Everyone knew it. It was as if, collectively, they were being forced by the tyranny of reason to watch helplessly as the black and greasy locomotive roared down upon them, even as that subterranean voice was screaming, Get out! Get out!

They sent two men across the bridge to set up security on the other side. Then they sent another two men, and those two set up security as well. "And then it's time for me to go across with my staff sergeant," Chris said. He was still carrying the radio. The reception was bad, so he put up the 10-foot-long antenna, "which I call the ten-foot 'Shoot Me' sign."

At that point in the conversation, Chris and I had finished our breakfast in the diner in Milwaukee and were sipping coffee. Chris was making his voice real high and singing, "Hey, come get me!" and people in the restaurant were turning to look at the big buff guy with the buzz cut and the bionic leg, this mad Terminator who was cackling and squealing, "Shoot me! Shoot me!"

Suddenly, he seemed to notice the people. He grew quiet and folded his hands on the table. He shot me a glance, like: Oops, sorry. Then he continued his story. He began to walk across the bridge, side by side with his staff sergeant. "It's a beautiful day," he remarked.

"Yeah," the sergeant said. "It's my daughter's birthday today."

"Aw, tell her I said Happy Birthday."

"Yeah, I'm going to get home and I'm going to call her," the sergeant said. "Home" meaning their base camp.

"Awesome."

"You know what, Lawrence. We're walking awfully close here."

"Yeah, you're right, Staff Sergeant." Chris slowed down and the sergeant sped up to put some space between them. "The next thing I know, I wake up in Bethesda, Maryland."

ABOUT THIS time in 2007, another Marine, Jessica Goodell, was hiding in a tiny apartment in a terrible neighborhood in Tucson and drinking just as much as she could manage. In 2004, when it looked briefly as if she might miss the war in Iraq, she volunteered to work in the first Mortuary Affairs unit the Marines established. The Mortuary Affairs unit is sent to gather the remains when a rocket or a roadside bomb kills someone. The bodies are frequently dismembered or even, as Jess later wrote, "mounds of shapeless flesh which we scooped out with our hands. . . . vaporized mush." On one such mission a tank had been completely blown to pieces, leaving nothing but "tiny scraps of tissue," she said, including ears and testicles. The unit's task was to leave nothing behind so that the entire solider could be returned to his or her family. They also wanted to eliminate the possibility that any remains might be desecrated.

Using body bags, they transported the parts to the bunker where they worked. There they prepared them for return to the United States. The work was so horrifying that the first time a body came in, Jess and her team froze and couldn't function. In an extreme emergency, the amygdala forces a response from the brain stem that's called defensive freezing. A predator is less likely to see you if you're not moving. Despite their training, they were unable to do anything until their warrant officer led them through the process step by step. They had to fill out paperwork for each person who had died. One page showed an outline of a body, front and back. Jess had to shade in black any body parts that were missing.

It is difficult to get a clear sense of how powerful the explosions were. Once Jess found a cord coming out of a young man and pulled on it. The blast had blown a radio handset clear inside the body. The temperature in the vicinity of an explosion can reach several thousand degrees Fahrenheit, so many of the dead were burned as well. At first, Jess couldn't place the familiar smell. Then she realized that it was the smell of grilled meat. Most of the soldiers in Mortuary Affairs stopped eating meat. Then they stopped eating altogether. Coming back from a convoy, they were so pumped up that no one slept either.

Another part of her job was to gather everything the person was carrying and catalog the items for shipping. Sometimes there were letters meant to be opened in the event that the soldier died. Often there were photographs of family. One man carried a sonogram of a fetus. The more she processed bodies, the more Jess began to see live people as nothing more than the pre-dead. Her old mental models of living people were gradually being overwritten by the dead. All her life she had seen only whole people. In this eerie process of blacking out body parts on drawings and of seeing body parts and filling in the rest, it had become almost reflexive for her to look at a live person and mentally disassemble the body so that she was dealing with a collection of sundered parts. The system for retrieving memories about the most important thing in the world, other people, was being wrenched inside out.

Jessica was sitting in the cafeteria one day, watching a Marine eat. He wiped his mouth with a napkin. It came away with a red spot of ketchup on it. For some reason, the soldier put the used napkin into his pocket. Jess envisioned processing him, writing down "one scrunched up paper napkin containing a red stain." Then she would send the napkin home to his mother and his mother would wonder what it was, thinking about it year after year: Why put a napkin in your pocket? Was the stain blood? Jess became obsessed with thoughts about what would be sent home if she were killed. Eventually, she couldn't put anything into her pockets except the mandatory Rules of Engagement. She began thinking of herself as a corpse that would have to be processed, so she kept her tent and belongings pared down to a minimum for easy cataloging. She made sure that her name was on labels in her clothing. She wouldn't let anyone borrow her clothes for fear that the person might be killed and Jess would be reported dead. She was protecting her parents. Thus do we begin to see the entire world through the lens of trauma.

. . .

THERE ARE special cells in the brain called mirror neurons that
fire when you perform a specific action. But they also fire when you
see someone else perform that action. As with emotions, some of
the responses of mirror neurons are innate and others are learned.
The baby is born with mirror neurons that allow her to imitate
the expression she sees on someone else's face. If you see someone
accidentally slice off the tip of a finger while chopping carrots, your
mirror neurons cause you to wince in pain. It looks to your brain
as if you're slicing off the tip of your own finger. Mirror neurons
make it possible for you to feel what someone else is feeling. They
are the reason that some people not only can play air guitar but feel
compelled to do so. These networks of cells are part of the complex
system of subconscious communication that binds the family and
community together. And mirror neurons are the reason you feel
pain when something bad happens to someone else.

Faces are the most powerful conveyors of emotion, of the very
information that we must have for our survival. The face is the only
place on the body where skin attaches directly to muscle. That gives
the face the ability to convey extremely subtle gradations of emotion and even supersecret microexpressions that we feel but cannot consciously see, because they happen too fast. In fact, the only
reason to have a face is to express emotion. Almost every day, Jess
had to look at the faces of the dead with their myriad expressions
of anger, of serenity, horror, terror. And that completely scrambled
Jess's emotional system and her mental models of faces in general.
The members of Mortuary Affairs tried to look at faces as little as
possible, but we are born ready to look at faces. The instinct to do so
is irresistible. So although Jess grew more used to the broken bodies, even as her weight dropped to 100 pounds on her five-foot-nine-
inch frame, she grew more and more sensitized to the heads. One
day they opened a body bag to find that it was filled with nothing
but heads. A bag full of faces.

As her emotional system tried to adapt, the dead began assembling themselves into animated beings and to populate the bun-

ker where she worked. It wasn't just Jess. "We all started hearing and feeling the souls of the dead," she wrote. "They were in the bunker with us." One night she was the only one awake, standing watch. One of her duties was to go outside and refuel the generators that ran the refrigeration to keep the bodies cold. As she crossed the barren ground in the black of night, she could hear the dead walking around her. She could feel their presence. On another night, she heard the door of the bunker open and close. She froze. Then she heard footsteps. She could see no one. One night her whole team slept in the bunker because there was supposed to be an attack. There weren't enough cots, so some people tried to sleep on the litters that they used to carry the dead. "We set them up and some of the guys tried to settle in, but none could. Suddenly, one Marine flew off his litter as though he had been catapulted. He swore he had been pushed off." They huddled together in a corner for the entire night.

We create the beings of others in our heads, our bodies. And much of what they are to us is represented in the subterranean parts of the brain, the frog and the rat. But this part of the brain also has access to the sensory and motor parts, so in abnormal or traumatic circumstances, those spirits (for that's what they feel like) can rise up to distribute sensory information, to give us smells and sounds and sights that are not necessarily happening in the world outside our bodies.

The members of Mortuary Affairs were considered pariahs. No one wanted to be near them. They smelled of death. Anyway, no one wanted to think about getting blown up. So Jess and her team dealt with the dead more than the living, and that etched an entirely new emotional landscape out of which they created the world of the dead that they were experiencing. Just when she thought she had seen the most terrible things possible, something worse happened. A body was brought in, and Jess and another Marine began preparing it. As they were working, she looked at the dead man and saw his chest move. He was still breathing. In a panic, she flew across the room and hid herself: It was one of the spirits come alive and it scared her quite literally out of her wits. She had no idea what to do.

After managing to calm down, they called the warrant officer and the doctor, who told them simply to wait and let the soldier die. Jess flew into a rage. But that's what they did. They let him die.

After eight months, Jess returned to the United States to find that everything had changed utterly. Nothing looked familiar. Everything was too bright, too loud, too fast, too busy and frightening. Everyone seemed fat and was eating too much. People were careless. They went headlong and heedless. They didn't seem to know how dangerous the world was.

Back at Camp Pendleton, she found that the men from Mortuary Affairs were not sleeping in their bunks. They were sleeping all together in a pile on the floor with the lights on. It made perfect sense with dead people walking around all night.

The flashbacks and nightmares started even before she ended her service as a Marine. She lay awake all night, sweating. She thought she still smelled like roasted flesh. She still couldn't eat. She felt crushing guilt over what she'd been a part of. She was not yet thinking explicitly about killing herself, so she did the next-best thing. She moved in with a boyfriend, a six-foot-two, 230-pound ex-Marine trapped in his own rage who might well do the job for her.

WHEN CHRIS LAWRENCE woke, he was surrounded by people who had strange accents. He drew the only logical conclusion: He was being held hostage. He began ripping out the tubes that had been stuck into him and fighting off the staff, trying to get up. It was his duty as a Marine to escape. Someone rushed away and returned with the commandant of the Marine Corps. Chris recognized him and the commandant talked him down, explaining that he'd been blown up in Iraq and was now back in the United States. Chris had been out cold for five days. Once he realized that he was in the National Naval Medical Center in Bethesda, he began frantically trying to find out what had happened to his boys, as he called them. He remembered nothing about his deployment in Iraq and just assumed that he'd been blown up while driving in a convoy, not on foot. But no one knew what had happened to him. He'd been airlifted to them as a casualty, and that was all. It was months before Chris learned the details.

Slowly, over those months, he pieced together the story that he now told me in that diner in Milwaukee with all the patrons stealing glances at the bionic giant. And he did it with such skill and insouciance that it seemed as if he'd never had amnesia at all.

That beautiful day in Iraq. That Caribbean island in the Euphrates that Chris wanted to buy when the war was over. The "not right" man they encountered had placed a bomb beneath one of the steel plates that covered the gaps between the pontoons. Another man was hiding somewhere, watching them. A third man held the remotely controlled detonator. "The radioman is always your best target," Chris explained, "because the person next to the radio is the most important person. Also if you take out the radio, they have no way to communicate." So if Chris hadn't been generous, if he hadn't taken the radio from the fat kid, he would not have been blown up.

As Chris was crossing the bridge, walking now some distance behind his staff sergeant, he put his left foot down on the metal plate and swung his right foot across the sheet of steel. When the bomb went off, Chris actually left footprints in the half-inch steel. The blast blew the heel off his right foot and liquefied the ligaments and tendons, shattering the bones into crazed splinters. The concussion destroyed the bones in his left foot and broke his leg in several places. As his comrades watched in horror, he was launched into the air as high as the tops of the palm trees, more than 30 feet. "They said it looked like somebody had just tossed a GI Joe into the air." Chris was actually conscious throughout. He saw himself falling toward the earth and put out his left arm to break the fall. That move probably helped save his life. The shock absorbed by his arm splintered all the bones, turning that arm to mush. He also suffered internal injuries and more broken bones on his left side. Once he hit the ground, the ingrained reflexes of Marine Corps training kicked in, those dark behavioral scripts: He tried to get up and get ready to fight with his rifle. But his rifle had simply ceased to exist. He was Rambo with an air guitar.

"They thought I was dead until they saw me get up and start screaming," he said. "I was insanely lucky. If they'd placed the bomb anywhere other than under a steel plate, I'd be pink mist right now." It appears that Chris actually took a ride on the blast wave, staying pretty much ahead of it. The mass of the steel plate slowed the blast's progress and protected him. His sergeant, on his way to wish his daughter happy birthday, walked some distance ahead of Chris, so he was more severely injured.

Just as Chris's injury had to be carefully constructed and meticulously orchestrated by combining many small details, so did his survival. The vehicles had just come back from a milk run and were still running. The soldiers in and around the vehicles still had all their equipment on, so they were able to rush over to give Chris first aid within moments of the blast. If the vehicles had been five minutes farther away, he would have bled out and died. Another piece of luck involved where Chris was standing when the bomb went off. If it had gone off a second earlier, he would have been launched into the water. He would have drowned. Through yet another remarkable piece of luck, a helicopter just happened to be orbiting overhead and was able to land within minutes. If everything went just wrong to get him blown up, then everything went just right to save his life.

AT BETHESDA, the doctors concentrated on Chris's internal organs, which were badly injured and threatening his life. He had suffered damage to his liver, kidneys, and spleen. He still had both legs at that point, and the doctors worked on the bones as best they could. His left arm was so bad that they considered amputating it, along with the left foot, which was completely shattered. But Chris was dead set against amputation. After three months, the Navy transferred him to San Diego to begin therapy. When it came time for him to start walking, his right foot fell apart. It simply wouldn't knit back together. But Chris was determined to walk on his own legs again and was adamant about saying no to amputation. He was going to tough this out. So the therapists gave him a walker.

"Twenty-one years old on a walker," he said to me with a shake of his head, as if to say: Pathetic. "I was messed up."

At that point, his ex-girlfriend showed up again and said, "Hey, let's get married!"

His attitude was: "Well, I'm in a walker. Nobody's ever going to want me, so I might as well get married."

Then something strange happened. "I began watching the amputees. They'd arrive in January. They were walking by March. And they were out by May. Five months. I'd already spent longer than that in the hospital. Then I saw them doing backflips and running on treadmills and tackling people, and I'm like: Wow. I've got two legs, they've got one. What the hell?" As he began talking to the amputees, he met people who had gone through experiences similar to his. The real leg was too badly injured. It would never get better. And Chris did something that is key to successful adaptation in the aftermath of trauma: He gave himself permission to be flexible. He agreed to have his right leg amputated in March of 2008. His left leg was injured badly enough that they had to cut the toes off. "I never regretted it," he said. He was fitted with the prosthesis in May. It was such a relief to have it that Chris was up and about almost immediately. He now considers it his good leg. His attitude was that his hand was messed up, but "good enough. Long-sleeve shirt and pants, you'd never know. I don't have any toes and my arm isn't all that great. I'm pretty broken down, but I can still do my job."

His physical injuries were under control at last. But he wasn't out of the woods. Almost as an afterthought, Chris told me, "I had a traumatic brain injury, PTSD, depression, and all that crap." He said that during his recuperation whole chunks of time, sometimes weeks, would disappear from his memory. He'd watch a movie and the next day say, "Hey, we should watch this movie." Because of Chris's exceptional intelligence, he has been more resilient in the face of traumatic brain injury. He has what Eagleman calls cognitive reserve. Some people with Alzheimer's disease never show symptoms of it because they have worked out their brains vigorously all their lives. They lose some brain power to Alzheimer's but have a lot in reserve, so they appear normal until autopsy. That reserve, wrote Eagleman, comes from "blanketing a problem with overlapping solutions."

In other words, Chris had more to lose and still came out above average. But it was because of the traumatic brain injury that he had no memory of talking to me on the phone and agreeing to meet that day in June of 2011. "My memory's pretty shot," he said. Iraq exists for Chris as bits and pieces. "About today: What I remembered was that there was something going on today. What is it? I'm going to keep myself open for that something. Short-term is pretty darned well toast."

Chris had debilitating nightmares at first. The dreams were so realistic that his mother had to come to the hospital and talk him down and convince him that he wasn't still in Iraq. "I didn't sleep for weeks," he said. "Everything sounded so loud. I had anxiety attacks." But he had practiced self-control for his entire life, so when his heart would race, he'd "keep it calmed down." He also suffered from depression for the friends he had lost. "Right after I got hit, we lost six people. And they were close friends." Chris felt that if he had been there, he might have prevented their deaths. The Marine Corps would have allowed him to go back to Iraq, but he chose not to. And he still wakes up every morning wondering if he should have gone. Yet in that deep and secret place of knowing, that sixth sense that Chris now trusted, he understood that if he went back, he would either be killed or injured so badly that he could never work or enjoy life. Of leaving his fellow soldiers, he said, "Sometimes I feel guilty."

On the subject of post-traumatic stress, he said, "You're never going to be the same. You've just got to learn to live with how you are and let it not interfere with your life. I still am very vigilant, but I keep it under control." I noticed that when we entered the diner, he chose a booth in the middle of the room, with his back to the door. That didn't seem like something that a man suffering from post-traumatic stress would do. When I asked him about it, he said, "I can hear the door fine, so if somebody comes in, I know it." (Bizarrely, the explosion did not destroy his hearing.) "I'm still just as vigilant, but I don't let my issues run me. I run them." But there are times when he still struggles. When he goes out with his new girlfriend (the marriage didn't last), "I'm worse," he said. "Because she doesn't see with both eyes. She does not hear with her ears. She's a civilian." Referring to his fellow soldiers, he said, "When I'm out with my boys, it's like, I'm watching, you're watching, so who cares?" But by contrast, his girlfriend doesn't understand why Chris won't take her to nightclubs.

At first, Chris couldn't go into such places as Walmart. They were too loud, too bright, and there were too many people popping out from around blind corners. Many veterans never get past that. Chris reminded me of Micki. He would not slip below his Personal Scum Line. He said, "I like to overcome things. I don't like backing down from challenges. Here's a straw: Suck it up."

When I met him, Chris was working as a counselor for Veteran's Village of San Diego, a nonprofit organization aimed at keeping veterans off drugs and off the streets. Chris worked with soldiers returning from combat and helped get them back into the world. He was coming to the end of the grant that supported his work. I asked what he wanted to do next, and he said he wasn't sure. He had wanted to be an engineer before he went to war. "But then I look at it after my boys died and so many of my friends are dying over there, and I think: The real problems aren't with machines. The real problems are with society. The real problems are with people." He thought of going into politics but then realized that "most politicians get into it with the best of intentions, but then they lose themselves. You get past two terms and you have no soul."

He acknowledged that by all rights he should be dead and that the life he has is a gift. "I want to help," he said. "I just want to help people."

WHEN JESS GOODELL moved in with Miguel, the violent and abusive ex-Marine, she unwittingly put herself right back into the thick of the violence. One night, he hit her with a clock and shattered its glass case. On another night, he burst into their house in

St. Louis with an ax and threatened to chop up all their furniture. He told Jess that she hadn't been in the real war. He'd been part of the force that invaded Iraq in 2003.

It wasn't long before Jess was living in fear for her life and drinking all day long. She also began making subconscious preparations for suicide. Many times, people who are as yet unaware of their deeply hidden desire to kill themselves make a gesture of destroying something that represents the self. Jess buried her medals and ribbons in the back of a closet in the apartment. Because of how much her conception of herself had been wrapped up in those medals and in being a Marine, the act was like burying a proxy of her own identity. Reflecting on what she had done in Iraq filled her with shame. When the rage pathway runs long enough, it becomes fatigued, and you descend into depression. Miguel knew as well as Jess did that they couldn't go on. They parted at last and Jess drove east to New York State and crashed on her father's sofa. The nightmares continued to terrify her. She gave up sleeping. When her father couldn't stand to watch her destroy herself, Jess moved to her mother's house.

During the day, she'd find herself inexplicably back in Iraq, "processing an endless line of bodies that were no longer recognizable as such." She would drink so much that she'd vomit or black out on the floor. She'd wake with no idea where she was and no memory of arriving. Then drinking "became too much work," she wrote. So she switched to marijuana. She smoked all day long. And when that, too, stopped working for her, she turned to an activity long valued by her family. "I found my salvation in education," she told an interviewer in 2011.

She returned to Chautauqua, where she had grown up, and enrolled in college. She began filling herself up with knowledge, passionate to understand what was good and right and true. She read about war, nature, society. She read psychology and Socrates, Plato, Aristotle, and Thomas Aquinas. She began to see herself in the larger context of society and history. She began to see her problems as larger than herself. She began to look outward, for ways to help others who were suffering. She saw that "unearned self-esteem and narcissism . . . leave their victims anxious and depressed." In her struggles, she knew that she was not seeking normalcy. She just wanted to be able to get on with life, "to sleep and eat and work and, maybe, to one day laugh and love."

Jess started a group for veterans at school, and in taking that positive action, directed at a goal, she could feel a change within herself. She had actually taken control of something. The moment of vision in the survival journey may come to us in a way that we do not at first recognize amid the noise of our own anguish. We may feel it and let it pass only half noticed. But, like children, we store away what we cannot yet understand and then take it out in the fullness of time to examine it and to find the truth in it. Two years before, Jess had gone to a meeting of a group of veterans at the VA. Some of the men had poured their hearts out to her, and it had moved her deeply. She was so stunned and shell-shocked at the time that she hadn't been able to consciously absorb the significance of what she was witnessing. But now the stored emotional impact, the buried memory of what they'd said, returned to her in full force. In her own group of veterans, she saw that she could take sustenance from helping others like herself.

Jess Goodell is several years ahead of Chris Lawrence in the process of rebuilding. She still thinks daily of the torn flesh she held in her hands, the shredded bodies of sons and daughters, the things she shipped home to explode someone's life and then to expand in ever wider rings in a tsunami of grief and trauma. She was moving forward, but hers was a tentative progress. Yet she now seems to have found footing on a path that might sustain her. She is involved in a number of efforts to help others, including working at a food bank, helping refugees from Iraq get on their feet in Boston, and working with Marines at the hospital. She began to have good days when she could feel things she thought had been dead inside her. But a key component of her ability to rebuild was her commitment to deeply pursue education. Learning is its own reward as far as the brain is concerned. It deeply activates the dopamine reward pathways. As of this writing, Jess is on her way to getting a PhD so that she can help people who are suffering from post-traumatic stress.

It's too soon to tell how Chris Lawrence will do. He suffered a traumatic brain injury and Jess did not. As a result, it's an open question whether he could do the same educational work that she is doing. But he has all the qualities of character, all the strength and resolve, of someone who will use his experience to make him stronger. And he has the main characteristics of someone who can render his new life decipherable. He is able to laugh at himself. He is dedicated to helping. He has strong social support. He's acutely aware of how lucky he is, and he feels true gratitude. When he wakes up each morning, he knows that it's a miracle. He is humble and maintains his cool. He's willing to take risks to better himself (he had his leg cut off). And he does not strike me, nor did he strike the Marine Corps, as someone who will roll over and quit. As I left him in Milwaukee, he said he'd soon be heading back to San Diego. Then he was going to drive his motorcycle across the United States with some friends. He said he'd look me up in Chicago.

Looking ahead, I can imagine those two beautiful people nurturing the pieces of their selves back together and creating out of their experiences individuals who would otherwise not have existed on this earth. New people who are deep and wise beyond their years. And I see those two touching many other lives and making them better. What I see is not just hope but hope made real by action.

SIX

WANT IT, NEED IT, HAVE IT: OF PHANTOM LIMBS AND CHILDREN

LET'S SAY YOU have a five-year-old daughter named Grace. You're still asleep in the morning when Grace climbs into bed and snuggles up to you. Your heart leaps at her arrival, and the two of you giggle and laugh and kiss and then you settle down to read *The Travels of Babar.* Your emotional reaction creates a shape like a bell, a hill, a rise in the landscape of what you feel. Her arrival starts things happening in your body. It is a happy event, and yet the things that happen to you now look curiously like the things that happened to Eileen with the arrival of a crocodile or what happened to Micki when the shark attacked. Your muscles become more toned, cortisol enters your bloodstream, adrenaline, too. Your heart rate increases. Special chemicals called neurotransmitters are released in your brain to speed up your thinking and perceptions.

There are also some differences. Your eyes dilate when you see someone you love, and the room literally looks brighter. That's why people say, "Grace lights up the room." Oxytocin, the chemical of bonding and love, enters your bloodstream. Your reaction rises to the point where you and Grace laugh and kiss and begin to settle down. Then, slowly, all those physical and chemical processes return to the level where they began. Hippocrates pointed out that this is also the shape made by the course of an illness. The invading organism attacks. Your body fights it in rising action. The climax comes when the fever breaks. And then your body returns to its normal state once more.

Throughout each day, you experience that same emotional shape over and over. Most of the responses are small. You don't even notice many of them. Some are pleasurable: Maybe you find out that Copper River salmon, your favorite, has just arrived at Whole Foods. Some responses are the opposite: You might break a dish or stub your toe. Other events bring on a larger and more long-lasting response. You get a call saying your best friend is coming to town. You might feel good all day and then experience that feeling anew every time you think about it. You say your heart skips a beat, and that is the jolt of adrenaline you feel. But that's a happy jolt. It could be the very same jolt but with a very different interpretation if, for example, you fall and break your wrist. In addition to the pain and the inconvenience, you're going to need weeks of rehabilitation. You might ruminate on that, beating yourself up for not being more careful. You might get angry and decide to sue someone. But each response has a reassuring predictability about it. You know your own feelings and your left brain can easily come up with explanations for them. We like things that are predictable. Predictability is one of the most important factors in lowering stress. And while a little stress is good, too much can be poison, as we have seen.

We are born with certain emotional responses. We may call them reflexes or instincts. For example, an infant nuzzles and nurses from birth. That's the emotional response to the proximity of her mother. Scientists who study the brain make a distinction between emotion and feeling. An emotion is an automatic physical response aimed at survival. Most of the behaviors that we call instincts are actually emotional responses.

Feeling is our opinion about an emotional reaction. It's a bit mysterious how the same thing can feel so good or so bad, depending on circumstances. A racing heart can feel terrific if you've just seen your beloved rushing toward you across a springtime meadow. Or it can feel awful if you're hurrying to pick up Grace because someone at her school has called to say that she has a fever.

When the baby nuzzles and nurses at her mother's breast, she feels pleasure. Joy. Yum. That feeling marks the event, gives it an emotional label, the gut feeling that tells her its significance: This is good. That's what the neuroscientist Antonio Damasio calls a somatic marker. Everything surrounding the experience is labeled by the broad flashlight beam of the emotional system. The baby survives by repeating behavior that's been marked as good. The mother does the same. Allowing the baby to nurse stimulates the powerful system of rewards in the mother's brain. Dopamine. Oxytocin. And the body's own heroin: endorphins and enkephalins. This system is built on many of the same components of reward that inspired the mother to make the baby in the first place. Thus do mother and child build a new shared emotional system. They literally create each other. This is why the worst thing that can happen to you is for something to happen to your child.

A baby can imitate people from birth. A newborn baby opens her mouth when you open yours. She sticks out her tongue if you stick yours out. This is the first step in coupling memory and emotion as a way of investigating the world. It's remarkable, too, for a newborn to mimic facial expressions, since she has yet to see her own face. It's because of the innate ability conferred by mirror neurons. Mirror neurons bind people together into a society and create culture by forcing people to imitate each other. Mirror neurons are the biological substrate of empathy.

A baby is born understanding that it's very important to know about other people and to bond with them. At about three months, she begins flirting. She coos and smiles when you smile and talk to her. She even understands that talking requires taking turns. She listens while you talk and then talks while you listen. She tries to say the words you say but doesn't yet have the physical skill to get it right. She begins to match her facial expressions and body language with yours. About the time a baby learns to sit up, her horizon expands to include all the objects in her world. Her mirror neurons and emotional system begin to learn a vast array of new responses. They are mapped onto innate responses, such as grasping. Many inborn patterns of movement start to become refined by her will and her perceptions. She wants things. She needs things with a hunger that is mapped onto real feelings of hunger for food. She takes things. She learns what things mean. For example: The rattle excites her nervous system because it makes noise when she shakes it. The spastic quaking that besets her muscles even before birth is refined into the deliberate rhythmic shaking of the rattle. One of the very first coherent statements that my elder daughter, Elena, uttered was, "Want it, need it, have it." Said with all passion and intensity. And that statement pretty much sums it all up, not just for us as babies but for the rest of our lives as well.

At one year of age, she begins pointing. She looks where you point and expects you to look where she points. She's using people to find out about the world. If you put something new and interesting in front of a one-year-old, she first looks at you to gauge your reaction to it. Are you afraid of the new thing? Does it please you? Through mirror neurons that tell her how you feel, the baby takes your cue and acts accordingly. She shows great depth of understanding. Babies are not little Munchkins, cute but mindless pets. They are deep and serious. They are profound and very close to pure genius. A baby picks up a toy phone, pushes the buttons, and puts it to her ear, even though the toy phone does nothing. She even imitates talking on the phone. The conversation sounds like this: Da-da-da-da-da-da-da-da-da-da-da. Yet it is inflected like real speech. Babies know more than we can imagine.

In one experiment done at the University of Washington, Andrew Meltzoff showed a box to a one-year-old. When Meltzoff touched his forehead to the box, the box lit up. He took the box away. The child didn't see it for another week. But when Meltzoff presented it again, the baby immediately touched his forehead to it to make it light up. For a whole week, the one-year-old remembered and waited and was ready when opportunity presented itself. Through this continuous process, babies are making and storing new mental models and emotional labels for them at a furious pace.

Thus do we build and then rebuild our emotional systems. We make cognitive maps that embody people and objects. We connect them with emotional landscapes that tell us how we should feel about those objects and people and what they're good for. All of this activity is aimed at getting us around in the world, successfully, perhaps even joyously. And from the start, our brains and emotions and actions are intricately entwined with those of other people. We embody other people, especially those we love. We use them to learn about the world and then carry them through all our days while we do the things we do. They inscribe their emotional meaning on our brains and weave them into the fabric of our bodies, which respond with the feelings we have for those people.

NOW LET'S say that something terrible happens. Something so horrible and shocking that it is literally unthinkable, as in: You never think about it and perhaps have never even considered it as a possibility. This means that it is completely unpredictable. This also means that there is no way to prepare yourself for it. It comes like the crocodile out of the deep and takes your head in its jaws. It bites like the shark. It is the most stressful event possible.

Ann Hood is a writer. By chance, she and I share the same literary agent and publisher. In the spring of 2002, Ann's five-year-old daughter Grace came home from kindergarten one afternoon and lay on the couch, woozy and burning up with a fever. Ann took Grace's temperature. It was 105. She called the pediatrician, who told her to take Grace to the emergency room. Months later, Ann would wonder why the doctor was so quick and sure in her response. After all, Grace's symptoms sounded like the flu. The doctor told Ann that it was something in her voice. Ann had read something in Grace that was beyond logical thought, something from deep within the systems of unconscious memory. She knew something was seriously wrong, but she could not say why. Like recognizing keys by the tinkling sound they make, the doctor had read that same thing in Ann's voice over the phone. That shows the power of the unconscious systems are of mental models and human mimicry and the emotional contagion enabled by mirror neurons. Using the subliminal sensory systems that give rise to the sixth sense, we catch one another's emotional states. Ann's response was just like Chris Lawrence's when he said, "That ain't right."

But the hospital staff was not tuned into that stream of information. They couldn't see anything terribly wrong with Grace. They thought she had the flu. They gave her Tylenol and left her and Ann in a treatment room. Then Grace had a seizure, and the staff began to pay attention. They took X-rays, sampled blood and spinal fluid, gave her an EKG and an EEG, trying to eliminate as many illnesses as possible. They could find nothing wrong. Her fever began coming down. Although Ann was terrified because Grace wouldn't wake up, the doctors told her that it was normal. She'd had a high fever that had caused the seizure. Children sleep after such an episode. They told Ann that Grace would spend the night in the hospital and be back in school in a day or two. They moved Grace out of emergency and into a room of her own. But when they put her back on the monitors, Ann could see that her fever was rising once again. The nurse went to get more Tylenol.

While a baby is building her emotional system, watching, imitating, exploring the world through her mother, it's not a one-way process. The child is also building new spaces inside the mother's brain. Through their interaction, mother and child build these spaces. These are real physical spaces filled with neurons and cell assemblies that are dedicated to the child, that are owned by the child. It isn't one particular area of the brain that the child occupies. The child's colonies in the mother's brain are like an archipelago of neural networks that involve sight, smell, touch, hearing, and many more subtle and unconscious channels of communication, such as pheromones and the microexpressions of the face that pass too quickly to blossom into consciousness but are registered in the intense subterranean log of memory by the emotional system. This is the log to which the sixth sense refers. When Chris saw the man on the bridge who was intent on killing him, he was reading microexpressions on the man's face and smelling the stress boiling off of him. I sometimes call this channel of communication The Stream. This mutual, dynamic interaction, this sharing of space in the brains of mother and child, communicates important information—joy, happiness, sadness, pain, distress—so that the mother can respond appropriately to serve the baby. When babies flirt, they are involved in this mutual mapping. For the baby to be healthy and content, the mother must gaze upon her and communicate with specific body language. Mothers throughout the world tilt their heads in the same characteristic way when looking at their babies.

Thus do mothers appear to have extrasensory perceptions about a child. It's not extrasensory. It comes through the senses. But it's so finely tuned, it's so subtle and fast, it can seem telepathic at times, especially since it operates over the horizon beyond conscious thought. Now, looking at Grace in the hospital bed, Ann could tell that something was drastically wrong. But in the world of scientific logic that was the hospital, she had no way of articulating what she knew. The information she was receiving wasn't on that literal, stepwise channel of the frontal lobes. It was coming through the emotional space in her brain that Grace owned. It was coming through The Stream. Ann sensed the discord between their mutual emotional maps, the clash of mirror neurons. The mimicry they had practiced for years to synchronize their emotional systems was no longer working.

At that moment, a family friend, Andy Green, who was a doctor in that same hospital, stopped by the room. Dr. Green had spent a great deal of time with Grace and he, too, had a space in his brain for her, as he did for his own children and for Grace's brother Sam, a close friend of Dr. Green's daughter. When he saw Grace and then saw Ann, he immediately knew what Ann knew. He grabbed the phone and called the intensive-care unit, and moments later doctors and nurses burst into the room. Ann looked up and saw that both her husband and Dr. Green were weeping. This made no sense. It made even less sense when the attending physician turned to Ann and said, "Your daughter is not going to make it." It made so little sense that Ann laughed out loud.

One of the main jobs of the emotional system is to teach us the rules of our world and the best responses to it. In other words, it teaches us how to make decisions, whether they are conscious or automatic. We learn the things and the people in our world and how they interact, and we learn the rules of their behavior. Babies who are involved in this process find it satisfying and comforting and even joyful when the world behaves in those predictable ways. We grow up expecting that to continue. When the world doesn't behave by those familiar rules, we often laugh, as when we see something impossible happen, say, in a magic show or a circus. In the center ring, a dozen clowns emerge from a car that's no bigger than a washing machine. The impossible can seem funny.

Laughter can be part of an emotional response, but it can also interrupt one or hold it at bay. Laughter can be a defense against an emotional response to something that completely violates and undermines all the rules of the world that we've ever learned. It can be a signal to the self and to others that what appears to be an emergency is really a false alarm. (Laughing at slapstick is this sort of response. We know that the pratfall isn't really harmful.) Laughter quiets the amygdala. So Ann laughed at the impossible thing the doctor said. The unthinkable thing. On a neurological level, her laughter said: This is not happening.

When the doctor said "We need to intubate her," Ann shifted into a second defensive strategy. She was overcome by the eerie feeling that she was in one of those television shows about a hospital, *ER* or *Grey's Anatomy.* Ann knew her world. She knew all the rules and how everyone and everything in that world behaved. Since this could not be that familiar world, it must be make-believe. And the only mental models she had for such a pretend world came from watching television. Ann had literally found herself plunged into an alien landscape where there were no familiar landmarks. All her maps, her mental models, were suddenly rendered invalid. She was, in a very real sense, lost. As lost as one could be in a real wilderness with no map or compass.

Now her emotional system raced out of control, trying to match something in that alien world with her familiar mental models.

She heard her own voice scream, "What is going on?" And with that, the doctors and nurses wheeled her daughter down the hall and away.

Ann found herself in a trauma room in the ICU with teams of professionals working on Grace, urgently, futilely, throughout the night. When a doctor explained that he would have to operate on Grace, Ann found her mind incapable of even comprehending the words. The raging response from her emotional system was disrupting her frontal lobes, as rocketing stress hormones made it impossible for her to think. She literally felt that she could understand nothing anyone was telling her. Time passed as in a dream. Beyond the curtains, light came and went and came again as the entire world somehow went on out there.

Then something wonderful happened. "Something changed," Ann wrote. "The atmosphere in the room slowed." She heard a nurse laugh. Grace's blood pressure and her kidney and liver functions were all returning to normal. They referred to her as "out of the woods." The formerly grim doctor announced, "Your daughter's going to be fine." The drama was over. The shape of the normal emotional response, the shape of both drama and disease, seemed to have run its course, reached its climax, and was now on its way to subsiding.

Ann hadn't slept in two days. As relief washed over her, she fell asleep in a chair beside Grace's bed. She had no idea how long she had slept when the lights went on and people began crowding into the room again. She leapt up to find a nurse telling her, "We're losing Grace." She was forced out of the room and watched helplessly through a window as the team worked frantically once again. Then she heard the call for a cardiologist, the announcement that Grace's heart had stopped. The cardiologist came, but Grace was dead. She had died from a fast-moving form of streptococcus bacterium that invades the bloodstream and destroys the organs. Sweet and beautiful Grace, healthy, happy, active, smart. Dead at the age of five. Just like that.

. . .

THE ARMS are very important. The arms and the hands. The child in your arms makes the space in your brain. New connections form among neurons, new assemblies of cells that hunger to be occupied by the child. Your skin is a sheet of sensory nerve cells that burn their map, point to point, into the surface of your brain. Your fingers inscribe a map of the child that can be read, that must be read, by that sensing area of your brain. Those maps are infused with meaning through your emotional system so that the fingers and hands and arms crave the ecstatic touch of the child. This keeps mother and child together so that the child can nurse and live and build her own body, and, with it, an emotional system.

The brain has three general pathways for information: the What Pathway (what am I seeing?), the Where Pathway (where is it and where am I?), and the So What Pathway (is it good or bad?). The Where Pathway in the parietal lobe of your brain knows the extent of the child, where she is in space, and precisely where your hands and arms must go to hold her. You can lose your keys because they have no emotional claim on you. You cannot lose your child. Once those maps are engraved, you can't lose the child even if she's gone. Neurologically speaking, the child becomes another limb, an organ. The child's heart beats within you and the beating continues for life. The heat of the child's metabolism radiates through you and then shines like the sun upon you once she's born.

As the child grows, the space she occupies in you gradually changes. Physical changes take place in the parietal lobe to encompass the larger body, as motor and sensory areas record the new movements. The emotional system takes in a walking, talking child and illuminates those new behaviors with feelings of joy. You have less and less opportunity to hold or carry the child, but your brain follows her wherever she goes and accordingly redraws the map of her. Her sun still shines on you. She sits in your lap and your brain creates a new space for that, new maps of her size and shape, new mental models for the feel of her hair, the tingle of her smell. A special space holds her face, her voice. A group of cells in your temporal lobe waits like a flame tucked away in a transept. It bursts to life at the sight of her. She lights up the entire cathedral of emotion.

With the child alive and happy and walking around, robust with laughter, one joy seamlessly merges with another as the widely dispersed parts of the brain renew their sights, sounds, touches, smells, emotions, and feelings. The maps grow and fade and blend. They evolve. The child turns your brain like a kaleidoscope and the colored crystals shift, creating new patterns all the time. New spaces develop in the brain to contain the child in her new form. But what happens when, like a chain saw severing an arm by mistake, the child dies? Still small enough to hold in your lap. What happens to the spaces in your brain that she created? The arms are important because if the mother doesn't hold the baby, the human race ceases to exist. Mothers know this terrible truth without even thinking about it, because it exists in a place where thinking is afraid to go. Just as Aron Ralston was afraid to think how painful it was going to be to cut that last nerve connecting his hand to his brain.

Ann Hood said that her arms became the same as the phantom limbs that people find so excruciating after an amputation. The physical pain from her arms would wake her at night. The space in the brain that the child creates has such powers. It's not metaphorical. It's real. A good deal of the effect has to do with the way the parietal lobe makes maps of the body and of the body's interactions with the world. If you cut off a real arm, a brain scan reveals the profound changes that take place in the map of that arm. Just as you can't lose the child, you can't lose your own arm. The arm in the brain doesn't go away, even when the real arm is gone. If you decide to move your arm, a strip of cells on the top of your head called the motor cortex sends a signal to the arm: the intention to move. The same signal is also sent to the parietal lobe, which creates the image you have of your body and its orientation in space. The parietal lobe also helps correct mistakes and fine-tune the movements you make. This and other structures (including the cerebellum) are constantly helping track not only the body but the objects the body encounters. This system operates when you play golf, for example, and all the sensory feedback has a familiar place in mental models, ready and waiting in your brain: the heft of the club, the thrill of the grass, the smooth swinging sensation, the crack of the ball, even the smells involved in the game become incorporated into this elaborate complex of neural and muscular activities. The nervous system creates maps that include the golf club and ball and even the distance to the hole. An avid golfer learns to hunger for a game. That's because your nervous system grows, in effect, into the golf club the way a virtuoso's nervous system grows into the violin and the bow. The instrument exists in multiple maps in the brain, and those maps are entwined with the emotional system and other areas involved with appetites (which simply means meeting the demands of survival, such as satisfying hunger and thirst). This hunger is not a metaphor. It's real and physical. A veteran of the Vietnam War who suffered from chronic post-traumatic stress said, "I want to have a gun in my hands so bad at night it makes my arms ache." He would have understood Ann's pain.

With no signals coming from the amputated arm, the cell assemblies and networks in the brain that represented the arm hunger for the lost arm. The brain can still send signals telling the arm to move, but of course there is no arm. But the parietal lobe still listens in on those signals. It has no way to know that the signals aren't being sent to a real arm. The parietal lobe assumes that the arm is still there and that creates a phantom limb. The Where Pathway still knows where the arm is. When the real arm doesn't move and therefore doesn't send signals to the parietal lobe confirming its movement, it feels like a paralyzed arm. And that hurts like a never-ending cramp. V. S. Ramachandran, a neuroscientist at the University of California, relieves this pain in his patients by having them try to move the amputated arm while watching in a mirror as the intact arm moves. When an amputee sees the image in the mirror, it appears that he's actually moving the missing limb. That visual feedback confirms, at last, that the amputated arm is moving, and the painful sensation goes away. The useful illusion of a unified self is restored.

Five years of constant sensation from Grace through Ann's hands and arms were cut off with Grace's death. The complex systems in the brain that organized and watched over those interactions continued to do their work, creating the excruciating hunger and anguish and the real sensation of phantom limbs and physical pain.

In the case of a real amputation, no signals of feeling come back from the missing arm. But the brain won't simply let those landscapes of neurons starve. The sensory cells on either side invade the map of the arm and take it over, mingling their sensations with those of the absent arm. On the surface of the brain is a sensory map of the body, that point-to-point representation of the sheet of skin surrounding the body. The cells that allow you to feel touch from your head, hands, knees, feet, and every bit of your external body lie neatly arranged on a strip running down the middle of the top surface of your brain. The nerve cells that sense the hands are right next to the area for the face (perhaps representing fetal position). Many people who lose an arm begin to feel a touch on the cheek as a touch on the missing hand. The missing limb never really goes away. If the maps in your brain don't match the real things in the world, people think you're insane. Having a map in your brain of someone real who suddenly vanishes from the world will make you feel insane.

You want to get over it. You want to get through it to the other side, which you hope will look like the place where you started, the place before the bad thing happened. Because of the structure of the brain, the emotional system, that's not possible. Because we save everything, for better or worse. Memory accumulates, the bad with the good, the pain with the pleasure. It's all uniquely ours. Ann had gone through a wormhole, a tear in the fabric of space. She was now in a parallel universe.

WHAT IF everything in your life that once gave you pleasure suddenly became a source of excruciating pain? What if every joy turned, as if by an evil curse, into grief? Is that even possible? How would you cope with it if a warm and sunny day in April made you shiver uncontrollably and the sight of the first flowers in your garden made you want to run through traffic? Suppose that hearing the music you always loved sent you to bed, where you had to pull the covers over your head and spend the rest of the day hiding, sobbing. The maps that Grace created in Ann's brain had become intimately woven, like phantom hands, through all the things she loved. Touching any one of them set the entire system aflame. Her world became toxic and anything in it—a book, the sound of a telephone, nail polish, something glittery—could send her into a frenzy of grief and anguish. "Out in the world," Ann wrote, "there are only five-year-old girls holding their mothers' hands wherever I go."

How could Ann get on with her life? She was a writer and she couldn't sit down to write. She couldn't even read. She carried a diary with her. Someone said that keeping a journal would be a good idea. Ann sat and wrote the word "fuck" in it over and over. She had seen the grief counselors. She had been dragged to yoga and meditation classes. She'd talked to the ministers, social workers, therapists, and all the friends imaginable. Well meaning. Spouting platitudes. ("She's in a better place.") Piling food on her doorstep. All well and good, but nothing seemed to calm the alarm that was screaming in her head 24 hours a day. This is the animal howl born 10 million years ago in the African forestland. And a feedback loop in Ann's more complex and sophisticated brain caused that alarm to become stuck, like the car horn after the auto accident, so that now everything set it off. It was a cruel and bizarre twist of biology in which the emotional system, so good at identifying danger, had been given a chance to identify everything associated with Grace as lethal. So at the sight of a pair of leopard-patterned rain boots or the sound of a Beatles song, Ann was thrown into the cauldron of rage once again. She literally couldn't boil pasta, because that had been one of Grace's favorite foods.

A certain type of seagull goes mad if you place a red egg in her nest. This is because the color red sets off her rage pathway, while the shape of an egg activates her nesting instinct. She must simultaneously attack and nurture. And the brain, even the brain of a bird, is arranged so that it's impossible to do both at the same time. That sort of conflict was contributing to Ann Hood's misery.

The very objects of her world had been imbued with the nurturing instinct that she had so lavishly directed onto Grace. But now the attack on Grace caused those objects to set off the rage instinct that would protect Grace from harm, as Ann fought back as if against a shark, a crocodile. Fever and cancer.

With steroids and adrenaline flooding her system, Ann would fall asleep and be right back in the hospital in a nightmare. She would wake to her own screams. Her emotional system was trying to consolidate memory through dreams. If you don't dream, you forget. And although we may want to forget, the biological system that evolved for our survival insists on doing its work. The more information you are given in any given day, the more you dream about it. And in that hospital, Ann had taken on more information than she had ever been forced to swallow. Lots of rapid-eye-movement sleep, the kind where we dream, consolidates certain kinds of information better than deeper sleep (called slow-wave sleep). But memory was the major source of stress for Ann, and that stress was dumping more steroids into her system. Steroids interrupt sleep. The result: lighter sleep with less real rest and more nightmares, trapping her in another feedback loop. The combined effects of stress and sleep deprivation meant that her frontal lobes and hippocampus were both impaired: She couldn't think straight or remember new things clearly. Ann was faced with the horrifying prospect that she might never get out of that living hell. She could see no reasonable path. There seemed no fitting therapy. She had run away from her panic on a trip to San Francisco, to France, but the relief had been slight, temporary. The thing she battled was inside her. And then she tried something completely different.

"Knitting saved my life," Ann wrote.

Knitting?

When I first heard that, it seemed hard to believe. It seemed too trivial. Or perhaps a myth of pop psychology. In fact, the first time someone suggested to Ann that she take up knitting, she dismissed the idea. Anyway, she claimed, she was not good with her hands. But friends persisted, and she finally gave in. What she found was remarkable.

To understand how knitting could have saved Ann's life, it might help to know a little bit about Tourette's syndrome. That may seem too odd to be believed as well, but I'm going to suggest that there are important similarities between what afflicted Ann and what afflicts someone with Tourette's. Tourette's is part of the continuum of conditions involving obsession and anxiety. And in the wake of severe trauma, we tend to look like someone on that same continuum, obsessing and suffering anxiety just like someone with a real organic disorder of the brain. So let's see if we can make sense of a convergence of Ann Hood with a person who has Tourette's syndrome.

SEVEN

SEE ONE, DO ONE, TEACH ONE: THE SECRET OF SEEKING

IN 1825, THE FIRST case of Tourette's syndrome was described by Jean Marc Gaspard Itard in France. His patient was the Marquise de Dampierre. "In the midst of a conversation that interests her extremely," Itard wrote, "all of a sudden, without being able to prevent it, she interrupts what she is saying or what she is listening to with bizarre shouts and with words that are more extraordinary and which make a deplorable contrast with her intellect and her distinguished manners." Itard didn't follow up on that work. But some decades later, George Gilles de la Tourette continued the study of people who suffered from such symptoms. People suffering from Tourette's may experience involuntary grimacing, facial twitching, and blinking. They may lunge out spasmodically, punching and grasping, and walk with an odd, jerking gait. They might make unintentional noises, clearing their throats repeatedly, snorting, and even growling and howling. Sometimes those vocalizations involve strings of expletives. Tourette's is characterized by compulsions, mimicry, repetition, obsessions, and a tendency toward bizarre humor and play. Those with Tourette's may also be tormented by sexual compulsions and uncontrollable aggression. People with Tourette's are often imprisoned rather than treated.

Oliver Sacks, the renowned neurologist and author, met a surgeon named Carl Bennett who suffered from Tourette's. It should be
fairly clear by now that the words "surgeon" and "Tourette's" don't
seem to go together. Sacks traveled all the way to British Columbia
to see for himself how someone beset by such a wide array of involuntary physical movements could possibly function in the operating room. They met at the airport and Bennett drove Sacks home.
Sacks described the surgeon's "odd, rapid skipping walk, with a skip
each fifth step and sudden reachings to the ground as if to pick
something up." As Bennett drove, he displayed involuntary behaviors, such as smoothing his mustache, adjusting his glasses, aligning his knee with the steering wheel. Bennett would jerk his arm
out suddenly, and repeatedly touch the windshield while squeaking
and squealing in an odd high voice.

Ann, too, was beset by a variety of involuntary actions, such as
sobbing, writhing, startling, and flinching. Her symptoms were
certainly different from Bennett's, but her sphere of control had also
clearly been destroyed or distorted. For example, she did not make
a conscious decision to become dirty, yet her clothes and hair went
unwashed. She had no rational concept that led her to sit for hours
on end, unable to stop herself from working on a jigsaw puzzle. She
knew it was not like her to lie in bed all day watching *Sex in the
City*. Nor did she wish to drive to the cemetery and throw herself
onto the freshly turned earth of Grace's grave, "clawing at it, weeping." Something very like Eileen's crocodile and not totally unlike
Tourette's had taken over. Ann found herself screaming at people,
weeping in the grocery store, tortured by flashbacks of the hospital
and of her own shrieks echoing in the corridors. Something physical and completely out of her control had hold of her.

Sacks went to the hospital with Bennett to watch him treat
patients and perform an operation. Sacks saw Bennett lying on the
floor in the common room, discussing a patient who had neuro-
fibromatosis while lifting his foot up in a kicking motion. (Neuro-
fibromatosis is the condition that afflicted John Merrick, known as
the Elephant Man.) The other doctors knew Bennett well and took
this in stride.

Sacks scrubbed in for surgery beside Bennett, watching him lurch and reach, his hands darting out at everything around him but never quite making contact with any contaminated surface, even while he touched the people around him with his toes and cried out, "Hooty-hooo! Hooty-hooo!" How could such a man possibly perform a delicate operation?

In the operating room, Bennett studied the mammogram of the woman who lay anesthetized upon the table. Then he picked up a scalpel and began to cut. Suddenly, he was a different man altogether. The complex and challenging operation lasted two and a half hours and required that Bennett perform such intricate procedures as tying off blood vessels and locating fine nerve fibers that must not be cut. It went off with no sign at all of his Tourette's syndrome. Bennett's performance was astonishing because medical science had been looking for a treatment for Tourette's for more than a century and a half at that point. The only available drugs had catastrophic side effects. Yet here was something Bennett could do that turned off his symptoms like flipping a light switch.

A curious feature of Tourette's is that it does not feel like a disease to the person who has it. People who suffer from Parkinson's disease, for example, perceive the condition as an attack from outside the true self. All the bizarre behaviors that Bennett exhibited felt like a part of his real self, not something external that was attacking him. As a result, while drugs such as haloperidol may tone down the overt symptoms of Tourette's, they also erase the self.

The very concept of self is something that most of us take for granted until something (crocodile, war, death) comes along to shock us with the idea that it's not really what it seems. Indeed, the unified sense of self that most of us feel is a necessary illusion created by an intimate and delicate dance, a trick of neurological timing, that takes place constantly between brain and body, as well as among all the myriad selves that we all embody. The brain must constantly and dynamically represent the state of the body and what it is doing, how it is feeling, where its parts are. It must also monitor what is going on in the outside world, even while dreaming up the next right action to keep the trick going. The frontal lobes are home to the networks where information about the inside and outside come together. The brain is an organ of prediction. Since all kinds of information are coming from all over the place at different rates, the brain needs to synchronize this flow into a single thing. That thing is the self. "We know this centralization of prediction as the abstraction we call the 'self,' " says Rodolfo Llinás, a neuroscientist at New York University. Sometimes it doesn't take much to disturb that balance. And a self that is not unified can be profoundly disturbing. Motivation and joy wither. Bizarre feelings arise.

Apotemnophilia is a condition in which the map of the body is incomplete. Some part of the body—a hand or arm or leg—fails to be represented in that so-called Where Pathway. At least that's the thinking about this odd condition. People with apotemnophilia can still feel and use the limb, because it is mapped in the sensory and motor areas of the brain. The nerves are working. But those people feel a strange and disturbing sense that the limb doesn't belong to them, a feeling that Ramachandran calls "overpresence." A kind of memory is missing in these people: the inborn memory, or mental model, of that limb. The most remarkable consequence of this conflict between the innate need to occupy a unified self and this feeling of being strangely divided is that apotemnophiliacs want the offending limb cut off. In fact, half of them actually go through with the surgery and afterward report that they feel whole again.

The trick Bennett performed in the operating room is a trick of memory. When he operates, he said, "It never even crosses my mind that I have Tourette's." In other words, he is able to forget. He turns one system of memory off and turns another one on. The transformation of his personality, his self, is so complete that he can joke and banter with the staff even while his hands continue the procedure. Sacks described this as "another self . . . taking over the brain." And this is not so odd. Most of us have different personas for different occasions, being one person at work, another in bed with a spouse, yet another playing with the children. Each of these involves pulling up from memory one set of behaviors while suppressing another set. In other words, remembering one persona and forgetting the others. When you're playing with the children, you have to forget your erotic persona and remember your parental persona. You have to remember emotional states that are appropriate to playing with the children and forget ones that go with your spouse and your office and the ones that cloak the person you are when you're speaking convincingly at a PTA meeting about getting another crossing guard for a dangerous intersection. These don't have to be conscious acts of remembering and forgetting. They just have to happen in that vast array of seamless background processes that are always unfolding automatically in the brain. In a sense, this is the fundamental task we all face after traumatic survival: To selectively forget enough, hour by hour, day by day, so that we can go on with life. We can all learn a lesson from Dr. Bennett. The trick that he pulls off involves doing something physical to reset the contents of memory. And as we'll see, it may well involve activating a pathway in the brain that effectively silences another pathway, the one that bedevils us, the rage pathway.

NATURE DOES NOT tend to invent new things from whole cloth. Rather, she likes to tinker with what is already there. The rage pathway, that ancient mechanism in the brain that causes animals to scream and fight and struggle and bite when they are attacked, is normally held in check by signals from an area of the brain called the basal ganglia. Involuntary screaming, crying, thrashing, and grimacing are all characteristic of an activated rage pathway. When Ann Hood was writing the word "fuck" over and over in her diary, she was doing one of the things that the activated rage pathway typically does in humans. To the brain, swear words are not the same as ordinary language. When you injure yourself, they emerge spontaneously. If you step on your cat's tail, the rage pathway produces a characteristic scream. If you slam the door on your finger, you may well produce a string of expletives. You can think of swear words as screams educated by language.

The brain and body are possessed of a great many push-pull systems. The sympathetic nervous system excites us, while the parasympathetic nervous system calms us down. One hormone pumps steroids up, another brings them down. The amygdala excites an emotional reaction while the thinking brain inhibits it. The brain itself is a push-pull system balancing reason and emotion under normal circumstances. (And, in a sense, reason deals with the outside world while emotion deals with the inside you.) We have in essence two states, two jobs, two motivations and behaviors. Either we are drawing something to us—we are seeking, say, a bite to eat—or we are pushing things away from us or demolishing them (say, slapping a mosquito that's using us as a bite to eat). There's the reward system directed at encouraging us to get stuff and the punishment system directed at making sure that we get rid of certain stuff. Everything is a degree of those two reactions, mostly mild, sometimes intense. The rage pathway is activated when you're attacked, frustrated, or when an attack is directed at those people and things that have been mapped in your nervous system. I use Dr. Bennett as an example because that same pathway is activated inappropriately by an inherited disorder in his brain. By looking at Tourette's syndrome, we may better understand our own responses to the injuries that life inflicts upon us.

In Ann's case, the injury was to her daughter, who was richly represented in Ann's nervous system. So she experienced the death of her daughter as if she herself had been attacked. Ann needed to discover a way to get at that rage pathway in her brain, the push pathway, and calm it down.

Jaak Panksepp, a neuroscientist at Washington State University, has proposed another circuit or pathway that might embody the pull that counterbalances the push represented by the rage pathway. He calls it the seeking pathway or the seeking system. (Kent Berridge, a neuroscientist at the University of Michigan, calls it the "wanting system.") It's the same pathway that's involved (in cats, for example) in methodically stalking prey. "This system," Panksepp wrote, "supports expectancy, exploration, foraging and other . . . activities aimed at meeting a large variety of bodily needs." The seeking pathway uses some of the same areas in the brain as the rage pathway, but it is a distinct system, in Panksepp's view. And because it occupies some of the same areas, it appears that it may disable the rage pathway. The seeking pathway is involved in "assertive goal-directedness," says Panksepp. He and his colleagues also call this seeking behavior "assertive aggression," but it's not aggression as we normally think of it. It means what my daughter Elena first articulated at the age of three when she held out her hand and said, plaintively, "Want it, need it, have it!" It means attempting to acquire or accomplish something.

"Assertive aggression," Panksepp wrote, involves any activity that arises from what he refers to as "a dopamine-fueled" motivation. You might find yourself seeking advancement in your job. You might be in pursuit of a partner in marriage. You might be remodeling your home. All those acts of "assertive aggression" involve having a plan and carrying it out. In the great push-pull systems of the brain, this is the state in which you get the meal as opposed to the state in which you're trying to avoid becoming the meal. And I would suggest that this may offer a key in understanding why knitting worked so well to calm Ann's rage and blunt her grief: We want to gain a meal and we also want to avoid becoming one. *But we can't do both at the same time.* So perhaps the random chaotic neuromuscular storms produced by the rage pathway cannot take place while we are making a careful plan and following it step by step.

The marvelous thing that Ann discovered was that she could quiet herself through knitting. So it may be that to the richly associative human brain, the smooth repetitive physical activity of knitting is the equivalent of stalking. And stalking is a plan carried out by deliberate, careful action. Dr. Carl Bennett could induce a similar calming effect while performing surgery. So I ask, Could the two activities be employing similar pathways in the brain? What we know is that in study after study, activities with characteristics such as these (physical, patterned, repetitive, organized, directed toward a goal) have proved therapeutic for people suffering from trauma or grief.

Ann described the effect of knitting. She entered the knitting shop in Tiverton, Rhode Island, in the crucible of her grief. But she found that when she left after two hours of knitting, she had been unburdened for the first time and could actually breathe in and breathe out without "crying or cursing or reliving the horrible tragedy that had taken over my life."

When you first learn a skill such as knitting or surgery (or violin or golf), it begins as a voluntary, deliberate action that requires conscious thought. It begins in the frontal lobes as an idea. When learning a new skill, you have to think about it consciously. You have to make deliberate use of your body, step by step. Your eyes and the feeling of where your limbs are tell you if you're doing it correctly. It won't be smooth. You'll have to work at it. But as you practice, control migrates out of the frontal lobes into the lower parts of the brain and the activity becomes automatic. The basal ganglia become involved and your movements begin to flow. Your cerebellum and parietal lobe (the Where Pathway) begin to monitor what you're doing and correct errors automatically. You no longer have to think about it. Your body does it without your consent, so to speak.

But the basal ganglia have another important function. They constantly initiate many kinds of potential behavior.* The frontal lobes monitor and evaluate those courses of action. If you're standing in the kitchen, drinking a glass of water, the basal ganglia might suggest: Hey, let's throw that glass against the refrigerator. And the frontal lobes will say: Naahh. Not such a good idea.

In Tourette's syndrome, says Elkhonon Goldberg, the basal ganglia may "somehow escape from the control normally exerted over them by the [frontal lobes]." Carl Bennett's refrigerator was severely dented from things he had thrown at it. In Ann's case, there was a similar loss of control, and perhaps it involved a similar mechanism as well. Perhaps by activating the seeking pathway, her knitting forced the basal ganglia and frontal lobes back into an orderly communication. Panksepp refers to that type of behavior as expressing "psychic energy" and characterizes such activities as positive

---

* This is a stunningly complex system. But you don't need to know all the technical interactions involved to understand its effects on mood and behavior. For a more thorough explanation, see Michael Gazzaniga's book *Cognitive Neuroscience*, pp. 300–307 (see References).

aggressive. (Recall George Vaillant's "creative aggression" from the long-running Study of Adult Development.) Panksepp argues that as such, they compete effectively with the aversive kind of aggression: rage.

The neuroscience of this matter is by no means settled and there is much debate concerning the very nature of emotions and so-called pathways in the brain. In many cases, researchers disagree on such fundamental issues as what to call areas in the brain. As one scientist put it, neuroscientists would rather use one another's toothbrushes than their terminology. LeDoux, for example, calls undertaking activities that combat anxiety "active coping." He told me, "In general, states with stronger motivational significance tend to dominate. Animals that are being hunted by a predator don't have the luxury of eating and having sex. Postponing these activities is coping as well. [Conversely] behaviors that are successful in preventing strong emotional arousal are reinforced by the reduction in arousal." To be both brief and consistent, I'll take the advice of one of my friends who is a neuroscientist and use the term "seeking pathway." While much more research remains to be done in this area, what we do know is that active coping, planning and undertaking organized activities, does work to temper rage and grief.

ONE OF the worst effects of bereavement is that the rage or outrage that we feel at the loss cannot be answered. Ann could not bring Grace back. She could not right the wrong. So ultimately we tend to exhaust the rage pathway and fall into a helpless lethargy that looks a lot like depression. Anxiety and rage represent efforts to cope. Depression is the absence of effort. Anxiety and rage are about adrenaline. In an extreme form, such as post-traumatic stress, every car that backfires sends you on a rocket ride of panic. Depression is about cortisol (steroids). You're under tremendous stress with the brakes on so that you can't do anything at all. Stress and cortisol also prevent chemicals such as dopamine from making you feel good.

People who start out with a low level of cortisol are more prone to post-traumatic stress. Beta blockers, which stop the actions of adrenaline, might be able to prevent post-traumatic stress reactions if they're given right after a traumatic episode. People with high cortisol can become chemically locked into a state of giving up. And one of the keys to survival is: Never give up.

But where major trauma is involved, that's easier said than done. Often it cannot be done by main force. Many times, as in Ann's case, the cycle repeats and repeats, with the brain automatically seeking Grace and not finding her. A frustrated seeking pathway gradually transfers control over to the rage pathway. Then comes the explosive rage, the irrational behavior, the weeping and gnashing of teeth, and once again the fatigue of the pathway and the descent back into depression.

It seems like a never-ending cycle. And for some people it is. But by engaging the seeking pathway with a task that you can achieve, most people can break the cycle of fear, rage, exhaustion, and depression. Not only does the seeking pathway compete with the rage pathway and its effects, but it also connects with the reward system in the brain. Successfully activating the seeking pathway makes you feel good. When the basal ganglia can broker a successful action through this pathway, dopamine is released, so the very act of correctly completing a stitch or row of stitches activates the reward and pleasure pathways of the brain. Learning by itself promotes dopamine. This is one of the reasons that it was therapeutic for Jessica Goodell to immerse herself in study after the horrors of Mortuary Affairs. In terms of the chemistry of the brain, learning is its own reward. So the relief that Ann experienced from knitting may begin to make biological sense. In Panksepp's words, "It is not really possible to be extremely angry and methodically goal-oriented at the same time." And this could provide a key to switching identities, a possible reason that we can forget one persona and adopt another. Carl Bennett could not be the goal-oriented surgeon and the enraged Tourettic at the same time.

Remember the saying "Get organized or die." In the wake of trauma, "Work, work, work," as Richard Mollica wrote. He is a psychiatrist at Harvard who studies trauma. "This is the single most important goal of traumatized people throughout the world." The hands force order on the mind. The body controls the brain. In fact, neuroscientists increasingly believe that the only reason we have a brain is so that we can move the body. So quite naturally, what we do with the body is going to influence what goes on in the brain. Shortly after the attack on the World Trade Center, LeDoux wrote an article for the *American Journal of Psychiatry*. In it he described how active coping could physically redirect the flow of information in the brain away from the rage pathway (amygdala, pariaqueductal gray, and hypothalamus) back to the basal ganglia, thus leaving fear and depression behind and "getting on with life." Work done by Ann Graybiel, a neuroscientist at MIT, has shown that the basal ganglia coordinate the processes that go into forming habits (or learning new skills). And those habits include what she calls "habits of thought and emotion" as well. So by learning to knit, it appears that Ann was taking direct positive control of the basal ganglia, the very area that could shut off her rage.

When you engage the basal ganglia, you also engage another system that promotes well-being: the safety system. Eric Kandel, a neuroscientist and Nobel laureate, writes, "Our studies . . . point to a second system [other than the amygdala] deep in the brain that is concerned with positive emotions." He's referring to the fact that a lot of research has been done on fear and the amygdala but not as much on feeling good. "It is conceivable," he writes, "that by enhancing the signal in the striatum [part of the basal ganglia], learned safety not only enhances feelings of safety and security but also reduces fear by inhibiting the amygdala."

Kandel has explained that just as you can inadvertently train yourself to be afraid through the experience of trauma, you can train yourself to feel safe. And tellingly, a structure within the basal ganglia is activated during feelings of safety, reward, and simply feeling great. It's called the striatum and drugs such as cocaine set it off, but so does the learning of a new habit or skill and the performance of organized, patterned activities, perhaps even knitting. Perhaps ancient people made so many stone tools not merely because they were useful but because doing so activated the striatum and made them feel safe. Others watched, and mirror neurons allowed them to feel what it might be like to perform that activity. In a very dangerous world, it felt safe and good to perform those patterned, repetitive actions that entrained the seeking pathway. And the end result was a tool that could help in another activity that involves the seeking pathway: hunting.

THE PHYSICAL act of knitting wasn't the only influence that was helping Ann. She did her knitting in a group of supportive people. Social interaction causes the release of oxytocin, a hormone that helps people form bonds and even fall in love. That hormone is released during orgasm, in labor and childbirth, and while breast-feeding. It imparts feelings of well-being and promotes physical contact, which in turn releases more oxytocin. (Animals release oxytocin when they groom each other.) And when oxytocin goes up, the stress hormones go down.

Knitting is therapeutic in another way as well. It's difficult to do and the results are unpredictable. Sometimes you're rewarded and sometimes you fail, especially when you're first learning. Ann wrote that she was trying to knit a scarf and made a mess of it. "Jen pulled it off the needle and all my mistakes were miraculously gone." Gregory Berns, a neuroscientist at Emory University, wrote in his book *Satisfaction* that even though we like predictability, unpredictable rewards are most effective at raising the level of dopamine in the brain, the centerpiece chemical in the pleasure and reward system. (This is one of the reasons gambling can be so addictive.) It is also well documented that we respond more to a reward when we have to work for it than when it simply materializes out of thin air. And perhaps most significantly, the brain interprets the action itself, not the results of that action, as the reward. So Ann's scarf or hat or sweater was not the point of knitting. Knitting was the point of knitting. She had stumbled onto a continuous reward system with an overarching influence on the brain and body.

"We harbor mechanical, 'alien' subroutines to which we have no access and of which we have no acquaintance," wrote David Eagleman of Baylor University. "Almost all of our actions—from producing speech to picking up a mug of coffee," says Eagleman, are the output of this automated system. He says these behaviors arise from "zombie systems," and the systems are set up so that two conflicting behaviors cannot occur at the same time. One type of behavior precludes another. That may be part of the reason that knitting worked for Ann. The crazy screaming panic produced by every scene or object that she encountered began to quiet down, because the two states, the push and the pull, could not coexist. Some days she did nothing but knit. In fact, she once knit for almost eight hours straight and wound up unable to move her fingers. And yet the activity gave her an inner peace that was otherwise unavailable to her. "The quiet click of the needles, the rhythm of the stitches, the warmth of the yarn and the blanket or scarf that spilled across my lap, made those hours tolerable."

Ann's knitting and social bonding forged real physical changes in her brain and body that produced the calmer state, and that calmer state gradually became more and more the norm, something that her brain made room for in its endless cartography. She created a new set of cell assemblies that began to outshine the ones that had been spot welded in the acetylene flame of grief. During this period, Ann heard from the mother of a little boy who had gone to Grace's school. The woman called to say that her two-year-old son had just died. As the woman told her story, Ann found herself compulsively pacing the house, using physical activity to induce calm in the face of such horrifying news. Then she got a grip on herself and told the woman, "Come to my house. I will teach you how to knit." Ann was going to help the woman use her mirror neurons to catch Ann's newfound emotional calm. She was going to help the woman use her seeking pathway to quiet her rage. She was going to show the woman how emotional contagion and stalking behavior just possibly might save her life. And, like Lisette, who had comforted Ruth and Betty, Ann was finding someone worse off than she was, someone with a fresher wound, and was thereby becoming the rescuer who could replace the victim she had once been.

Some years ago, I became interested in neurosurgery. I was lucky enough to have as friends two neurosurgeons who let me watch. I saw a lot of skulls get cut open during that period. But I also discovered how the students learn to become brain surgeons. They have to watch someone perform an operation. Then they have to try doing it themselves. And then, to solidify the learning, they have to teach someone else to do it. Roberta, one of the surgeons, put it this way: "See one, do one, teach one." Of course, it's more than one, but that phrase always stuck with me, and the more I learn about surviving survival, the more I see it as a formula for healing: See one, do one, teach one. Mirror neurons help you read the intentions and emotions of another person. They allow you to watch her do something and then to imitate that action. This can even happen in your imagination. And in that process, they allow you to engage the seeking pathway, the safety system, and to adopt that person's emotional state, to catch her contagious calm. Emotion is all about the body. The body is all about feeling. Doing the right thing helps you feel the right way. Knitting was so influential in Ann's life that she went on to write a novel about it called *The Knitting Circle*.

Knitting, like surgery, also has a payoff that the chaotic emotional responses of grief and rage do not have. In prolonged grief or extreme anxiety, the energy of suffering is not patterned in any satisfying way. Your responses to the world become like seizures, chaotic and unpredictable. But knitting follows the pattern of an emotional response: You start, you work, you finish, and everyone in your knitting circle smiles. Your mirror neurons make you smile at the smiles, and your own smile forces you to feel better. Each row is like a little emotional bell shape. And then the entire job of knitting the hat or scarf or sweater forms a larger emotional shape. The nesting of these emotional bells makes a beautiful fractal pattern. And beautiful patterns make us feel good.

In ancient days, maybe everyone had some form of anxiety disorder. After all, life was short and every day you really did face the possibility of being eaten alive. Hence all the drumming and dancing and ritual. Rituals mark and manage events. Rituals contain uncontainable emotions. They tell your emotional system to feel bad on this day so that you don't have to feel bad on all the others.

On what would have been Grace's sixth birthday, Ann Hood got a tattoo. She marked the day and the day marked her.

The next year, when Grace would have been seven, Ann and her husband, Lorne, made the decision to adopt a baby. Ann was forty-four and could not have another child herself. They had already tried. Three years after Grace died, Ann and Lorne received the call. Their baby girl was ready to be picked up in China. "For the first time in almost three years," Ann wrote, "something like joy was creeping at the edges of my heart." In one of those remarkable coincidences that seem to bind the universe together, the little girl's birthday was April 18, the date of Grace's death. They named her Annabelle. As they rode the bus toward their hotel, the baby looked at Ann and laughed, and Ann had what can only be described as a mystical experience. She achieved joy again, and it settled in to coexist with her grief. You create the world by your belief in it, so it's important to believe this: There really is a path. It takes you not back to your old life but onward to the new one.

DR. BENNETT forgot that he had Tourette's syndrome while he was doing surgery. If he was interrupted, he would suddenly remember and his tics would return. Doing surgery for a couple of hours could not make his Tourette's disappear for the rest of his life. He had a neurological imbalance that could not be corrected. Nor could Ann make her grief go away altogether. "Grief isn't something you get over," she wrote. "You live with it. You go on with it lodged in you." Ann's challenge was much different from Eileen's, as well. The crocodile had damaged Eileen's physical body. Ann's physical body had no marks on it. Maybe it would have been easier if she could have seen the scars like Lisette's gunshot wounds. Maybe that's why Ann had to have the tattoo. Moreover, Eileen could embrace the idea of forgetting the crocodile. Ann could never forget her daughter, nor would she want to. Lisette's trauma was even more multidimensional, cutting across her own body and the lives of her children. These three distinct kinds of trauma elicited different strategies for adaptation. But they all involved using the body to change the structure and meaning of memories. They all involved doing *something*. And they ultimately involved doing it for someone else: See one, do one, teach one.

If we look closely at ourselves and those around us, we might find that there is no normal. All of us are making accommodations in some way. We just don't have a name for the condition. Or perhaps each of us does have a name for it. Ann Hood has Ann Hood's syndrome and Lisette Johnson suffers from and enjoys (depending on the day of the week, the hour of the day) the condition known as Lisette's chorea: her dance of life. There is no ideal state of being alive, just as there is no ideal of beauty, though we like to imagine both. Our constant compensation is inherent in being a creature that must move and seek and imitate and learn. And rage at times as well. In an ever-changing environment, we must live within a narrow range of conditions just to stay alive. If we get too cold, too hot, too dry, too wet, we'll die. Our bodies are constantly chasing those moving targets. The chasing of ideal conditions that we never achieve is what we call life. If we ever reached the ideal, we would do nothing, want nothing, and have no motivation. From the outside, we might look like a patient with sleeping sickness. To be alive in any functional way, we must strive. Striving means struggle in the endless push-pull of pain and pleasure. Raging and seeking.

Mark Vonnegut, son of Kurt Vonnegut, was diagnosed as schizophrenic when he was in his twenties. He was hospitalized several times, given huge doses of major tranquilizers, and set off like a bottle rocket with electric shocks to his brain. He went on to get better (he actually had manic-depressive illness). He graduated from Harvard Medical School and has had a successful career as a pediatrician. He wrote that it makes perfect sense that if you're dealing with a lifelong disease, you should take good care of yourself—eat healthful meals, get enough sleep, avoid smoking. Those are all the things you ought to do anyway. But, he said, "somehow having a disease makes them easier to do. A human without a disease is like a ship without a rudder." Nietzsche wrote, "As for sickness: Are we not almost tempted to ask whether we could get along without it?"

We don't want to invite misfortune into our lives. But when it comes, we can choose to act, and in the act we can rise above the trauma and even above ourselves. Looking back years later on her own survival, Lisette Johnson put it well when she said, "I sleep through the night in the room where it happened and nightmares are infrequent now. I touch the scars and tears aren't automatic. My heart doesn't pound like it used to when I hear a siren. . . . There are times still, though, that I am thrown back in as though it were yesterday."

Years after the event, Ann wrote that even now she could "hear a song or glimpse a little blonde-haired girl, and my knees will still buckle." She has now learned to see the blunt attacks of grief before they arrive, "to recognize the early signs: the inability to concentrate, the jangling nerves and short temper, too many hours staring at daytime TV." When that happens, she leaves the country for the most exotic place she can find. And as we'll see in Chapter 10, travel is an excellent way to fool the brain and relieve it of its horrors.

EIGHT

"PLEASE, GOD, LET ME KILL HER": DISMANTLING THE SELF

MICHELE WELDON IS a writer. She's educated, smart, funny, and talented. She grew up in a suburb of Chicago in an upper-middle-class home with a large, happy family. Her parents loved each other and openly displayed their affection. Michele's entire family was fun. She loved her mother and adored her father. When she was in graduate school, she talked to her parents on the phone every day. She graduated and took a job as a marketing editor in downtown Chicago. She was twenty-five when she met the man she would marry. Call him Evan. Michele wrote an entire book about him and never once used his name. In fact, she didn't even give him a pseudonym. He haunts the pages like a ghost.

Evan seemed like the ideal choice for Michele. She described him as "attractive and charming, accommodating and sensitive, effusive and engaging, unassuming and honest." She added, "He was a great kisser." He could even dance. Evan, too, was twenty-five years old when they began dating. In college, Evan had been a championship boxer. In Michele's view of the world, shaped largely by her happy childhood, she didn't need to know much more before deciding that Evan was the right guy. "If there was a warning sign there," she wrote, "I couldn't see it." She expected all men to be like her father and brothers—good, stalwart, uncomplicated. "Men with no surprises."

Ten months after they met, Michele landed a job writing features for the *Dallas Times Herald.* Although it was exactly what she wanted to do, Michele was torn about leaving Evan. She was happily surprised when he quit his job and moved to Texas to be with her. In Michele's mind, this was the beginning of everything she had always dreamed of: the wedding, the children, the holiday dinners, the anniversaries. They would be just like her parents. It was a moment in her life that felt perfect. Everything was in its place.

They moved to Dallas and she loved her job. They lived in separate apartments but spent all their free time together. Then one night after work, Michele went shopping on a whim. When Evan couldn't reach her, he became frantic and called all her friends. She arrived home to find that he'd left six messages on her answering machine. Michele told herself that he just cared so much about her.

They had been together for a year when Evan proposed. He had to arrange every detail of the proposal, right down to the setting, the kneeling, his grandmother's ring in the blue-velvet box. They planned the wedding for October. They had an engagement party. Then six months before the wedding, Evan told Michele that he couldn't go through with it. He left.

Michele had no idea what was going on. Nothing had happened between them. But as the weeks passed, she began to rationalize. Friends told her that cold feet were common. Michele decided to make it work. She got in touch with Evan and told him that she would wait six months, no more, for him to decide. When the deadline came, Evan asked her to wear his grandmother's ring again. They set a new date. They picked out patterns for china and crystal. Evan, a staunch Catholic who had once been in the seminary, insisted on a church wedding, presided over by three of his friends who were priests. Michele wrote it up for *Brides* magazine. *Town & Country* ran their photograph. "He will be the perfect husband now," Michele thought. "There will be a happy ending." But

Michele noticed something odd at the ceremony. During the vows, Evan shot his hand into the air "in a fist and held it there, the defiant, jubilant conqueror."

As soon as they had settled into their new home, Evan informed Michele that every day when he returned from work he expected to see a nice pattern on the carpet from the vacuum cleaner. He let her know that her writing, her ambitions and aspirations, were nothing more than a distraction from her rightful place, doing the housework and caring for him and the children they would have. They were married in August 1986, and before the year was out, Evan punched Michele in the chest with such force that she had to wear high collars to conceal the deep bruise from a professionally thrown blow. Before their first year of marriage was over, he physically attacked her again. He was a championship boxer. The damage he did was not trivial. He beat her so viciously that she couldn't eat, because of the cuts inside her mouth caused by her own teeth. His rages grew to the point that he bit through the skin on her arm during one attack. Michele made flashbulb memories of "his eyes before I closed my own. Cold blue, pale as stone, the pupils wide, black chasms, his dark eyebrows arrows aimed at my face, his teeth gripped hard to his mission." And each time the attacks came, she told herself with relief, "This has to be the last. This can't happen again." But it did. He hit her when she was pregnant with their first son, Weldon. He beat her up on Christmas Eve.

Michele lied for him. She told people that one of her boys had hit her with a toy train. Or something. Anything to avoid admitting that she had married the wrong guy. It was unthinkable. Anyway, her friends told her how wonderful her husband was. People called them the perfect couple. Lies create shame, the dissonance between the self you project and the one you conceal. And in that torment, that exhausting tension, a kind of paralyzing despair sets in.

On more than one weekend night, when they were preparing to have friends over, Evan tormented her psychologically, saying, "Psycho Wife" over and over in a vicious singsong voice and calling her "Loser" right up to the moment the friends arrived to find him beaming and her looking emotionally numb. Then Evan would toast Michele and tell everyone how much he loved her. She could feel the classic traumatic split beginning. One voice said, "I'll do everything perfectly. . . . He won't have to do anything. We can be happy." But another, more rational voice began to creep in, whispering, "He's dangerous. Get away from him."

In *Deep Survival*, I described several instances of survival that played out over days or weeks or even months and that put the victims under a tremendous burden of stress. When Steve Callahan was castaway at sea and nearly died of thirst and hunger, his personality began to split in two. The severe abuse to his body was sending unfamiliar signals to the areas of his brain that map the body. This began to distort the body image to the point that he couldn't fully recognize his normal self. That mismatch caused two distinct selves to emerge. One was the self that he called the Captain, the cold rational self, mediated by the frontal lobes, the will, the intention to survive. The other was the Steve who whined and complained and asked for more than his set ration of water, the emotional self. Many survivors talk of this sort of split and even report hearing what they call "the voice," which tells them what to do. The abuse to Michele's body was having the same effect on her brain as if she'd been set adrift at sea. As if she'd been attacked by a shark.

The attacks could start from any point on the compass of their lives. A discussion of the kids, money, a party they'd been to, dinner, the garden, housework. He flew into a rage because Michele was cleaning the floor while he was reading the newspaper. She slept soundly only when Evan was out of the house. She began to dissociate and leave her body. When Evan attacked, Michele began to feel as if she "was swimming underwater, without sound and without weight, body-less, soul-less, unable to breathe or speak or remember." In that state, she escaped "to the mountains inside me, the paradise he couldn't poison or devour with his words. I would find again the haven where I kept the kaleidoscope of colored drawings, where I could hear the songs inside me sing again."

She developed asthma, a common reaction of battered women. It grew severe enough that when she heard his footsteps on the stairs, she would reach for her inhaler. Yet the two voices continued. "I am not a battered wife," she told herself. And then for a big Halloween party, Michele insisted that Evan dress as O. J. Simpson. She dressed as Nicole. She even bought Evan a big bloody rubber knife to brandish. Nicole Brown Simpson had been murdered the previous summer, and Michele was trying to tell everyone what grave danger she was in. She couldn't bring herself to say it out loud, but this was her cry for help. Her friends just thought she was being morbid and tasteless, but her mind was screaming: "You're missing the point. She and I are the same. My husband and O. J. are the same, too." The rational voice inside her, growing louder and louder, was becoming harder and harder to ignore. Then one night during an attack, he muttered under his breath, "Please, God, let me kill her." And she knew. She understood that Evan might really do it, just as O. J. Simpson had. He might kill her sons. He might kill them all. It was real.

She saw a counselor, who said, "Get a plan. If he ever hurts you again, you have to take the children away."

She packed a suitcase and kept it under her bed, ready to go. The voice said, "He bit me on the arm as Weldon, two, watched and I held Brendan, then nine months old, in my arms." She would be driving down the street and suddenly she would hear his voice, as clear as if he were sitting next to her, saying, "Please, God, let me kill her." She was having flashback hallucinations, nightmares. She felt as if her mind might explode at any moment. She couldn't even remember who she was before he sank his claws into her.

SEVEN ATTRIBUTES combine to give us what we perceive as self, says Ramachandran: unity, continuity, embodiment, privacy, social embedding, free will, and self-awareness. When Evan repeatedly attacked Michele, he severely disrupted six of those seven attributes. Michele had gone into the marriage believing that Evan was one person, when in reality he was more than one. The smiling public Evan had an evil twin. Michele had already undergone the traumatic split that survivors experience, the rational and the emotional. She had lost the first attribute of the self: unity. Now she was forced to view herself as two people in another way as well: the one who chose well and the one who chose badly. Her feeling of being one person was disrupted. How could the Michele she knew and trusted have made such a terrible mistake?

His attacks also disrupted continuity in Michele's life. From one moment to the next, one year to the next, we feel our lives unfolding in a continuous ribbon of time. We can trace our lives backward in a smooth catenary arc and forward into a future that we plan and hope for. Unpredictable violence from someone you love shatters that continuity. It literally interrupts your life and even makes chunks of it disappear into memory holes caused by the high levels of stress that impair the hippocampus, the cartographer of memories. Michele's dissociation shattered the continuity of her life, as parts of her memory floated away. She'd lost the second attribute of self.

Under normal circumstances we feel embodied, or as Ramachandran put it, "at home in your body." Trivial things, such as mirrors and illusions, can temporarily disrupt the body image, as he showed in his laboratory when treating patients suffering from phantom-limb syndrome. As we saw with Eileen and the crocodile, physical attack plays havoc with body image. For one thing, it causes physical changes in the body, such as swollen lips, bruises, and aching ribs. The Where Pathway of the parietal lobe is disrupted because the parts of your body are no longer in their correct position in space. In Michele's case, physical attack also caused her to leave her body and to feel as if she were no longer its owner, its occupant.

This goes back to the idea that a violinist can grow his nervous system out into his bow, the blind man can see with his cane. This may seem theoretical or metaphorical, but it's more than that. When Ramachandran was trying to treat phantom-limb syndrome, he found that he could make experimental subjects feel sensation in a rubber hand. The illusion was achieved by hiding the subject's real hand while he looked at a rubber hand that was positioned where he expected to see his own hand. Then someone stroked both the real (hidden) hand and the rubber (visible) hand in the same pattern of movement. Soon the subject became convinced that his feelings were emanating from the rubber hand. Ramachandran was even able to create the same sensory illusion using the surface of a table as a proxy for the subject's nervous system. Ramachandran stroked the subject's real flesh-and-blood hand, which was out of sight. Simultaneously, he stroked the surface of the table where the subject could see the stroking being done. The subject, a student, soon became convinced that he could actually feel sensation in the table. His nervous system had grown out to occupy the lifeless table.

It was no mere parlor trick. If someone were to smash your hand with a hammer, in addition to feeling pain, your blood pressure would shoot up, steroids would pour into your bloodstream, and your galvanic skin response would rise sharply, to name just a few of the changes that your body would undergo. (Galvanic skin response is a fancy way of saying that you sweat more under stress. GSR is measured by attaching electrodes to your skin as with a lie detector.) Once Ramachandran had established the illusion and the student could feel the fingers stroking the table, Ramachandran whipped out a hammer and smashed it onto the table. Despite the fact that he had hit an inert table with the hammer and had touched no part of the student's body, his instruments measured a sharp rise in the student's galvanic skin response. The student had allowed his own nervous system to map the table, to grow out into it, and therefore had registered the threat as if the hammer had hit his own hand. This is the trick of neurological timing, as Damasio calls it, that helps create the illusion of a stable and unified self. Because things appear to happen at the same time (stroking sensation on hand while you see the fingers stroking the table), they bind together. Cells that fire together (that is, at the same time) wire together. Normally, that sort of assembling of the senses is used to bind the parts of the self that represent your real experiences of the world. Ramachandran simply tricked this natural system into binding the nervous system with the table. (This phenomenon is part of the explanation of road rage: If your nervous system grows out into the body of your car, then threats to the car may activate your rage pathway.)

By the same token, when your body is changed, it disrupts your sense of self. No longer at home in her body, no longer at home in her home, Michele had lost embodiment, the third attribute of self. As Jonathan Shay, a MacArthur Foundation fellow, put it in his book *Achilles in Vietnam*, "Severe trauma explodes the cohesion of consciousness."

Through physical violence, Michele was robbed of the attributes of both privacy and free will. When someone enters the realm of your personal space, it feels intrusive unless it is in the service of love and affection. When someone attacks you, he controls how you feel and what you think. Above all, you feel pain, and you can't think when fear is that intense. Since you have no control over what happens, your autonomy is wiped out in a single blow. It has been suggested that free will might be seated in the supramarginal gyrus, a part of the brain that allows you to imagine many things you might do, and in the anterior cingulate cortex, which allows you to choose one course of action based on what you're thinking with your frontal, rational, brain. A blow to the face takes those parts of the brain out of service as the amygdala takes over to initiate a response for your own survival. Evan literally disabled the parts of Michele's brain that gave her free will, privacy, and autonomy.

And for someone to have self-awareness, she must have a coherent self to be aware of, so the seventh attribute was also destroyed by the attacks. The only thing Michele had left was social embedding. She still had her children and could still have some normal emotional responses to them. She still had her siblings and her friends. She still had meaningful work as a journalist. "Being able to be creative every day helped," she told me. But she was gradually being separated from friends and family by her secret. She couldn't tell them the dark truth about her life. And her increasingly strange feelings and states of mind were in large part due to her sense that her self as she had always known it was breaking into unrecognizable pieces.

The self is also about memory. J. Douglas Bremner, a professor of psychiatry at Emory University School of Medicine, wrote, "Identity can be thought of as a collection of memories." As we've seen, those memories are colored with emotional significance and a wide array of associations. Explicit memories, the ones that are conscious, are formed and retrieved through the hippocampus. Any time you disrupt the hippocampus, you are doing something to that sense of identity. When Bremner gave people a drug that blocked activity in the hippocampus, they felt as if they were outside their own bodies in a dreamlike state. Time was distorted and colors seemed exceptionally brilliant. These are very similar to the responses of police officers in situations where they have to shoot someone. Time slows down. The senses go through radical distortions. Some are sharpened while others are muted, as the supercharged emotional system tries to take in huge amounts of information in an effort to sort out what is important and what's not. One officer, for example, had to fire at a man who was attacking his partner. He "saw the muzzle flash and some smoke," but "the shot sounded real muffled," he reported. In spite of that, he heard the ejected cartridge tinkle onto the windshield of his squad car. Another officer, defending his partner from attack, said, "My vision changed as soon as I started to shoot. It went from seeing the whole picture to just the suspect's head. Everything else just disappeared." He said he could actually see the bullets hit the man's head as he shot him and described each shot in great detail. This last perception may have been imagined in the same way that Micki imagined seeing the shark's teeth when she hadn't actually seen them. When recalling memories of extreme events, we tend to embellish, as the brain tries to bring from the past anything that might help with the present emergency.

When Aron Ralston came out of that slot canyon in Utah with his hand cut off, he attracted worldwide attention because our mirror neurons went: Eww! Yuck! And then a little voice in the back of our heads said, *I wonder if I could have done that.* . . . As the boulder fell toward him, he wrote, "Time dilates, as if I'm dreaming, and my reactions decelerate." He described the incident as happening "in slow motion." It's the brain's adrenaline-fueled attempt to take in as much information as possible, as fast as possible. Absorbing that much information usually takes longer, so the passing of time seems slower in comparison when we recall those events. And of course, since we can all identify with this sensory distortion, it works well in movies. Slow motion in movies often signals that something is taking place very fast or with very high emotion.

Similar distortions can also happen in less extreme circumstances. For example, you could be at a party and see someone across the room. It's love at first sight. And all at once there is no one else in the room. You can't hear the crowd, the music. All you see is that other person's face, especially the eyes, as you make that first connection. Love can be stressful, too. It does, after all, lead to the most important act of survival.

EACH TIME Evan beat Michele, he apologized, sent flowers, bought her clothes at Ann Taylor, went to counseling with her, and professed his love for her anew. Once he even gave Michele a two-year-long break from the beatings. She began to believe that the counseling had worked. She began to tell herself that it had all been a bad dream. She'd almost forgotten about the suitcase when one night she happened to notice it under the bed. She thought: "How foolish of me to be so . . . dramatic." They celebrated their seventh anniversary with dinner and a night at a hotel downtown. She felt that they had succeeded at last. But the split in her was what had succeeded. She kept a part of herself in the suitcase, under the bed. "The suitcase," she wrote, "had become a sacred symbol of the . . . part of me he couldn't convince, brainwash, or manipulate with his affection. . . . Even if I acted as if I believed him, no matter how desperately I wanted to believe him, I knew enough somewhere inside to have an escape plan, a trapdoor, for the boys and me."

Then Evan closed their joint bank account and cut Michele off from all their money. To buy food, she was reduced to selling gold chains, gifts that her father had given her. She stood under the shower to cry at night so that the boys wouldn't hear her. And the voice in her head grew louder, telling her that her husband was "a vicious, controlling, abusive man." The attacks began occurring closer together. There was the very real possibility that Evan might kill her. He already knew that he wanted to. He had already said so. But Michele had been brought up in an Irish Catholic world where no one got divorced. Marriage was for life. You patched up your problems and went on. Anyway, she could no longer reason clearly enough to get away. She was moving in two directions at once. She took the winter clothes out of the suitcase and packed summer things, larger clothes for the growing kids. She told herself she'd never need them.

In 1995, Michele and Evan spent the Fourth of July weekend with his parents in Wisconsin. They were in their bedroom when his fist slammed into her jaw. Her mouth filled with blood. Her head hit the wall so hard that she had a lump the size of a softball. She sustained a deep bruise on her arm where he'd grabbed her. Her lips were grotesquely swollen, lacerated by her teeth. By then, she had remained silent through nine years of terror. She had closed her eyes when she knew an attack was coming and had held her breath and gone deep inside herself to withstand the violence. "I would cry without a sound," Michele wrote. But this time she screamed, and Evan's parents rushed to the room to see their daughter-in-law bloodied and weeping. Michele stumbled into the bathroom and began vomiting blood.

In the aftermath, Michele's sisters photographed her and found her a lawyer. An emergency order of protection was issued. Michele was forced to write down all the instances of violence and was astonished at how much she had endured. She could see the pattern, how the attacks were moving closer and closer together in time, the damage growing more severe. Her state of mind was shattered. Her memory was full of holes, and she was unable to concentrate. Now that she had fully admitted what had happened to her, she felt physical pain well beyond her injuries, a "pain that touched every cell of my body." She was experiencing sensory distortions. She was shaking visibly when she appeared in court. She could barely whisper. Her face was so swollen that the clerk asked her to take the gum out of her mouth.

"I don't have gum in my mouth," she said.

The court reporter began to cry.

Even after appearing in court, Michele still had difficulty grasping the reality of her situation. She told the lawyer that she and Evan had an appointment with the counselor that night. "You're not going to the appointment tonight," he said. "It's too late." Alone in her house with her children that night, she thought: "It was easier to be hit once in a while." But as confused as she was, she would hit upon a strategy that would not only usher her back into the world, it would give her career a new direction.

NINE

SEARCHING FOR FRANKENSTEIN: KNITTING WITH WORDS

"**WRITING HELPED TO** save my life," Michele wrote. "My own words were my own salvation. Writing helped me recover from divorce, rebuild my life, regain strength, and move past the pain." Writing wasn't the only strategy Michele employed in adapting to her new life and in building her new self. She went to weekly meetings at a shelter for abused women and learned by telling her story. She learned lessons that many survivors in the wilderness have learned. For example, that fear can be transformed into an anger that is powerfully motivating. It was a slow and difficult process. The sight of a father with his son at the park could fill her with longing for what might have been. She had nightmares and flashbacks just like a veteran of combat. But she had taken the first step in her new journey of survival: perceive and believe. "It is the first Herculean task," she wrote, "to accept the truth."

Then she began going through the steps: Stay calm. Think, analyze, and plan. Take action. She got rid of the clothes he had bought her as gifts after beating her. She had her hair dyed and cut short. She celebrated achieving these small goals and rewarded herself. She took long baths and wore blueberry mud masks and bought sexy new bras. She had a sheer white canopy put over her bed and reveled in the thought of how much Evan would have hated it. She began having better dreams, about old boyfriends and people she knew in high school. People who knew who she was before she became the catatonic abused wife. Before the shattered self, the dissociation. The dreams were part of the process of learning.

Michele's mother encouraged her to write about it. Writing lifted Michele out of the past by carrying her through it and giving her control of it. She found that writing calmed her. The flow of words with the clicking of fingers on the keyboard did something real to her nervous system. Writing holds a special place among the activities that people use to calm and heal themselves. It is physical, patterned, organized, rhythmic, and directed at a goal. But it is more. It also creates meaning as it flows. If the self is made of memories, as Bremner says, then writing lets us redraw the map of our memories and redefine the self.

Trauma continues to torment us even after it has ended, because it interrupts the narrative of our lives, the essential storytelling of the left brain. Tilmann Habermas, a psychologist at Goethe University in Frankfurt am Main, wrote that memories are strung together into a "coherent, ongoing narrative" to create what we know of as identity. From the age of about ten, the left hemisphere of the brain begins to create that narrative, arranging it in episodes and giving it coherence as adolescence ends and we enter our adult years. Trauma breaks that coherence and leaves the story in shambles. That's why we have to invent a new narrative. One of the reasons that writing is therapeutic for many people may be that the act of writing combines storytelling with a patterned, directed physical activity that engages the seeking pathway and with it the system of dopamine and reward.

Many people can enter an altered state of consciousness when they write or knit. It resembles a state that we ordinarily achieve only in sleep. Indeed, we rewrite our memories during sleep. Robert Stickgold, a psychiatrist at Harvard, enlisted volunteers to play a game called Tetris, in which animated geometrical pieces must be turned so that they fit together by the time they've fallen to the bottom of the computer screen. As the participants practiced the new skill, they began having dreams in which they saw the pieces falling and could even manipulate them in their sleep. Their skill improved rapidly. Normal sleep takes place in three stages. The first is a hypnagogic state between waking and sleeping in which we can experience a mixture of reality and dreamlike perceptions. The second is deep slow-wave sleep. And the third is REM (rapid eye movement) sleep during which we dream. Dreams can be thought of as conversations between two parts of the brain, the hippocampus, which creates short-term memories, and the neocortex, where long-term memories are thought to be stored. During training, networks of neurons in the hippocampus fire together to encode the learning (they fire together so they wire together). When you go to sleep, the hippocampus plays back those patterns to write a permanent record of them. At the same time, the amygdala becomes active and helps bestow emotional labels onto those memories. Whenever the memory is retrieved, an assembly of cells representing its good or bad qualities also becomes active and gives emotional meaning to the memory. If you sleep another night while learning a new skill, your performance improves even without any more actual practice. Sleep alone does the trick.

As you're falling asleep, you tend to replay sensory images of whatever activity you've been involved in. When I was a boy in Texas, we spent many summer days at Galveston beach. My brothers and I played in the surf all day long. At home in bed at night, in that hypnagogic state before sleep, I felt the slow pull and heave of the waves so profoundly that I sometimes pushed against it and fell right out of bed. When I was learning to fly aerobatics, I could see the world turning and feel the G-force as I ran through my routine while falling asleep.

When my daughter Amelia was four or five years old, I was teaching her to ride a bicycle. That process is always frustrating, so I took her aside to have a little talk with her. I said, "Look here, Pooch. One night you're going to go to sleep; and while you're asleep, you will have a dream. In that dream, you'll be riding your bicycle without training wheels. You'll ride like the wind. It'll be like flying. And the next morning, you're going to get up and you'll be able to ride. You'll see."

During the next week, I didn't push her to practice. She rode with training wheels, and I ran behind her, shouting encouragement. Then one morning, she shot out of bed and raced up to my office. "Pop! Pop!" she said. "I had the dream. Take the training wheels off."

We went outside. I unbolted the training wheels and threw them onto the lawn. Amelia mounted her bicycle, and I steadied her as she started off down the block. I ran with her for a few steps and then let go. And she raced ahead, shouting, "Pop! I can ride! I can ride!"

This was long before the research about the consolidation of memory. The reason that I told Amelia about the dream was that dreams had always played a part in my writing. That may be why I write early in the morning. For me, writing is like entering an unknown territory where I have no idea of what the hazards will be, how I'll find my way around, how or even if I'll get back again. Sometimes I become completely lost and have to give up. As with knitting, I have to rip out all the stitches and start over. But when I have been stuck at some crucial point in my work, a dream has always shown me the way forward.

Dreams and dreamlike states are a real and necessary work space in many types of pursuits, because a vast landscape lies beneath our conscious, deliberate lives. It's the emotional system, those subcortical areas that Dr. Carl Bennett described as tormenting him with their storms. It is as if we stand on the bow of a great ship with no idea who the captain is, nor what his intentions are, nor what powers far beneath the deck are taking us from place to remarkable place.

People from many walks of life have known about this phenomenon for a very long time. Friedrich August Kekulé was a German chemist who worked out the structure of the benzene molecule, an achievement that proved to have a profound influence on applied chemistry. For years he had been studying the way carbon and hydrogen atoms bind to each other. He described what happened shortly before he wrote his most important paper on benzene in 1865:

> I was sitting writing on my textbook, but the work did not progress; my thoughts were elsewhere. I turned my chair to the fire and dozed. Again the atoms were gamboling before my eyes. This time the smaller groups kept modestly in the background. My mental eye, rendered more acute by the repeated visions of the kind, could now distinguish larger structures of manifold conformation; long rows sometimes more closely fitted together all twining and twisting in snake-like motion. But look! What was that? One of the snakes had seized hold of its own tail, and the form whirled mockingly before my eyes. As if by a flash of lightning I awoke; and this time also I spent the rest of the night in working out the consequences of the hypothesis.

Benzene, of course, is a ring that looks like a snake biting its own tail.

In the "wet, ungenial summer" of 1816, Mary Wollstonecraft Godwin Shelley was visiting Switzerland with her famous husband. Lord Byron and his personal physician were her neighbors. The four were confined to their houses by rain. After some days of reading the books of ghost stories that the Shelleys found in their house, Byron suggested that they each write an original ghost story. But Mary could not think of anything to write. During those long and fruitless rainy days, she listened in as her husband and Byron discussed philosophy and entertained questions such as "the nature of the principle of life, and whether there was any probability of its ever being discovered," as she later wrote. After days of frustration, she experienced that hypnagogic state that comes just before sleep. "When I placed my head on the pillow I did not sleep, nor could I be said to think. My imagination, unbidden, possessed and guided me, gifting the successive images that arose in my mind with a vividness far beyond the usual bounds of reverie." Then she saw "the pale student of unhallowed arts kneeling beside the thing he had put together." The student, of course, was Dr. Frankenstein and the "thing" was his monster. And the idea that she had been searching for through all those rainy days became the novel *Frankenstein*. Her brain had nimbly and unconsciously assembled the tale, incorporating into it the philosophy she had heard discussed.

Stickgold's research, along with that of James McGaugh at the University of California at Irvine, among others, suggests just how deep and how far beyond deliberate conscious attention that creative process lies. Some of Stickgold's experimental subjects were amnesiacs who could form no new conscious memories at all. From one day to the next, they couldn't remember what the game of Tetris was. But they, too, dreamed of it, and their skill improved. They would even approach the computer and put their fingers on the correct keys for playing the game, though they had no idea why they did so. The subcortical parts of their brains had learned what their conscious minds could not reach except in dreams. This is the realm of Chris Lawrence and the sixth sense. This is The Stream.

Those dreamlike states play a part in helping us solve all sorts of problems in real life. When Aron Ralston was trapped by the boulder, it did not occur to him at first that he could cut off his hand to free himself. He tried all sorts of tactics to get the boulder off his hand, a very different approach to solving the problem (offending rock, not offending hand). It wasn't at all obvious that he should forget about moving the boulder. Indeed, even when he thought of cutting his hand off, he considered it impossible on two counts. It seemed like suicide: If you slash your wrist, don't you bleed to death? Moreover, he had no tool that could cut through bone. Exhausted, sleepless, dehydrated, Aron described what happened on the fifth day. He had already resigned himself to the fact that he was going to die there. He had taken out his knife and scratched his epitaph onto the wall, the dates of his birth and death. He understood that he would not make it through another freezing night in shirtsleeves. And as he waited, he must have dozed slightly, for he went into just such a hypnagogic state as I've been describing. He saw himself step away from his own body, which was pinned by his hand beneath the boulder. Then he had the vision of his future son; and as their eyes met, Aron realized that he was going to escape the canyon and live. And in that moment, the idea came to him of how he would escape.

In our hypnagogic states we gain special permission to enter the emotional life of memory beyond the realm of conscious thought. If we write and if we're lucky, there words are wed to the feelings of the body and given their cryptic power to move us to tears or laughter. There our inspirations and dreams are made manifest. The ideas that emerge from that secret place surprise us, because we ourselves do it. We must. We're alone. Yet we can't perceive ourselves doing it. Or else, like Aron, we perceive ourselves as other, as outside our normal selves. Aron's inspiration, like Kekulé's or like that of a great poet, seemed to spring full-blown out of nowhere. We can't achieve those states deliberately. We can't aim for them. We must act by indirection.

The *Tao Te Ching* says:

Fill your bowl to the brim
and it will spill.
Keep sharpening your knife
and it will blunt. . . .
Do your work, then step back.

That is what I mean when I say to trust the process and let go of the outcome. As Michele began to write her story, she felt the deep stirring within her: *This is who I am.* She had always wanted to be a writer. She had worked as a writer. And a man had tried to destroy that in her by stealing who she was. Now she was staking a claim on what was hers. "I was hurt, but I am still here," she wrote. "And I am good." An important part of the process of moving forward after trauma involves accepting yourself and what it means to be you in the aftermath of the event, whatever that event may be. I was attacked by a crocodile. I lost a child. I married the wrong guy. This is me, and I am still here. Writing it down binds it in The Stream of your subterranean memories.

. . .

VIKTOR FRANKL, the author of *Man's Search for Meaning*, said that to achieve success, we have to stop aiming for it. "The more you aim at it and make it a target, the more you are going to miss it." We must be doing something else with passion and a true heart, and only then will the thing that we call success present itself. In the 1920s, the German philosopher Eugen Herrigel studied the Zen discipline of archery in Japan. In his book *Zen in the Art of Archery*, he wrote that his master admonished him by saying that an art such as archery had no purpose at all. Herrigel's master, whose name was Kenzô, said that the harder he tried to hit the target, the worse he would do. He said that Herrigel had "a much too willful will." At the heart of his troubles, said Kenzô, was that Herrigel thought that "what you do not do yourself does not happen."

It is difficult to let go of desire, especially when it is a desire to be rid of something that torments us. It is difficult to let go of will and intent. But in letting go, we open up a space in which something brilliant can emerge from below. This is true of writing but also of many other pursuits. Archery. Knitting. Golf. When Aron admitted to himself that he would probably die, when he let go of that concern, he had the vision, became convinced that he would live, and was inspired to break his own bones. Thus do we invert what we consider the normal order of things. The part of the brain-body complex that ordinarily remains out of reach is suddenly thrust into the foreground. The logical processes of deliberate thought and action are not so much eclipsed as they are enlisted into subterranean service. That is why people lose track of time when they engage in these repetitive patterns of physical activities that induce dreamlike states. In *Anna Karenina*, Leo Tolstoy described Konstantin Dmitrievitch Levin going into such a state while cutting grass with a scythe. As he fell into the rhythm of swinging the scythe, he "lost all sense of time." He went into a very pleasurable dissociative state in which, though he didn't even know what he was doing, he was doing it with great skill and precision. Moreover, if he suddenly became conscious again of what he was doing and tried to pay attention to it, his performance deteriorated. It was only in the magic of oblivion that he could achieve transcendent perfection.

Not looking at the target, entering dreamlike states, can lead to inspiration: the voices and images that come from beyond consciousness. In moving on in the aftermath of survival, we can train ourselves to enter that secret neurological landscape described by Kekulé and Shelley and Tolstoy. It is the same place that may be reached through meditation, the place where the brain and body are one and where we can discard the concept of mind, because we've become a being that is no longer divided.

Most people have a way of entering that state of flow, what Aldous Huxley called deep reflection. Mihaly Csikszentmihalyi, a psychologist at Claremont Graduate University, coined the term *flow* and referred to it as an "optimal experience." For some people, as we'll see, it comes on the golf course. For others, while swimming, playing an instrument, cooking, knitting, or even ironing clothes and doing housework. For Michele, it came while writing.

Ann Hood wrote that knitting was a form of meditation. She said that she and the women with whom she knitted all entered what she called a "still place." The world outside vanished and all their attention was absorbed by the singular act of knitting. Knitting, like writing, is a form of prayer.

I love writing because I can be completely in the moment. My attention is full. Nothing else seems to exist, and I can feel the flow of energy going through me, entering somewhere that feels like the top of my head and churning up the very substance of my center and then drawing that substance up and out through my fingers and shooting it out my eyes like a beam of light. It feels like the wind on a hot summer day that comes down cold from 20,000 feet as a thunderstorm is building. Flying aerobatics gave me that same sort of feeling as I drew figures in the sky with a high-performance plane, like writing with a great pen, doing Cuban eights and seeing the earth swirling up at me in a gumbo of green and yellow and knowing that I could yell and scream and praise the Lord, but only the skill in my own two hands and the calmness in my heart could bring me safely home again.

I wanted to know the unknowable and my father, the scientist, the professor, could not tell me. My mother could because she read fiction and fantasy. But it was coded so that it appealed to a part of the brain beyond consciousness, so it carried the feeling of being a right answer without any way to articulate it, in the same way that an aroma of gardenias can reach inside you and find its rightful place, its confirmation, and yet remain out of reach of some literal explanation of its effects. The scent of a gardenia is true even if you can't articulate it. Or, as Edna St. Vincent Millay put it, "It is a thing that exists simply, like a sapphire, like anything roundly beautiful; there is nothing to be done about it."

Peter Ilych Tchaikovsky, the Russian composer, described "the germ of a future composition" coming "suddenly and unexpectedly" upon him. "It would be vain to try to put into words," he said, "that immeasurable sense of bliss which comes over me directly a new idea awakens in me and begins to assume a different form. I forget everything and behave like a madman." It is the very bliss of this madness that is our salvation in the aftermath of trauma. For it is a madness within which we can remain sane. A madness that takes over the instruments of emotion and redirects them away from our agony and toward something meaningful, useful, something purposeful, and even blissful. Art, science, sport, learning are all effective responses to trauma.

A CANADIAN psychologist named Michael Persinger decided to stimulate the temporal lobe of his own brain electrically to see what would happen. The temporal lobe contains the main structures of the emotional system. It labels the world of mental models with emotional markers to guide our behavior. When Persinger turned on the current, he experienced . . . God.

Andrew Newberg, a scientist at the University of Pennsylvania, studies the biological basis of religious and mystical experiences. He scanned the brain of a mystic who was in a trance induced by meditation, the state of nirvana, so to speak. The scan showed a sharp decrease in activity in the parietal lobe, the Where Pathway, which, as we've seen, tells you where things are in space, including your own body. It gives you an image of your body, so that you know where your limbs are and can do physical things with the substance of the world around you. The parietal lobe makes clear what is you and what is everything else. The mystic had turned off his parietal lobe through meditation, which put him in a state where he had lost his orientation in space, as well as the boundary between himself and the outside world. In sexual ecstasy, we lose our boundaries, both figuratively and literally. To reproduce, we have to violate the covenant of the immune system, that only what is us can be allowed to remain inside and all other organisms must be killed. To reproduce, two immune systems must reach a truce, however brief, to join two sets of genes. Sex transcends the Where Pathway, which helps define what is us and what is not and which end is up. That's why it's possible to feel head over heels in love. The chemistry of love can turn us upside down.

Ramachandran wrote of "temporal lobe storms" resulting in "deeply moving spiritual experiences, including a feeling" that God is visiting you personally and suffusing you with his message and his love. The temporal lobe contains the hippocampus and amygdala, among other structures. In a lecture he gave at the TED conference, Oliver Sacks said that temporal-lobe hallucinations can also transport you in a kind of super déjà-vu fashion to a specific time and place in which you experience all the sensory perceptions from that past experience. Sights, smells, sounds, feelings, all come rushing back to you enriched by the appropriate emotions. That ability to transcend the humdrum logic of everyday life bears on how well we deal with the most brutal experiences. The transports that artists experience during the most intense moments of creation may be kin to temporal-lobe seizures.

It may be no coincidence that some patients with chronic temporal-lobe seizures develop a condition called hypergraphia, in which they compulsively write hundreds and hundreds of pages of text. Like my mother's German grandmother, who would get up from the table during a meal and say, "I have to go write now," and then disappear into her own secret world. When we enter that occult landscape where ecstasy and invention meet and mingle with our wordhoard and with all our worldly experiences that give words their textures and flavors, we are in a terrain that is similar to the one we enter during sex. The networks in the brain and body that are involved in mystical and transcendental states are the same ones that are responsible for sexual bliss and orgasm. In fact, women may have orgasms during temporal-lobe seizures. (No men have yet reported this.)

Susan K. Perry is a social psychologist who wrote a book titled *Writing in Flow*. One of the writers she interviewed said, "After a really good writing session, I feel very sexual. . . . Sometimes after writing, I'll masturbate." She's not the only writer to report that, either. Writing requires a state of arousal that for many people is readily interpreted by the emotional system as having sexual overtones. And, of course, writing is sexual because the dramatic shape of a well-wrought story mimics the emotional shape of an orgasm, the ultimate emotional response.

Writing is also a social behavior. It is a form of communication that can initiate emotional contagion, bringing together and synchronizing two emotional systems, the writer's and the reader's, and making them resonate as one. When Michele engaged in writing to move herself beyond trauma and grief, she entrained the deepest parts of her battered emotional system in the construction of her new self. Many survivors when lost in the wilderness begin talking to the animals they encounter there. Lost in her emotional wilderness, Michele was doing something similar. And when you think about it, writing is a lot like talking to someone who isn't there. It's a lot like prayer. Michele prayed a lot, too.

TO ACHIEVE emotional reserve, we do as Eagleman said of cognitive reserve: Blanket "a problem with overlapping solutions." Michele employed overlapping strategies to propel herself forward. Her children, for example, were an important part of her adaptation. For one thing, they made her get out of bed in the morning. She took solace in cooking, a physical activity involving patterns and ordered steps that lead to a goal. "The process of mixing and kneading or stirring and adding was quieting to me." She celebrated her small successes. "Some days a triumph was defined by bottoms of cookies that weren't black."

The reminders of violence lurked in Michele's house. The sight of the coatrack at the back door gave her chills because that's where Evan had been standing when he said it: "Please, God, let me kill her." That visual cue set off the same terror and dissociation she had experienced during the actual event. After she had gotten the court order to bar her husband from the house, her son Weldon asked, "Can we please live somewhere Daddy hasn't been?" Michele moved her family to a new house. The smells were different now. They didn't jolt her into flashbacks of having a fist slammed into her face. She painted rooms, hung new curtains. "With dozens of different textures of rags," she wrote, "I rubbed and rolled the paint in varying intensities, washing, smooshing and spreading my soul in every inch of wall in that room until I felt the best I had in years." We map our surroundings using the hippocampus so that we know where we are, vital information for survival. By changing her surroundings, Michele was forcing that system to create new maps that did not match the ugly memories. In painting the walls, she was painting over old memories.

Like so many survivors, Michele developed a mantra. Echoing Montaigne (*Que sais-je?*), she asked, "What do you know to be true?" She wrote: "Some women paint, others sew, some run, garden, or master a skill. Still others hold their pain inside them, hoping it will not leak all over the carpets and the new furniture in the middle of the Christmas party with all the relatives present. I write."

If we are to survive beyond our own experience of survival, we must all become artists in some sense, the artists of our own lives, in possession of the keys that allow us to enter that transcendent state that will remake us.

TEN

LESSONS FROM ISHMAEL: THE NEUROPHYSIOLOGY OF TRAVEL

IN THE SUMMER of 1988, Kathy Russell Rich, a writer and editor who lived in New York, suddenly knew that she had cancer before she was even diagnosed. She called it a "sharp, instinctive knowledge that I had cancer." She knew it with her sixth sense. She knew it in The Stream.

When she was finally diagnosed, confirming her intuition, her chemotherapy was devastating. It distorted her body image until she could barely recognize the self she had always known. Her words should have a familiar ring by now: "I kept trying to dive back in, but my old life wouldn't have me." She found that she simply could not put the cancer behind her. It was part of her. She tried running away to the Caribbean. It was a relief, but it didn't last. She would lie out on the beach and close her eyes. Suddenly, she'd be back in the green room where she'd been burned with radiation. The technicians had placed marks on her skin so that they could aim the beam at the same spot each time. The marks were tattoos. They were permanent. Those tattoos were still on Kathy's chest, and each time she opened her eyes, she saw them and received another jolt of traumatic memory. She realized that she was lying on the sand with one arm thrown over her eyes, the exact position she'd adopted during the treatments. Reliably, the body had called up the nasty memory that matched her posture. Then the arm itself gave expression to what she was going through: It swelled so severely with lymphedema that she couldn't get her bracelet off.

Eerily, she also knew that the cancer wasn't gone. She had the intuition again. She compared it to being in a store that had just been robbed and knowing that the gunman had not yet left the building. She was having the same odd feelings that she'd had before the first diagnosis. The emotional system, which we reach through our hypnagogic states, speaks to us in a foreign language and not in the language of the neocortex. We are multiple selves, and one covert self really does know what's going on in the body, if only we can listen. Kathy's body began tormenting her with dreams to try to get her to pay attention. In her journal she wrote of one such dream: *Danger's coming.* She had nightmares about nuclear explosions and about being led through a museum of death.

Just when she was supposed to be getting over it and getting on with it, a scan revealed that the cancer was "everywhere" in her bones. She had tumors in her skull. Her oncologist gave her "a year or two" to live. Her only hope was a bone-marrow transplant, a risky procedure that killed most people at that time. It involved destroying the immune system and replacing it with a new one through transplanted stem cells. (This type of stem cell comes from bone marrow.) Since the immune system defines what is you and what is not, this would represent the ultimate rewriting of the self.

It was around Christmastime that Kathy entered her apartment, gathered her mail, and dropped a piece of it on the floor. When she bent to pick it up, she felt something tear in her back and actually heard the bone collapse. She fell to her knees. She managed to grab her cordless phone and make it to bed. She wouldn't stand again for two months. Deep into that night, three in the morning, she had to pee so badly that she used a nearby water glass. In the morning, she called a friend to summon an ambulance. In the hospital, X-rays revealed that two vertebrae in her spine had collapsed into mush. And in the hospital, an orderly dropped her and crushed a third. Kathy actually grew shorter. As the cancer broke her bones, it entered her spine. She was within a few days of the time when it would sever her spine and paralyze her. She was going to die if they didn't begin the transplant immediately. Meanwhile, nothing could control the pain.

Kathy was thirty-two years old when she was first diagnosed with breast cancer. The cancer came back and began eating her bones when she was thirty-seven. After two years of being treated with different hormones, she was ready for a bone-marrow transplant, her only hope of living much longer. The doctors started her on six months of chemotherapy in preparation for what she called "four high-dose chemo bombs." The plan was that they would nearly kill her and then just at the last moment, snatch her back from death's door. Kathy found that her mental state had become "fighting mad." She was recruiting her rage pathway in support of what she would have to endure. There are times when you want to shut that pathway off when the crisis has passed. But the crocodile's teeth were sunk deep into Kathy and she needed to scream and fight. She had been working on being happy before. But by the time of the transplant, she was deep in, working the survivor model just as Steve Callahan had in a raft on the open ocean. "I can only afford success," he told himself at crucial moments. "Don't hurry. Make it right."

The chemo bombs attacked her immune system and gradually destroyed it. I think of the emotional system as an extension of the immune system, since both are essentially concerned with defining and defending what the self is. The immune system detects foreign invaders. The emotional system detects what would harm the self as well as that which can maintain it, such as food. As Kathy's immune system dissolved, depression set in. It makes sense: By killing the immune system, a bone-marrow transplant actually kills off an essential boundary of the self. You awake a stranger to yourself. With an injection of bone-marrow cells, her immune system would rebuild itself. But Kathy had to take drastic measures to build a new emotional system, and thereby create a new and integrated Kathy Russell Rich.

Once again, she found her answer in The Stream. Her intuition spoke to her. Only this time, it told her that she was going to do well. The gunman had left the building, as she put it. "Intuition," Kathy wrote, "is crucial to healing." She stayed on her task of survival, imagining a future in which she was alive, robust. Survivors who are shipwrecked at sea tell of keeping themselves going by daydreaming of what they'll do in the future. Kathy began planning a bicycling trip through Turkey. And when the weight of her illness was too overpowering, her friends conjured the future for her. Everything made her cry. She was, at the last, like a survivor at the end of the Holocaust, "keeping myself going largely on reminders that there would be an end." When it arrived, it was all anticlimax.

All of a sudden, she found herself at home, alone, in an apartment that looked like an alien landscape. It was October and the furnace had not yet been turned on. She felt so cold that she practically lived in the bathtub. Her senses were so raw that she described the dripping faucet as sounding like gunshots. She was in the bathroom so much that she couldn't avoid catching glimpses of herself in the mirror. Kathy said that the only parts of her that looked familiar were the soles of her feet. Months passed before she was strong enough to go outside. Kathy responded to noises as if she suffered from post-traumatic stress. And she thought longingly of death as if she were suffering from depression. But her white-cell count rose, and her body grew stronger, and one day she admonished herself: She could not have a procedure that cost a quarter of a million dollars and then think about killing herself. It wasn't allowed. It would have been grotesquely un-American. She found that thought funny enough to make her smile. And the smile made her feel good.

In January, she went back to working half days. February made her less susceptible to pain. March sent her shopping. April: She began to grow real hair. Midsummer: She had a crew cut and a mountain bike. She'd bought tickets to Turkey. And it was good and it helped and it gave her confidence. But her self had been irretrievably altered. Try as she might, she could not slip back into it. It would not have her. So she did something brilliant. She went to India to spend a year learning to speak and read and write in Hindi. Yes, I had the same response as when I heard that knitting had saved Ann Hood's life.

Hindi? Maybe she means Indy, I thought. You know. Where they have that car race?

TRAVEL IS a time-honored strategy for healing. That may be the real reason that ancient people migrated out of Africa: As the human brain grew into the speculative and contemplative organ that it is, our capacity for grief grew as well. I doubt that we had to leave Africa because it was full. Travel may have been an early adaptation to profound grief. It forces the unconscious reorganization of a number of areas in the brain, especially those involving the hippocampus, which has the special function of creating spatial maps. Every time you travel to an unfamiliar environment, your brain undergoes an important transformation. In going to India, Kathy rendered all the mental maps of her surroundings invalid, including the ones she'd made for her apartment and the maps of her neighborhood and the less detailed ones of Manhattan and even her position on the North American continent. Having an accurate mental map of your environment is extremely important if you're an animal that likes to do things such as eat and avoid predators. Without an up-to-date mental map, you might as well be dead. In fact, your emotional system sets off alarm signals when the map in your head doesn't match the environment. When your emotional system is disrupted by trauma, all that activity can have a salutary effect.

When Kathy arrived in India, her temporal lobes, including her emotional system and hippocampus, concluded that she was lost. Those structures in the brain did not evolve with an interpretation of the world that includes the concept of tourism. The emergency of being lost is frightening. Your emotional brain considers it an urgent business. So your brain gets very busy when you're in an unfamiliar place, but busy in a way that you can't perceive at a conscious level. You can feel it getting busy, but you don't know quite what you're feeling. You may simply say that it's exciting to travel, because even while the amygdala is trying to create an emergency response and the hippocampus is trying to take in all this new information for its cartographic endeavors, the conscious and rational part of your brain knows that you're safe. So even as the unconscious part of your brain is working as if it's an emergency, your frontal lobes are putting a damper on the response with the aid of reason and logic and the reassuring knowledge that you're safe. It is the tension, the struggle, between these two parts of the brain, that lends an air of fun and excitement to travel. What Panksepp said about the seeking pathway can also be said of the process of making new mental maps: It "supports expectancy, exploration, foraging." Moreover, when you're in a new place, you don't have the same cues to set off your troubling emotions, those accidental conditioned responses that can be so painful.

Making new mental maps is merely one job the brain has to accomplish in such an unfamiliar environment. The language, the food, the music, the smells and sights and sounds are all different. The neural pathways of the brain are busy sorting through all that information to create and catalog new mental models. Then once you've been in the new place for a while, the hippocampus actually does wire up a new mental map and sends signals to the emotional system that you're not lost anymore. The emotional system obediently calms down.

At the beginning of *Moby-Dick*, Ishmael says, "Whenever I find myself growing grim about the mouth; whenever it is a damp, drizzly November in my soul; whenever I find myself involuntarily pausing before coffin warehouses, and bringing up the rear of every funeral I meet; and especially whenever my hypos get such an upper hand of me, that it requires a strong moral principle to prevent me from deliberately stepping into the street and methodically knocking people's hats off—then, I account it high time to get to sea as soon as I can."

Yossi Ghinsberg was lost and nearly died in the jungles of Bolivia when he was in his twenties. Although he survived, his best friend did not. When I told his story in *Deep Survival*, it ended with Yossi's rescue. But of course, that's not really where the story ended. It has not ended yet.

For a time, Yossi had no aftereffects from his traumatic experience. "I never had a nightmare and never suffered any fear or anxiety whatsoever," he told me. He returned home to Israel and went on with his life. He went back to school, got married, and entered into his career. But a few years later, he said, "I felt a great sense of confusion, a sense of alienation, not belonging at home and in my society, not interested in my career." He said he felt like a modern-day Fisher King. "All I could do to find solace for my pain was to get on the road and travel again, this time without destination or time frame. I left everything behind and set out on this journey that never stopped." As he wrote to me, "Initially I was seeking answers and understanding. Why am I alive, and my best friend who was a better person is dead? Who spared my life and what does it mean? What is my purpose for existing in the world?" Yossi literally wandered the world, leading a Bohemian life, studying religion, the occult, meditation. He threw himself into the deepest places of wilderness that he could find. As he put it, "I found home everywhere." He finally put it all behind him. He traveled it out of his system until he was no longer searching for answers. He began giving talks about his journey. That act of sharing became his "identity and purpose." Travel can help many of us. And the more intensely challenging the activities you include with it, the more effective it is as therapy.

Various terms have been used for mental models. I've mentioned several of them. "Sparse coding" is another one. It means that only a small amount of the total information is stored at any given location in the brain. That's why incomplete bits of sensory information can light up the entire network. A circle with a curlicue in the center makes many people think of a pig. You have a lot more detailed information in your brain about pigs, but those marks are enough to call up a generalized pig. The hippocampus is doing this all the time with everything you perceive through the senses and through whatever rises up out of memory.

The hippocampus also encodes what are known as place cells.

Those cells fire when you're in a particular place. Some researchers think that originally the hippocampus may have been for nothing more than encoding maps of the environment. Gradually, it may have been taken over for creating other kinds of memories. Whatever you put into the hippocampus, out comes a map. As with identifying a pig from sparse information, the hippocampus can identify places from scant information. You can paint your walls and change all the furniture and still know where you are in your house. But if you move to a new house (or nation), your hippocampus has to map everything about the place and push the old maps into long-term storage. They'll probably fade over time, so that you might not be able to quite remember where everything was.

As you move around in your environment the hippocampus makes a grid of it. It does this by firing at regular intervals what are known as grid cells, thereby making landmarks. When you go to a new place (India in Kathy's case), the grid cells are turned on instantly while the place cells in the hippocampus take more time to wire up. If you go in a straight line and don't cross your own path, your hippocampus won't encode place cells and you won't wind up with a mental map of your environment. You can physically create a mental map by walking around or you can do it by rehearsing the space in your head, say, by studying a road map. The reason people offer to give you a tour of their homes the first time you visit is that they understand at an unconscious level that the emotional system craves a reliable mental map, and walking around makes one. Movement is necessary for making maps. Since the same pathways are responsible for making memories, movement is required for making memories as well. It may be imagined movement, but to the brain it looks the same.

So-called theta rhythms arise in the hippocampus when you move around and navigate, making your mental maps. They pulse at about 8 to 12 times a second. (Our muscles pulse at this rate, too, and voluntary movements are timed to be in phase with those pulses.) This holds true even if you're only navigating your own memory, and the rhythms are sustained as long as you continue doing it. "Theta oscillation is also the hallmark of REM sleep,"

György Buzsaki writes of his work in neuroscience at Rutgers University. So, in a real sense, walking around, navigating, can help put you into a hypnagogic state that opens onto that vast subterranean landscape we are privileged to view during sleep.

Moreover, to the brain, taking a long walk and remembering stuff look very much alike. Place cells arise at junctions. Maps and memories are consolidated in sleep and transferred to the neocortex for long-term storage. Ultimately, Buzsaki says, "Episodic and semantic memory . . . may have evolved from mechanisms serving dead-reckoning and map-based navigation, respectively."

So Kathy's intuition that going to India to study Hindi would help her was spot-on. Travel was good medicine in itself, and for Kathy, an American New Yorker, India represented high-dose travel. She was, after all, living in a place where she might encounter a leopard. But the combination of travel to sweep away all her old mental maps and the necessity of learning an entire universe of new mental models, including words, was an inspired way to create the new self she needed. It made her a child, a beginner at life, one of those little people who routinely build new immune systems and emotional systems from scratch. At the same time, learning the language engaged the habit-forming cerebellum and basal ganglia that are involved in helping new skills become automatic. As a beginner at Hindi, she had to occupy her hippocampus and neocortex in deliberately storing explicit memories of how things are said or how they look on the page. She had to deliberately steer her hand to knit the snaking letters with pen and ink.

Language is a special form of what Rodolfo Llinás, at New York University, calls a fixed action pattern. He also calls such patterns motor tapes. David Eagleman calls them mechanical, alien subroutines or zombie systems. In the past, I've referred to such automatic actions as behavioral scripts. A simple example of a behavioral script is the act of tying your shoe. When you are four years old and try to learn, it takes all your concentration. Once you've learned, it takes no concentration at all. In fact, as Tolstoy's Konstantin Levin saw, concentrating on such an activity can mess it up. Behavioral scripts are controlled by memories that are not available to the conscious mind. When something in the environment sets them in motion, they run their instructions automatically, making you perform whatever behavior is encoded in these memories. They do not ask for your permission. They evolved because they're efficient. The novice burns energy like mad. Experts use very little energy. (I experienced this while trying to learn to play racquetball. My opponent beat me by forcing me to run all over the court, chasing shots, while he stood calmly in the center, barely breaking a sweat.)

An infant is born with the ability to produce innate movements. They come from central pattern generators in the spine. These are essentially neuromuscular explosions, small neuronal storms that set off spasms of the muscles. The neuromuscular system is a complex system, and those explosions are emergent phenomena. That means that there is nothing controlling the system. It's like weather: It organizes itself. And the patterns that emerge are not designed, they just happen—hence the term "emergent." Thunderstorms are the emergent expression of a complex system known as weather. And like neuromuscular explosions, no two thunderstorms are exactly the same, though they all share general features.

The emergent movements that infants make are chaotic and undirected at first. But through seeing people do things (mirror neurons) and through the Want-it-Need-it-Have-it process, the randomness of those movements is gradually reduced until they become coherent, directed, intentional. You can see this when a baby learns to walk. At first, the central pattern generator is simply producing bursts of jerky motion in the muscles of the legs, giving toddlers their odd marching gait. But as the baby practices, the cerebellum detects errors and irregularities and begins correcting and smoothing the walk until it becomes fluid. The action gradually develops into a behavioral script, a fixed action pattern, and it can play out with no need for conscious thought or deliberate effort.

Practicing a skill such as playing the piano follows a similar process. Once the action moves out of the conscious, step-by-step parts of the brain and into the unconscious parts, it can give rise to movements with a speed and accuracy you can't duplicate consciously. Buzsaki cites Glenn Gould's 1955 recording of the *Gold-*

berg Variations. Some of the passages are at the upper limit of speed for muscular movement, about 10 or 11 movements each second. Once learned (no mean feat), such an action becomes ballistic. That is, like a bullet fired from a gun, once it is set in motion, it requires no sensory feedback or further guidance. It becomes the equivalent of the neuromuscular storm of an explosive serve in tennis. Such an action is truly out of the thinking and even the sensing brain and is driven one-way by the cerebellum and basal ganglia in a power storm of activity. These types of actions represent the berserkers of skills, literally going naked into battle without any of the adornments of thought or sensory reflection. That's what happens when we learn language. The production of speech itself becomes an explosive and emergent behavioral script. We may think that we deliberately and consciously say whatever comes out of our mouths when we talk, but that's an illusion.

Robert Sapolsky told me, "My father had a pretty severe dementia late in life, and while he eventually couldn't tell you what decade it was, he could give a 10-minute lecture on the history of flying buttresses. [He was an architectural historian.] And then, 30 seconds later, give the same lecture again, verbatim." The reason he could do that is that the lecture, the act of speaking those words, with all their subtle inflections, had become a fixed action pattern, a behavioral script that would run automatically. This works much like a conditioned response in which assemblies of cells that fire together wire together.

James McGaugh, one of the top experts on memory in the nation, wrote, "[We] all have a private world of learning and memory that is not accessible to conscious experience." He illustrated that with the story of a Hungarian colleague of his who was at work when he received word that his mother had suffered a stroke and was in the hospital. The doctors reported that she was speaking complete gibberish and they couldn't understand her. He rushed to the hospital to find that she was speaking Hungarian, her native language. Even though she hadn't spoken Hungarian since she was a teen, the stroke had wiped out English and left her with the fixed action patterns of Hungarian.

So, in learning Hindi, Kathy was tapping into an extremely powerful physical engagement of not only her seeking pathway but of her entire emotional system and its relationship with the body and the control of movement.

FLASHES OF her old life came back to her unexpectedly in that new place. When she sat to receive a henna tattoo, the cold wet sensation of the dye on her skin sent her into a panic, because it felt exactly like the swab of alcohol before a biopsy. In receiving the tattoo in that setting, she was able to rewire that part of her brain. "Rips turn to hearts turn to flowers," she wrote. Kathy found that even the syntax of Hindi was helpful in constructing the new self. "The courtly politeness of Hindi filters into my English. . . . It leeches my American personality, makes me feel I've gone pale. . . . We are how we speak." Indeed, learning a new language deeply changes the way you speak your own native tongue. You will never speak quite the same way again. The effect of her bold undertaking was immediate. A month in, she wrote to a friend, "I've never been so happy."

Words stake out territory in your brain just as people and objects do. Indian people have looks, gestures, body language, and facial expressions that are dramatically different from what we see in the Western world. Because we are human, we must mimic what we see. Through this mimicry, Kathy was able to begin feeling what the Indian people felt: emotional contagion. Indeed, the same areas of the brain that are involved with language are involved in the system of mirror neurons. That system and the innate reflex of imitating others make us effective as social beings: If you live in groups, you have to know what's going on with the others in the group. And language is an extension of that system for knowing what's going on: You can ask. You can tell. So the new language and the culture in which it was embedded gave rise to new emotions that Kathy had never felt. This served to reorganize the landscape of her brain and body even further. A. L. Becker, author of *Beyond Translation*, has shown that your face is actually reshaped by learning a new language, which requires recruiting new patterns of activity in your muscles. So Kathy could look in the mirror and see the new self taking shape.

Being in the new place where you're learning the language makes you doubly lost. And when you wish to rebuild the self, lost is good. When dealing with trauma, the more lost you can be, the better. Being lost in this sense is akin to the hypnagogic state. It carries the meaning of losing yourself in a good book or in the task of knitting or doing surgery. You're lost with a plan. Or, as my brother Philip says, "Learning starts with a willingness to be lost."

Your brain wants to learn whatever language it hears and learns it despite you and even beyond your ability to discern that you're learning. Lee Osterhout at the University of Washington did brain scans of students who had just started studying French. After they had practiced for just a few hours, Osterhout discovered that they couldn't tell the difference between real words in French and words that were made up and just looked like French. But their brains could tell. That is, even though the students were not yet able to speak the language, Osterhout and his colleagues could measure electrical signals in the brain that responded in the same way that a native speaker's brain would, showing recognition of the difference between real words in French and fake words that merely looked French. Although the students' brains showed this signal of recognition, they couldn't articulate that recognition consciously. It was strictly on the level of the sixth sense. Nine months into the course, the students were much better at speaking French, but their brains were processing the language like native speakers. Learning a language forces you to get out of your own way.

Kathy found that the harder she worked, the worse things got. Only when she finally gave up did she begin to make real progress. At some point in the process of learning, you have to back off and let the brain do what it knows how to do. This is related to the Zen concept of Beginner's Mind. As the Zen teacher told Herrigel, who was trying so hard to learn archery, you do not hit the target by trying. Practice, practice, practice, yes. But then let go of the outcome and trust the process. This is why great ideas often occur in the shower: You're not trying very hard when you're taking a shower. You may not even be thinking about your task. Osterhout's students teach us something else as well: We know much of our lives in that same way. Like Chris Lawrence, like Kathy Rich, we know more than we know we know. The brain is learning faster than our conscious minds can keep up. Remember the blind person who can point to the light. Remember the frog and the rat. Remember The Stream.

It takes children about 10 years to become expert speakers of their native language. With much room for variation, that's roughly how long it takes to become expert at anything physical (violin, tennis, golf). When you say or read a word that denotes movement (pinch, punch, grip), the area of your brain used for making that movement becomes active, as if you're actually pinching or punching. Many scientists believe that language arose from sign language, and when you learn a language, you learn the gestures that go along with it. Learning a new language requires a new set of physical movements. They are not just random motions. They're bound to the words, and when senility begins to steal language from you, it steals the gestures as well. Indeed, learning a second language and practicing it every day, along with your native tongue, can put off senility by years.

HALFWAY THROUGH her stay in India, Kathy realized that her old self was fading away and being replaced. "The values of the place I was from . . . had come to seem, when I encountered them now, galling and strange. In turn, I'd begun to feel I wasn't myself." The way Kathy took in the world changed while she was living in that small town in India. One day she happened to see a tourist, a westerner, and was astonished at how strange the woman looked. Her gait appeared to Kathy as if she were stomping on something. She was shocked by her bare legs, "hard and knotted as a laborer's." Indian women never showed their legs in public. (In fact, a husband in India might never see his wife naked.) Kathy even tsked at the tourist as she passed by, shocking herself with her own prudery. "It was as if I'd been possessed, and I have been: by words."

By the time she returned to the United States, Kathy found that she was reflexively able to switch into the new self at the slightest encouragement from the environment. She was on the phone with a call center and found herself arguing with a man who wasn't giving her the service she expected. She felt suddenly strange and out of character and stopped to ask where he was from. Bangalore, he said. His slight accent had done it. "It had taken only a hint of Indian prosody, the faintest singsong, to trigger in me a whole neuronal constellation of a self that had formed the year before." This was precisely the effect that Oliver Sacks saw in Carl Bennett when he performed surgery and lost all trace of his Tourette's syndrome: a switching of selves, forgetting one and remembering another.

"Dreaming in Hindi," Kathy told me of the book she wrote, "is all about how you bring yourself back to life after you've been assured you were going to die imminently and then didn't. But could any minute. But don't. And now here you are."

We're all here by chance. One day while I was writing this book, I went with my wife, Debbie, to visit her mother. She drove on the return trip. We were stopped at a light near our favorite ethnic grocery store when we heard that unmistakable sound, at once high and low, the shriek and moan of tortured metal, and I saw something black go rocketing across the intersection. I had not seen the impact, because we were three cars back and the view was obscured by a white van. At first I couldn't tell what the black object was. Then I realized that it was a badly crushed motor scooter. I leapt out and ran to the intersection to see if I could help. People in the cars around me were on their cell phones. I came around the white van to find a man lying on his back on the pavement. He wore a motorcycle helmet, but one look at his expression, his body, told me that he was dying. His face was contorted and his breathing came in short and labored bursts punctuated by soft animal groans. His penis, hanging out of a tear in his pants, looked so vulnerable I felt my heart collapse. That poor pilgrim, frozen in an attitude of such extravagance in his last moments, curled in on himself as if in deep concentration on the task of passing through that hard door of escape from this vale of tears.

I immediately saw what had happened. He had been clipping

along, secure in his helmet, when a car turned left in front of him. He hit the car without even braking. Now a woman was shrieking and screaming, "I didn't see him! I didn't see him!" Her hands over her ears as if to block out the sound that she would hear, waking or sleeping, for the rest of her life. Thomas W. Hensel died on the scene. He was fifty years old and had a wife who was a doctor and two young children. He lived in a fine house in an affluent suburb and was just out running an errand on a nice sunny day. The scooter probably seemed like a good idea to save gas, a trivial decision in the great scheme of things.

When you see how fragile and dependent upon chance life is, you begin to think like Kathy Russel Rich and Micki Glenn and Chris Lawrence. We're all in the same position. We're all riding on the back of Tom Hensel's scooter. And we'd all do well to become true believers.

ELEVEN

THE BEAR:
ONE FLEW EAST,
ONE FLEW WEST

IN THE FALL of 1983, Patricia van Tighem and her husband, Trevor Janz, were hiking the Crypt Lake Trail in Waterton Lakes National Park. At twenty-four, Patricia was just out of school and had been working as a nurse in the hectic surgical ward at a hospital in Calgary. Trevor was a third-year medical student. They hit the trail in the early-morning chill, moving easily under bright autumn sunshine past rock outcroppings overgrown with wind-sculpted pines and covered with soft moss and grass. Waterton-Glacier International Peace Park is the great engine that whips up the weather for the rest of the continent and sends it howling down toward Fargo and Minneapolis. It embodies some of the last true wilderness in the lower 48 states, a place of beautiful hazards.

As they moved up the switchback trail, they met other hikers and stopped to take photographs. But as they passed on into a dense pine forest, Patricia was beset by a sense of foreboding. Something was not right. Trevor called her paranoid, but Patricia wanted to stop and rest and take in the scene. She could not say why. While they sat on a rock, she took some pine needles in her hands and crushed them to intensify their aroma. She loved the smell of pine. They resumed their climb, passing four hikers going the other way. They could see the snow forming at higher elevations. Cold descended as they passed a group of 20 children accompanied by adults. It was a popular trail. There seemed no reason for concern. Yet as they came into view of a waterfall, Patricia stopped again. An awful smell hit her, but Trevor dismissed it. A bighorn sheep had died just off the trail. And though she didn't know that fact, she could smell its decomposing body, and somewhere deep within her, unconscious memory traces were drawing conclusions about that and trying to signal to her that this matter needed attention. She was in The Stream. Chris Lawrence would say that the universe was trying to speak to Patricia. Her amygdala instantly picked up the smell and a single word rose to her conscious mind: *bear.* Once again, the brain always knows more than we consciously know. Patricia's subtle inner guess was correct. She voiced her concern about bears. But Trevor's enthusiasm won out and they pressed on up the trail.

That night, the camp was cold, despite a fire that some other hikers had made. Patricia and Trevor joined them. Snow began in the night and was still falling when they woke. Soon they were back on the trail in a beautiful landscape of pine trees laden with snow. Trevor rushed down the trail ahead of Patricia, eager as always to plunge onward, in contrast to his wife's more cautious approach to the world. He disappeared around a bend and Patricia hurried to follow. But as she came within sight of him, the world she saw did not match the model in her mind. Something was out of place. It was so out of place, so unthinkable, that it took a moment before she could comprehend what she was seeing. A tremendous blond shape, a concave face, the humped back, moving improbably fast, and then Trevor was down and the bear's jaws were around his leg. The atavistic roaring reached her, turning back the clock a hundred thousand years.

An extreme rush of adrenaline bestows superhuman strength. Homer described this in the *Iliad*, when Achilles went berserk and "in rage visited indignity on Hektor." This state, both horrible and transcendent, can come upon us when we're faced with certain death. The amygdala steals all restraint from the frontal lobes, and the rage pathway reduces us to a paradoxical state that is both bestial and godlike. Going berserk, we can lift boulders and tear apart the solid world. Patricia split in two, and as one part of her reflexively scrambled up a tree, the other part observed that it was physically impossible for her to climb a tree that way. The snow continued falling as silence descended on her, frozen with terror in the thin high branches.

The bear charged her so fast that she could scarcely comprehend it. Their eyes met for a moment. Then the bear was up the tree and Patricia was falling. On the ground, the bear took her head in its mouth and began chewing. She could feel its teeth scraping across her skull. She could feel its slobbering tongue and smell its rotten breath as it peeled her scalp off and crunched out her left cheekbone, ripping away her eye and half of her face. Patricia tried to hold still, to play dead, as the crunching and scraping continued. Her lips were all but ripped off. Then she thought of her mother and of all the people who would be destroyed by her death. A strange deliberation overtook her and she reached up and twisted the huge black nose before her. The bear barked and stood aside. It began pacing in front of her, rocking, turning like an imbecile, watching her with its pig eyes and making low drooling sounds. Patricia played dead.

Silence fell at last. She lay immobile, trying to think what would happen next, what she should do. She could feel the panic begin to rise within her as anger and fear ebbed and flowed, exchanging places. She began to stand and felt that something was wrong with her head. There were voices. She was on her knees. She realized that she was blind. She was in the snow, hypothermic, and near death, when hikers came rushing to her aid. Somehow they managed to get her down the trail and to find a search-and-rescue team. Not until she reached the hospital did she learn that Trevor was expected to live. When at last she felt the morphine slide into her vein, she went into a dreamlike state.

Her stay in the hospital was a torture of surgical procedures interrupted by shrieking hallucinations, flashbacks, and nightmares. The bear was in the hall, stalking Patricia in her dreams. She locked herself in the bathroom and the bear was just outside the door, "breathing and snorting and woofing . . . its long claws scratching." For weeks she was completely blind, adding to her feeling of disorientation. The bear took not only her skin and scalp but the muscles of the neck that held up her head. The surgeons took part of her latissimus dorsi and grafted it in place as a substitute. Skin from her buttocks was taken to cover her neck and head. That procedure alone took 12 hours. As the weeks wore on through excruciating pain, her only respite was in drugged sleep. She was informed that her left eye, where the bear had eaten away the cheekbone, would never see or move again. The bear had also ripped off the eyelids.

A month after the attack, Patricia and Trevor were able to go out for the first time. Her parents picked them up and took them home for a visit. On that outing, it first became clear that Patricia and Trevor were about to take radically divergent courses. Patricia's response was terror and shame at her grotesque disfigurement. She felt weak and vulnerable, apprehensive that the car would crash on the way home. She now experienced the world around her as an intensely hazardous place. Arriving at the home where she had grown up, she felt overwhelmed. "I am a stranger in some way," she said, echoing the now familiar sense of those who survive severe trauma. And indeed, a part of Patricia could now live only in the wilderness, wrestling forever with the bear.

Trevor was disfigured, too, his head and face crisscrossed with stitches, his jaw broken, his leg ripped open and sewn back together. The bear's teeth and claws had come within millimeters of severing both his carotid and femoral arteries. Either one of those wounds would have ended his life before he reached medical help. And yet, as they left the hospital that day, he was singing, despite the fact that his jaw was wired shut. Again and again, he said that he felt lucky and grateful to be alive. One evening in the hospital, he smuggled a wheelchair to Patricia's room and sneaked her out of the ward. He jammed open a back door with one of her slippers so that he could take her outside in the cold air to see the beauty of Mount Lougheed in twilight. (She was able at last to open her one good eye and see.) Trevor seemed able to admit how bad his condition was, saying, "What a wreck," when he saw himself in the mirror, and: "We really took a beating." But that night he also said he wanted to get out of the hospital and go ice climbing. In his mind and his emotions, he was rapidly moving on from the experience. By contrast, when he said they were lucky, Patricia thought, "That word has no place in my vocabulary just now."

It is as difficult to trace the origins of such different reactions as it is rare to have two people who are so neatly matched in their experiences. Both had been exposed to trauma before in their duties as nurse and doctor. In her year of work as a surgical nurse, Patricia had seen bowel resections and mastectomies, appendectomies and the removal of gallbladders. In other words, her emotional system had been primed for big reactions to trauma. Witnessing trauma can cause high levels of stress and anxiety, as we saw with Jessica Goodell's experience.

Michael Ferrara had a 30-year career in search and rescue in the area around Aspen, Colorado. He had been forced to deal with charred bodies from plane crashes and the blue-and-bloated faces of victims who had drowned or been crushed by avalanche debris. He was considered the toughest rock star of search and rescue, as well as of his own thrill-seeking pursuits that included racing motorcycles and climbing in the Himalaya. Nevertheless, he wound up with full-blown post-traumatic stress just from watching the effects of trauma on others.

Yet Trevor saw the same things as Patricia. His experience in surgery and in emergency rooms might have been worse. But it did not seem that his emotional system had been primed, for it never really went off at an extreme level, even though they had been attacked by the same bear in the same setting. Generally, people who have already experienced trauma can be expected to respond more readily and more powerfully to insults in the future. Emotional priming works like this: If the puppy makes a mess on the floor while you're trying to prepare dinner for the 12 guests who will soon arrive, you're more apt to yell at your six-year-old when she spills her milk. That effect goes away. In a little while, you won't be so irritable. But extreme events can leave you permanently primed. Put another way, you're more at risk for developing post-traumatic stress if you've already been exposed to extreme stress one or more times. This works on all time scales. The example of the puppy is on a short time scale. You'll probably get over it by the time the guests arrive. On a larger time scale, if you experienced intense combat in World War II, you are more likely to have attacks of anxiety in the face of an event such as the collapse of the World Trade Center. (Post-traumatic stress can remain hidden and suddenly emerge many years later, as we saw with Yossi Ghinsberg.)

But those are general statistical correlations and people vary widely in their individual emotional reactions. As well matched as Patricia and Trevor were in their experiences, the differences in their responses, like two diverging pathways, grew greater and greater over time. Patricia simply longed for the return of a normal life. Trevor's response seemed to be: I'm a new man. Let's see what this new guy can do. Neither Patricia nor Trevor could eat solid food at first. But while Patricia grew thinner, Trevor took a blender to the hospital and put everything in it, including ice cream and lasagna, so that he could ingest enough calories to gain weight.

By the time they were able to leave the hospital, their different reactions had begun to wear on them. They would argue, because Trevor was losing patience with Patricia for reliving the accident and being so down all the time. But she was responding to cues that set off emotional memories that Trevor either had not stored or was able to suppress. The big whiff of pine needles she took on the trail left her with an abiding panic reaction in the presence of the smell that she had once loved. The sight of pine trees with snow on them made her physically ill.

As in a chess game, the strategy after survival is trivial at first. You can try whatever you like. But as the consequences of each act, each tactic, each move, pile up and reverberate in the complex systems of memory, the commitment to a single course becomes deeper and deeper, until at some ill-defined point, you are unable to go back and try another strategy. This is your life.

. . .

AFTER LEAVING the hospital, they stayed at Patricia's parents' house in Calgary at first. She would sit in the living room, watching out the window, vigilant, literally expecting at any moment to see the enormous blond shape of a grizzly bear heaving into view. Trevor and her parents went out for hikes, but Patricia was too afraid of the woods to join them. Exasperated, alone in the house, she was experiencing the split between the old Patricia and the new. She would shout out loud at herself, "There is nothing out there! Stop it. Stop looking!" This is precisely the split that Micki Glenn experienced in the aftermath of being attacked by a shark. Just as Micki did, Patricia hated the new wimpy self that was controlling her life. And although she may not have known it, Patricia was behaving just like a veteran of heavy combat.

"I haven't really slept in twenty years," said one veteran of the Vietnam War. Like Patricia, he continually checked the doors and windows, and then checked again. At night, instead of sleeping, he got up time and again "to walk my perimeter," as he put it. Patricia had also begun to feel that alienating sense that veterans have, that no one understands, not even her husband who seemed so cheerful and optimistic and active. Patricia couldn't concentrate either. Another classic symptom. Her frontal lobes had been scrambled by the hormones of stress.

She and Trevor sought help from a psychotherapist. Trevor voiced his frustration with his wife's refusal to go cross-country skiing, her obsessive writing about the bear. They had tried to take a hike together, but after 15 minutes, Patricia was ill with trepidation and had to turn back. That night, she had terrifying dreams. But their experiences had been different in one crucial way. Trevor had had no premonition about the bear. Patricia had ignored the clear warning she had felt. Now, like Kathy Rich, Patricia needed a complete change of scene. She needed something to wipe out all her mental models. She needed an emotional system transplant.

Trevor had nightmares, too. But his attitude toward them was: *Yeah, you might have some bad dreams, but buck up: Life is good.* And:

The only way to deal with the attack is to get on with it. His response
was not to think about it. He just got busy and put it out of his
mind. Vaillant in his Study of Adult Development found that this
type of suppression was straightforward, practical, and it worked.
"Of all the coping mechanisms," he wrote, "suppression alters the
world the least and best accepts the terms life offers." Contrary to
what many psychologists would have you believe, he says, simply
suppressing a traumatic experience and getting on with business is
"the defensive style most closely associated with successful adaptation." Trevor forced this hard-nosed logic to dominate over emotion, telling his wife in frustration, "We won't be attacked again,
Trish. We're predisastered." (In quoting from the movie *The World
According to Garp*, he was employing one of the best strategies for
successful adaptation: humor.) And for the lucky person who can
take that adaptive approach, Patricia's reaction would certainly
seem nonsensical, perhaps even perverse. In the midst of the attack,
Trevor recalled feeling distant and philosophical about it. He had
seen the bear attack Patricia and was under the impression that she
had been killed. When the bear returned to attack Trevor for the
second time, he later told his wife that he was convinced he'd die,
but his only reaction was curiosity. He thought: "So this is how I
die." Patricia's response to the bear was pure panic and terror. And
Trevor's calm indifference merely fueled her anger and frustration.

At the most basic biological level, we need to see our emotions
mirrored in other people, especially those we love. Those we depend
on. Mirror neurons, with their deep connections to the emotional
parts of the brain, force us to feel what the other person is feeling,
whether or not we want to. It is a fundamental feature of being
human. Mirror neurons and mimicry make emotions contagious.
People become fast friends and even fall in love when they discover
this emotional resonance. They call it "chemistry." They say, "We
just clicked." But that process involves a complex of subtle and even
secret channels of communication. Those channels include everything from the fleeting facial microexpressions I've mentioned to
our ability to detect another person's major histocompatability complex, which embodies molecules of the immune system that tell us

how closely related we are to the people we encounter. So it made sense that Trevor and Patricia were frustrated with each other. The chemistry they shared had been altered by trauma and they no longer matched each other. When Patricia looked at Trevor, she did not get comfort or confirmation of what she was feeling. Even apart from the physical changes wrought by the bear, his enthusiastic grip on life clashed with her intense and deeply physical belief that something terrible was going to happen again. When Trevor looked at Patricia, his happiness and openness was greeted by a guarded and fearful pessimism and by a sadness, even an anger, that he could not help feeling and rebelling against. We think we can rationally overcome these silent systems of communication, but we can't. People who have had botox treatments are unable to produce certain facial expressions. That renders them incapable of recognizing the emotions represented by those expressions, because they can't imitate them. Even if we know something, we have to imitate it, however subtly, to feel it. Such a clash of emotional signals is so distressing that it can be fatal to a marriage.

There is nothing morally better or worse about their differing responses to trauma. They are both natural. For Patricia, snow had become an emotional cue for panic. And she lived, of all places, in Canada. Trevor was simply lucky that he hadn't forged that connection. J. Douglas Bremner, a physician and research scientist whose specialty is post-traumatic stress, wrote, "With extreme frights in some people, the system never really works again." Research with laboratory animals shows that certain conditioned responses can be extinguished, to use the psychologist's word. If a rat is exposed to a light and then receives an electric shock, it learns to react with fear when the light goes on. If you stop giving it the electric shock, the rat continues to panic for a time when the light goes on. But it gradually learns that the light is not harmful and the fear goes away. That is what happened to Micki when her husband put the shark on the screen of her computer. The researchers who do this kind of work believe that when the shock no longer follows the light, the brain forms a new kind of memory to mask the old one. The original memory doesn't go away. The emotional system is primed but quiet. The panic is just hidden, waiting for the next electric shock. If there is another shock, the fear returns even more powerfully. Then the response to the light becomes even harder to extinguish. It seems that when the emotional system is primed, it can stay primed for a very long time. And with a sufficiently large trauma, the response can't be extinguished at all.

Patricia was able to get her moods under control at times. She could sometimes see the beauty and feel grateful for her husband and for being alive. Sometimes she could allow herself to catch some of Trevor's emotional state and feel, as she put it, "a certain degree of happiness at seeing myself in the mirror." At one point, she told him, "Some people are left with nothing. Now I actually feel a little bit lucky." But she could never predict when the screaming terror might return. And that kind of unpredictability is stressful. Making matters worse for Patricia, we all carry a fundamental unconscious assumption that we are in control of our cognitive and emotional states, at least to some workable extent. Having those elements of the self slip from your control is terrifying, because it means that you can no longer trust the self you've known all your life. You literally don't know who you are or who you might be in the next moment. For Patricia, the attack had disrupted the most basic attributes of the self, her unity and continuity, her embodiment and privacy, her free will and self-awareness.

Moreover, Patricia had a problem that Trevor didn't have, one that may explain some of the differences in their responses. She had been more severely injured than her husband. She continued to have one surgery after another, along with chronic pain. Each new surgery, each new pain, told her body that it was being attacked again. You can't harm the body without getting the emotional system involved, and any hope she had of reorganizing her emotions around something positive was upset by the next wave of pain and cutting.

Because the bear bit into her face, she had repeated operations on her sinuses. Within weeks of each surgery, infection would set in. More surgery would follow. Her head and face ached all the time. She had surgery on her nose, surgery on her good eye, and then suffered the removal of her dead eye, which had begun to rot in its socket from disuse. The surgeons tried to install metal pins in the bones of her face so that she might wear a synthetic eye socket with a glass eye in it. But the prosthesis was hideous and the pins caused chronic infections. She was on antibiotics for years. She needed to experience her body healing to make progress, and that just wasn't happening. Unable to escape the thing that was attacking her, Patricia had no chance to make positive memories to mask the conditioned fears.

A decade had passed since the attack. Patricia and Trevor now had children. He was a doctor working in the real world, while many days she lay curled up in her room with a blanket over her head, unable to function. Trevor had attacked the world in much the way Micki had, by seeking new pursuits. When he was in the hospital, Trevor had sustained himself in part by dreaming that he would one day go ice climbing. He made that dream a reality. He went mountaineering and started a garden, which won him awards. He stayed busy all day. He bought a sailboard and went wind surfing. He bought an old wooden boat to rebuild and sail. Trevor built a house to live in and built the furniture for it. He became an expert at the trait that Vaillant calls sublimation, channeling negative emotional energy into positive pursuits. And in addition to his career, he became, in effect, a single parent in charge of the household. Patricia wrote, "I think of suicide for the first time." She had been sick for so long that she couldn't remember what it felt like to be well. She sounded like Kathy Rich at the lowest point of her journey.

ONE OF the casualties of Patricia's trauma was her core identity. Although trauma can disassemble the self and necessitate the building of a new one, a core of the old self usually remains, like the skeleton on which, with sustenance and exercise, we might flesh out who we're going to become. In the worst cases of post-traumatic stress, even that core appears to be damaged. Patricia wound up a patient in the hospital where she had worked as a nurse, and when a doctor she knew failed to recognize her, she said, "I *want* him to remember. I *know* he knows me." When he recognized her at last, it confirmed something deep inside her, that the old Patricia she knew was still in there somewhere, the self that she had feared might slip away. But Patricia was finding it increasingly difficult to hold on to that identity. As we've seen, so much of what we communicate and feel depends not on what we say but what we do with our bodies and especially our faces. Now Patricia no longer knew what her distorted face was saying. She was reluctant to talk to the doctors because she didn't trust her face to do its job. And after more than a decade, the memories and meanings that defined the self had become those of someone who was chronically ill. She had lost the memories and emotional markers that defined the old Patricia. The new person she saw appeared grotesque and alien.

Part of what tells us who we are comes from the confirming sensory signals we receive from our bodies. These match the sensory and motor maps that we've built since childhood. With her head so swollen and her neck without proper muscles, Patricia felt that it was not her own, and a crucial element of selfhood fell away. She was having a sensory discord not unlike that of an apotemnophiliac, the person who wants to have a perfectly good limb cut off. A look in the mirror confirmed that this was not her head and that she was not the Patricia she had known. What she saw didn't match the visual map of herself that she had always relied on. And if you feel crazy when the world doesn't match your maps, you feel even crazier when you don't match the map of yourself. You feel depressed. And frightened. You want the offending limb cut off. And the offending limb is you.

Patricia, who had been perfectly normal and well-adjusted before setting out on the Crypt Lake Trail in Waterton Lakes National Park at the age of twenty-four, now began her passage through a series of mental hospitals, through electroconvulsive therapy, through drugs and therapy and more surgery, through more and more pain and depression. The assaults took their toll on Trevor, as the circle of insults spread outward to those she loved.

The fifteenth year passed, yet nothing could quench the crucible of her dreams. "Horrifying noise, of bones breaking. Smell of thick bear fur, horrible bear breath." Patricia read obsessively about bears and people being attacked by bears, and wrote compulsively about her experience. She also had a big family and good social support from her many siblings and friends. But their well-meaning attempts to cheer her up ("At least you're alive") merely sent her into a rage. When her book *The Bear's Embrace* was published, it became a best seller. She was celebrated on television by *National Geographic* and the BBC. Yet despite temporary relief, none of that could right the foundering ship of emotion. Nothing seemed able to create the new and powerful memories that she needed to mask the old and remake the damaged self. She knew something that many people never have to face: The world really is dangerous.

Patricia's temperament actually might have prevented the accident. When they were going up the trail, she had sensed something in The Stream. She smelled the dead sheep and knew it was a warning signal. She was correctly interpreting it, too. She was consciously afraid of bears at that moment. (The grizzly was feeding on the dead sheep and attacked Patricia and Trevor in an attempt to protect its find.) It turned out that Patricia was naturally very sensitive. During her second pregnancy, she was quick to say that she was carrying twins. An ultrasound technician checked and told her that she was wrong. But just as Kathy Rich could read her own body signals and knew that she had cancer, Patricia was in full communication with her subterranean self: She said that she had felt herself ovulate on both sides before she conceived and insisted that the technician take a second scan. The technician found the twins. The thought of twins made Patricia apprehensive. Trevor felt thrilled with its implications of challenge and excitement. Two distinct personality types emerge. Patricia was cautious and very sensitive. Trevor was bold and open but seemed not to perceive the same sorts of subcortical cues that Patricia perceived. Both sets of traits could be adaptive under the right circumstances. On the trail, Patricia was picking up signals that were below the level of consciousness. Combined with the smell of the dead sheep, those warnings gave rise to the foreboding she felt. A gut feeling. Chris

Lawrence's "It ain't right." The concept of a bear. Left to her own devices, she might well have turned back.

To live, we must sometimes go to dangerous places. But at other times we need to heed our intuitions, our inner voices. In Chris Lawrence's case, military logic won out and he crossed the bridge. In Patricia's case, Trevor's bold personality, along with logic (Bear? What bear?) won out. They pressed on up the trail. Although they missed an opportunity to bail out, Trevor's personality proved much more resilient in the aftermath. And Patricia's apprehension, the very caution and sensitivity that might have saved them, became her greatest liability in the years to come.

WE EVOLVED to live in small groups of 150 or so people. Within those groups, we lived in even smaller and more intimate groups of 30 or 50. And nesting within those, we lived in smaller groups made up of our extended families and friends. There was a kind of stability in this manner of living that we don't have in the modern city, where we're constantly exposed to hundreds or even thousands of strangers. Faces upon faces. The mirrors and mimicry of millions. The judgments and perceptions of those strangers influence us, sometimes assault us, and it takes a hardy individual to withstand it. Fortunately, most people are hardy. But when we come back from an experience of survival, we may need the security of the small caring group that we evolved to live in. We may need an environment that is quieter, perhaps even monastic, as we'll see in the next chapter. After trauma, throwing ourselves into the fray of a modern city can be devastating. Sometimes it simply can't be done. One veteran of the Vietnam War said that when he returned and his wife wanted to enjoy a simple pleasure, such as taking the kids out to dinner, he just couldn't do it. On one such occasion, he agreed to go against his better judgment. Against his gut feeling. His sixth sense. When they arrived at the restaurant, the hostess wanted to seat them in the middle of the crowded room. That was not going to happen. He had to be in a corner so that his back was to the wall and there was no one behind him. As he stood with his family, waiting for the right table, sweat was pouring off him. Half an hour later, the table became available. As he walked through the restaurant, his heart was hammering, and he was drenched in sweat. Before they reached the table, he said, "I gotta go," and dashed from the restaurant. He hurried up to the second floor of a nearby parking structure, where he could "have a real good line on everything going on." His wife and children ate without him. Although it would have been more adaptive for him to get used to going to restaurants with his family, he could not manage it. His entire emotional system, his self, his identity, his very body had been reshaped in that ancient mold that required him to be in smaller groups, quieter places. He was locked out of the bustling city life he had once known. War had taken that from him. Being attacked by a bear took that from Patricia.

Sometimes people faced with such a monumental challenge reinvent themselves by joining a Zen monastery. Kathy Rich decided to plunge into the chaotic world of India and to learn Hindi. Still others find their way in life through a new career, a religious conversion. Perhaps Patricia simply needed to change everything. Perhaps her struggle was the most heroic of all, keeping herself alive for more than two decades after the attack.

It would be irresponsible of me to tell only the stories that have happy endings. That would seem to say that some of us are good and some of us are not deserving. That if you just set your mouth right, you can plunge ahead. Sometimes the trauma is just so large, so relentless, that superhuman strength is required to endure it. Even Mollica, the psychiatrist at Harvard who works with victims of the Killing Fields of Cambodia, one night imagined himself jumping out the window to end his own mirror of their suffering. Sapolsky wrote, "Take a sufficiently severe stressor and, as studies suggest, virtually all of us will fall into despair. No degree of neurochemical recovery mechanisms can maintain your equilibrium in the face of some of the nightmares that life can produce."

On December 14, 2005, Patricia van Tighem checked into a hotel in Kelowna, British Columbia, and took her own life, leaving behind Trevor and four children. She had fought the bear for 22 years.

TWELVE

THE BRICKLAYER:
THE LONG WAY HOME

THE NAVY CRUISER USS *Indianapolis* was plunging through 15-foot swells somewhere between the Philippine Islands and the Marianas Trench when the first torpedo blew away some 65 feet of the bow. It was just after midnight on Monday, July 30, 1945. The second torpedo hit a tank that held 3,500 gallons of fuel and created an instant inferno. More than 300 men were killed outright. Within minutes, almost 900 men were plunged into the Pacific Ocean. The surface of the water was thickly coated with noxious oil.

A series of chance occurrences saved Don McCall's life. He had just gotten off his watch at midnight, a few minutes before the attack. "It was blazing hot," he told me. At the age of twenty, he was what he called "an old salt" and he had learned some tricks. He knew he'd never get to sleep in the sweltering air below deck. So he had stashed a blanket behind a 20-millimeter gun and found himself a place to sleep on deck in the open air. Of course, it was against the rules, but ever since his father died when Don was ten years old, he had been living by his wits, not by the rules. He had just gotten comfortable when the first torpedo hit. "I thought a boiler had blown up," he said. A moment later, the second torpedo struck, and he knew that something terrible had happened.

From where he stood on deck, he could see men stumbling out of the smoke so badly burned that they were shedding their skin as they came at him like ghouls in a horror film. As the ship listed and began going down by the bow, he grabbed his sheath knife, cut open a bag of life jackets, and began passing them out. Within minutes, the ship had rolled 45 degrees to starboard, and Don saw that he was going into the water one way or another. "I followed everything I learned at Great Lakes Naval Station," he told me. He tucked himself into a ball and launched into the night. He later guessed that he had fallen 70 feet. When he hit the ocean, water was forced up his nose and into his stomach, along with the floating scum of oil. Choking and vomiting, he swam as hard as he could so that the ship wouldn't suck him down as it sank. When he turned to look back, the fantail was standing straight up out of the water, and he could see by the light of the moon that the screws were still turning. Men were jumping off and hitting the propellers on the way down.

He turned away and swam again and came to a young kid sitting on a cork floater net. "He was petrified, just scared to death," Don said. He saw that the floater net was still rolled up. Many men in the water had no life jackets, and Don saw that if they unrolled the net, more people could sit on it. While some of the men distracted the hysterical kid, Don and another man dumped him into the water. Once the net was unrolled, Don helped the kid back on and several other sailors joined him. Collecting himself, Don understood how lucky he was. He had a life vest, so he didn't need to sit on the net. Moreover, he was uninjured. Many others were so badly injured that they stood little chance of surviving. Others were suffering various degrees of agony. But Don was virtually unscathed. He spent the rest of that night just getting used to the idea that he was going to have to survive this. He tried to relax and conserve his energy. He remembered that his instructor at Great Lakes had said, "Don't swim; you're not going anywhere." With the coming of dawn, he could see the vast panorama of dead bodies floating and heads bobbing in the water, and the full import of what had happened descended on him. With it came the question, Why weren't they being rescued?

By the end of that first full day, things were even worse. Constant sunlight just 12 degrees from the equator was burning and blinding the men. Thirst was driving some of them to drink saltwater. Others had begun to hallucinate. Several swore that they could see the sunken ship just 10 feet beneath the surface and dove down to get fresh water from the ship's stores. They drank their fill of seawater and returned to the surface. Soon they began foaming at the mouth. Projectile vomiting and madness followed. They imagined that the other men around them were Japanese and began attacking with their knives.

Don had initially thought that his chances would be better in a group. But now he drifted away from the chaos. "There was nothing I could do for them," he said. "I had to look out for number one." He was constantly thinking ahead. He decided to leave the group during the daylight hours and to move closer during the night so that he could take comfort from hearing the men talk. He realized that the life jackets were meant to last only 72 hours, so he took one from a dead man and tied it on top of his head. Not only did that protect him from the sun, but it dried out the kapok seed pods that gave the vest its buoyancy. When the jacket he wore became waterlogged, he could switch the two.

The next day, Tuesday, the sharks began attacking. Don could see that others who were huddled together in groups were thrashing to try to keep the sharks away, but they were attacked anyway. Don deduced that staying still was a better strategy. He pulled himself into a ball and floated, motionless, whenever sharks came near. "The sharks swam right by me," he said.

As the days went by, he continued to concentrate on strategies for survival. At one point, a rubber life belt floated by and he grabbed it. He had heard that the Japanese would use aircraft to strafe shipwrecked Americans. The life belt could be blown up through a rubber tube. He cut the tube off and kept it, reasoning that if the Japanese spotted them, he could slip under water and breathe through the tube. He was planning ahead. He had a future in his mind, and good survivors always concentrate on the present but plan for the future. Thus, taking it day by day, hour by hour, and sometimes minute by minute, did Don McCall endure. He prayed. He refused to drink seawater. He endured the incandescent pain brought on by dying of thirst. He soothed his ravaged emotional system with thoughts of home. Don was in the water for more than four days. When rescue came at last, it came by chance. A pilot who was flying around trying to fix a radio antenna happened to spot the oil slick and called for help. Don McCall was nearly killed when a lifeboat dropped from an airplane and almost landed on top of him. Instead, he was the first survivor to climb aboard.

In all, 880 of the crewmen from the USS *Indianapolis* died. Of the nearly 900 who went into the water, only 321 were rescued, and four of them died before they could get sufficient medical attention. The story of why no one was sent to rescue the men of the *Indianapolis* lies in a confusion of messages ignored and false assumptions made about the whereabouts of the ship. It was essentially a systemwide screw up of monumental proportions in which no one person was to blame.

I SPOKE with other survivors of the *Indianapolis*, including Jim Jarvis and Paul Murphy. Both men agreed that they had lived relatively normal, happy lives after the war and were not plagued by nightmares or morbid thoughts and fears. "I think," Jarvis said, "the main thing is we just wanted to get home and go back to what we were doing before. I kept busy enough that it didn't ever bother me much."

Although he wept at times as we talked, Murphy agreed that his experience was similar. He said that most veterans of World War II wanted to get back to work as quickly as possible, "so they didn't have to talk about it." Murphy's own children knew nothing about his experience in the war until 1985. Jarvis and Murphy began going to reunions with the survivors of the *Indianapolis* about that time, and although they now talk freely about their experiences, neither seemed particularly bothered by it. It had not disrupted their lives in any significant way. In fact, as we sat and talked on a rainy spring day in a conference room in a hotel in Indianapolis, Indiana, they both began citing instances in which other soldiers were worse off than they were. Murphy said the guys freezing in the trenches in Europe had a much rougher time. Jarvis said the guys in the jungle had it much worse, adding, "I think the water's a little easier on you." As we've seen so many others do, they were finding people who were worse off than they were and offering them the only help they could: empathy. The *Tao Te Ching* says, "Because I am compassionate, I can be brave."

Yet I found their level of equanimity remarkable. I was witnessing firsthand what Vaillant had found in the Study of Adult Development. As Trevor Janz had done after being attacked by the bear, these sailors were using suppression, "the dun workhorse, the mundane Volkswagen of the defenses," as Vaillant put it. Essentially, Jarvis and Murphy put the experience away and went on with life. They were able to turn their minds away from the trauma and go on with other things. They had the advantage of having grown up during the Great Depression. They had the gift of adversity that Micki had.

DON McCALL'S experience was radically different from Murphy's and Jarvis's. As a child in the area around Mansfield, Illinois, he had worked on farms from dawn to dusk for a few pennies or, when he was lucky, a nickel. He took the money home to his mother, who was dirt poor. He often worked for just a meal and was always pleased when a family invited him to eat with them. He had few prospects for a better life ahead of him. But when he joined the Navy in 1943, at the age of eighteen, his life changed completely.

"I had the world by the tail," he told me. "I got three square meals a day, a bed to sleep in, clothes to wear, and they paid me. I never had this before in my life. I was happy." But as soon as he completed his training, he was shipped out on the *Indianapolis* to work as an air-sea lookout. His first battle was at Tarawa, which was also the first campaign of the war in the central Pacific. When they pulled in at Tarawa, it was a beautiful paradise. "It looked like an emerald in a blue sea," McCall said. Then the United States Navy shelled, bombed, and strafed the small island with 4 million pounds of high explosives. As the landing craft hit the beach, they were met by withering fire from the 4,500 Japanese soldiers who were dug in. "With my binoculars," said McCall, "I could see the Marines hitting the beach and I was shocked to see such an inhumane thing happening." It was a slaughter. During the next 76 hours of continuous fighting, McCall watched as almost 6,000 men were killed outright. When they departed from Tarawa, it was nothing but blackened stumps of palm trees and a pall of smoke. They went on to attack Saipan, Tinian, Iwo Jima, and Okinawa, and McCall watched through his binoculars at each battle and was aghast at the senseless and appalling slaughter of those young boys. The horror of those battles never left him.

In two years of service, he received eight stars for the major campaigns in which he participated. He grieved deeply at seeing someone's son, someone's father or brother, die right in front of his eyes, over and over again. "It just tore me up. I saw women jumping off of cliffs with their babies. It's horrible." He was referring to the attack on Saipan, when the Japanese started the rumor that American soldiers would kill all the women and children. Many of the women, seeing the invasion on the beach, threw their children off the cliffs and then jumped to their deaths after them.

For Don, the sinking of the *Indianapolis* was just the final blow. And in some ways, it seemed worse to Don that he could no longer stay in the Navy, which, along with his mother's influence, had been one of the main organizing forces in his life. "I was thinking about making the Navy a career," he said. "But I couldn't go back to sea. When I came home on the *USS Hollandia*, I never slept. To this day, I have trouble with water. I don't take baths, I take showers. I am afraid of water."

When he reached home, his mother still had nothing. At that

time, she lived in a run-down house in Champaign, Illinois. His sister had married and his brother had taken a job out of town. Don returned from the war an angry and restless young man. He couldn't sleep. He was filled with rage. "I was looking for trouble. At the drop of a hat, I'd fight anything." After one incident, the police came to take him home. They already knew him well by then. When they put him into the car, he went right out the other side and they had to chase him down. When they got him home at last, he sat on the front porch, half naked in his undershorts. He spent most days drunk. Don's post-traumatic stress was not unlike the disease known as rabies. The rabies virus enters the temporal lobe and sets off the rage pathway. Since that behavior involves biting, the virus uses the salivary glands to spread itself to any unlucky victims. McCall was behaving like a mad dog for a good reason. Trauma had tampered with his temporal lobe, the seat of his emotions, the citadel of defensive rage, which serves to protect us from attack by predators.

But then Don met the woman who would become his wife, and the chemical changes that her love wrought in him saved him from himself. He told me that he was sure he'd have been dead if he hadn't met her. "She was the best thing that ever happened to me." He was working doing odd jobs at that time, "anything to make a dollar," as he put it. It turned out that the only thing other than booze and fighting that could take the edge off his anxiety was hard work. Then he was hired as a laborer for a masonry contractor who was impressed by his energy and doggedness and made him an apprentice bricklayer. There was something about the patterned rhythmic mechanics of laying bricks that soothed him, the heft of the hod, the slap of wet mortar, the swinging motion of the trowel, and the block-by-block building of something tangible, something outside himself that he could stand back and see and say, *I built that*. And of course, this is the perfect type of activity to engage the seeking pathway in the brain. The direction, the goal, the organized rhythm of it, all served to begin dampening his rage. Soon Don was admitted to the union and began making top wages. "I loved what

I did," he said. He gave his wife his paycheck each week and she took care of everything else. She paid the bills and protected him from the world. "I didn't deal with people well." If they went to a party, she would watch him carefully. When she saw signs that he was about to panic, she'd go up to him and quietly say, "Okay, Don. Time to go."

Don also credited his mother with being the primary positive influence in his life. He said that after his father died, the family had been very poor, but his mother worked hard doing domestic chores for others and raising chickens and a big vegetable garden to feed her family. She had shown him the value of work. So Don went to work.

In his spare time, he built a house for his wife and children. He discovered that he could live well in the way that Tolstoy put it: "To work for the person one loves and to love one's work." He worked, in his mind, for his wife, then for his children when they were born. And he loved his work. When I met Don McCall in 2010, he was eighty-five years old. He told me, "That's how I coped with this all these years. People think it's weird. They say you ought to get over this stuff. But watching those guys get killed. I have never gotten over it."

When I wrote *Deep Survival*, I was attempting to deal with brief intervals in the lives of people, the times they've had to muster all their resources to live through a specific, isolated event. But now, as I look at entire lives spanning many decades, I can see them as a series of journeys through survival, like moving through the swell of waves, some towering, some small. There is no resting place. Things are not settled until death. There is only the question of whether we will have the depth and poise, the grace, to sail through the next storm.

Don had reached that place when he organized his ongoing survival around his work, his wife, his children. Like Micki Glenn with her farm, Don had a routine that kept him busy *all the time*. He used sublimation, channeling all his waking energy into something useful. He used suppression, refusing to think about the trauma of war most of the time. He lived in a monastic way, buffered from the antic world of overload. He rose at six in the morning, ate breakfast, and worked all day. Then he went home and worked in the yard. As many traumatized people do, Don made a beautiful garden for the family. When his children were old enough, he took them on camping trips. He coached basketball and Little League. And his wife was always there, looking out for him. But in 1975 the next traumatic journey of survival began for Don. His wife died of leukemia.

"I was lost," he told me. "Absolutely lost."

He was working as a bricklayer at the Kraft Foods plant at the time. He would finish his regular workday with the masonry contractor on Friday, then start work at Kraft at four in the afternoon and work straight through to midnight. Then he would put in another 12 to 14 hours on Saturday and Sunday. He was making double-time pay and, for a tradesman, he was rolling in dough. But he was still emotionally lost. He had no idea what to do. As we've seen, sometimes you just have to mark time. Aron Ralston's "active option" of waiting or Ann Hood's knitting for eight hours straight represent this sort of strategy in the face of what is otherwise unendurable.

During this period of grief, Don said, "I'd take off and I'd walk 10, 12, 15 miles." Walking comes from the ancient central pattern generator deep within the spinal column and lower brain. Walking is soothing and engenders positive emotional states. It increases cortisol and dopamine in mild amounts. It also facilitates problem solving. Great scientists, writers, and artists have used walking as a way of organizing their thoughts and stimulating new ideas. Newton and Einstein were both compulsive walkers, as were the scientists at Los Alamos during the Manhattan Project. Wordsworth, Thoreau, Dickens, Whitman, Coleridge, and Henry James all used walking to induce altered states of mind. Remember that walking around and navigating can induce theta rhythms in the hippocampus and hypnagogic states that look like sleep.

In Don's case, walking also happened to offer a chance encounter that changed his life. "One day, I walked by the golf course, and I said, 'I wonder if I'd like that game.'" Curiosity brings opportunity. Paying attention may deliver us. He rented a set of clubs so he could try his hand at the game. He found the physicality of golf, the periodic organization of it, mesmerizing. "I got hooked on that game," he said. And significantly, it was an activity that combined his natural impulse toward long walks with a patterned and structured endeavor that would activate the seeking pathway and basal ganglia with the learning of a new skill.

In discussing golf, Don described the altered state of mind it induced. He said that even when he's playing with other people, "It's just me and that little white ball." Don found another blessing in golf. After a long day on the golf course, he could actually get to sleep. When Don said, "It's just me and that little white ball," he was describing the hypnagogic state that Ann entered while knitting, that so many writers enter while writing, and the state in which Dr. Carl Bennett could forget Tourette's and perform flawless surgery.

It took Don another 14 years before he remarried, but he did. He can't take his long walks anymore, because his knees are bad. But he plays golf using a golf cart. He reads a lot of history. "I read about the war," he said. "And one of the things I hang on to is that all of my kids have done fine." His children have stayed close to him. His three sons drive several hours from southern Illinois, St. Louis, and Indiana to take him to the doctor. His daughter, Peggy Campo, lives nearby and looks out for him. "He's very independent," she told me, "even now at age eighty-six." She was there the entire time I interviewed him. And all researchers agree that solid social support is one of the most important elements of surviving survival. Indeed, social support influences every element of our lives.

Don McCall shows us by his example that not everyone gets over it. Though most of us can live with them, some experiences live with us forever. Most people can find a strategy, or a series of strategies, that allows them to be whole, to survive again, and even to find joy.

"I enjoy my life," Don said. "I really do."

Peggy told me, "His strength came from his background, because after the death of his father, he grew up in poverty during the Depression. He loved being outside and he hunted and fished to help provide food for his family. He had to be resourceful."

"I'm not a hero," Don said. "I'm a survivor."

THIRTEEN

THE COURAGE TO SUFFER: IF HE CAN DO IT, YOU CAN, TOO

WHEN HITLER'S ARMY invaded Poland in September of 1941, Leon Weliczker was sixteen years old. He was an upper-middle-class kid with two brothers and three sisters. His father was kind, literate, sensitive. Leon's mother was a dark intelligent beauty. In March of 1942, Leon was taken prisoner and sent to the Janowska concentration camp, where he was put to work. From the window of the workshop, he could see gangs of workers in the yard, slaving under the constant blows of the truncheons wielded by the guards. The Nazi officers used the prisoners for target practice, shooting their rifles from the windows of an office building. The idea was to be skillful enough to shoot off a single finger or a nose without actually killing the person. But when practice was over, an officer would go among the crowds of workers and finish off the wounded with a pistol shot to the head. "A wound on the finger sufficed as justification for this treatment," Leon wrote in his memoir, *The Death Brigade.*

Leon turned seventeen in the camp, witnessing these atrocities and enduring constant beatings, freezing weather, starvation, and illness. The sentries amused themselves with sadistic games. They caught Leon one night as he went to the latrine. He was forced to lie on the ground with a group of men while the guards lashed them with whips for three hours. Then, he described, "Each of us had to urinate across the heads of the others. . . . There was one night when they refined their treatment by making each man urinate into another's mouth."

After three months under such brutal conditions, Leon and a group of about 180 others were marched out of the camp to an area of open ground known as the sands, where the Nazis buried their victims by the thousands in mass graves. Leon and his fellow prisoners were forced to strip naked and were given shovels to dig their own mass grave. This was to be the end for them. When the grave was ready to receive them, Leon watched as the guards directed two men to climb down into the hole and lie side by side. A guard shot each one in the head. He then directed two more to lie across the corpses at a right angle. When the guard had shot those two in the head, two more went down to continue the neat crosshatching of cadavers.

Leon waited, knowing that there was nothing he could do. At seventeen, his life was at its end. As Leon's turn approached to lie down in the hole, a Russian defector who was working for the Germans as a guard directed him to put his clothes back on. The Russian led Leon back to the camp, where a dead man lay on the ground near the kitchen. The Russian told Leon that the corpse was going to be put into the mass grave "with the rest of you." Leon began dragging the body behind him, following the guard. But the guard walked briskly and Leon was too weak to follow. As the distance between them grew, Leon was seized by a sudden insight. The methods the Germans employed embodied the seeds of their own downfall. If the Russian guard were to lose a prisoner who had been under his control, the Germans would shoot the Russian on the spot. So quite naturally, he would never report such a loss if Leon were to escape. The guard would have to keep his mouth shut. Leon then used his anger to drive action. Powered by a surge of adrenaline, he dropped the corpse and bolted back into the camp to vanish in the crowd. That night, he slipped away and returned to his home. He had shown the traits of a true survivor. Sick and weak, he had experienced despair at the mass grave. But once he was pulled aside by the Russian, he was ever alert to opportunity and inspiration. The guard, powerless to expose him, reported Leon as shot dead to cover his own carelessness and avoid execution.

Refusing to collapse into despair, Leon immediately found himself a job. He was engaging himself in useful action, constantly moving forward, doing the next right thing. But in the coming months, German sweeps of the Jewish ghettos caught more and more members of his family. While he was at work, the Germans took his three beautiful sisters, along with his Aunt Hannah, her two children, and Leon's grandmother. Leon learned that they had been beaten as they were forced to march 12 kilometers to a train station. They were made to stand naked for 48 hours before being driven in cattle trucks to Belzec. Upon arrival, they were put to death in gas chambers, even his little seven-year-old sister Bina. Leon learned that his father and mother had also been murdered.

The Germans gradually concentrated the Jews into smaller and smaller towns, the better to locate and exterminate them. Leon found himself living with 12 people in a single room. Despite the horrors that this once middle-class teenager faced, he was maintaining a positive attitude. He saw good where he could find it. Compared with a concentration camp, he said, "Our life was quite tolerable."

When the next roundup came, Leon took to the woods to hide with a friend. There they lived like animals, constantly on guard against the sound of distant gunfire. They feared Germans, Ukrainians, and Poles alike. During the day, Leon lay under camouflage in a hole he had dug in the ground. At night he would scavenge in farm fields and villages for something to eat. After two weeks of this savagery, overcome at last by loneliness and longing for his family, he set out for the town of Lvov, walking in bare feet through snow because his shoes had worn out. Along the way, he learned that his uncle, another aunt, and their four children had all been murdered.

In a daze of hunger and exhaustion, Leon stumbled through the streets of the ghetto in Lvov, staring around him in horror with no idea what to do. It was about four in the afternoon. Then he saw his brother Jacob coming down the street toward him "as if in a dream." Jacob took Leon by the hand and led him to a house where he was staying: broken windows, torn-up floorboards, threadbare beds, a wobbly table. "I sank into an indescribable melancholy," Leon wrote. But when his fifteen-year-old brother Aaron came in, Leon was suddenly filled with love and a feeling of responsibility for the two boys. He was shedding the cloak of the victim in favor of the role of the rescuer. Terrence Des Pres, in his book *The Survivor*, makes the point that in the journey of survival, helping someone else is as important as getting help.

When he asked his brothers why they weren't in hiding, they told him that they had given up and didn't care whether they lived or died. They had sold all the family's belongings and used the money to buy sweets. After gorging themselves, they just sat and waited to be captured.

Leon instinctively knew the cardinal rule of survival: Get organized or die. He flew into action, cleaning the room, bringing in a barber to cut the boys' hair, and generally imposing order on their lives. A chaotic environment breeds stress. Neatness is predictable because you know where things are, and predictability lowers stress. The worse the situation, the more important it is to make every little detail count for something. So they survived for a time in the ghetto of Lvov. But the German noose was tightening inexorably. More and more people were swept up in the *Aktions*, wholesale roundups of Jews that represented the final phase of the liquidation of humanity in that city. A specialist in genocide named Head Sturman Grzymekw was brought in to finish it off. A fanatic about order and cleanliness, Grzymekw strutted about the city, shooting anyone he thought wasn't neat enough. Sick people were required to turn themselves in at the hospital, where they were immediately murdered. The city was completely encircled by Heinrich Himmler's Schutzstaffel. Despair was epidemic. By mid-February 1943, people were selling cyanide openly in the streets.

That summer, the SS entered Lvov, drove all the people before them at gunpoint, loaded them into trucks, and took them to the camp at Janowska. Leon stood with Jacob and Aaron amid 8,000 others arrayed on the parade ground under searchlights, surrounded by SS and Russian sharpshooters. Anyone who moved was shot. Leon's attitude, as always, was that of a survivor: positive to the end. "I felt happy," he later recalled, "that I was able to spend these last hours with my brothers."

They stood on the parade ground all day and all night. As the SS began dividing the people into groups arranged by age, Jacob made an attempt to hide. He crept to the fence and tried to curl up in a ball, hoping not to be noticed. The SS shot him dead while Leon and Aaron looked on. When there were a mere 800 people left on the parade ground, all between the ages of fourteen and thirty, they were once again divided into two groups and Leon was separated at last from the only remaining member of his family, his brother Aaron. As they led Aaron's group away, the fifteen-year-old boy turned to look back, his cheeks smooth, his eyes shining. Leon met his gaze for one last time. Leon never saw his brother again.

VIKTOR FRANKL says that the tasks of life represent the real meaning of life. Sometimes the task is simply to "accept fate." He goes on: "When a man finds that it is his destiny to suffer, he will have to accept his suffering as his task; his single and unique task."

As a prisoner in Nazi death camps, Frankl took comfort in such thoughts and used them to help develop his will to carry on. He realized that no one could suffer for him. He realized, in fact, that his own suffering was an opportunity to do something active on his own behalf: to suffer well and to suffer in his own unique way. That was the process he and his fellow prisoners trusted, even as they let go of the outcome. This is what's known as survival by surrender. They knew they would probably die. But they had decided to stand up to their suffering and to embrace it as their job. He called this attitude "the courage to suffer." Kathy Rich knew it when facing almost certain death from cancer. Lisette Johnson understood it when she faced her husband's murderous rage. Chris Lawrence embraced it when it looked as though he'd never walk again. Their stories illustrate a concept expressed by Dostoyevsky: "There is only one thing that I dread: Not to be worthy of my sufferings."

SINCE LEON'S first imprisonment in Janowska, the brutality of the place had increased. Children, the elderly, most women, and anyone who was ill were executed upon arrival. The others were organized into work brigades and were worked, quite literally, to death. Sometimes an entire brigade would be abruptly marched out to the sands and executed. The atmosphere in the camp had taken a turn that made it, if possible, even more bizarre than before. The head of the camp was adamant that the inmates appear happy. So he installed an orchestra that played whenever the brigades left for work or returned to camp, as well as when a group was taken to the sands to be shot. (The prisoners called this the Death Tango.) The inmates were also forced to sing as they went to and from work. The roads on which they walked were paved with gravestones that the Germans had stolen from Jewish cemeteries.

One day, Leon's work brigade was led out to the sands, where, he assumed, they would all be killed. As they approached, he could see thousands of corpses burning in a great open ravine. Smoke and the smell of burning flesh rose, choking the men, as they were led down into the ravine and among the bodies. As the fire snapped and hissed, he saw that many of the corpses appeared to be reaching up with their hands in a beseeching gesture. The men found themselves standing in pools of blood surrounded by flaming corpses. Two men sat on a rise above the ravine, pumping gasoline and oil from a tank onto the corpses. On the rim of the ravine stood guards with machine guns. But mingled with Leon's horror at the appalling scene was an even stranger sensation. For instead of executing the 42 men in his group, the guards marched them back to the camp. And instead of being led to their regular barracks, they were taken to an isolated section of the camp that Leon had never seen before. There they were installed in new barracks. Leon was still certain that they were being prepared for execution. But then a group of women brought them water so that they could wash.

Dinner normally consisted of a watery gruel with little nutritional value. But now the women brought them generous portions of rich soup along with bread and marmalade.

It gradually dawned on Leon that they had been initiated into an elite group of prisoners. They would be responsible for erasing all evidence of what the Germans had been doing there for more than two years. Each day, Leon and his brigade were well fed and marched out to the ravines to dig up mass graves and burn the bodies. He began to realize how the Germans planned to conceal from the world what they were doing. He worked out a secret method for keeping a diary, with the idea that if he somehow got out alive, he would have documentation of what had been done. He knew that he'd be shot on the spot if his diary were discovered. But he was employing a solid strategy for survival: He had a purpose and he had an activity that made sense in the midst of the horror. He had one thing he could control where there was no control. He was fighting back.

Today, he wrote in his diary, *our brigade is opening a mass grave that contains 1,450 bodies. Many of today's corpses don't have bullet holes in them. They have open mouths with projecting tongues. This would indicate that they had been buried alive.* The workers pulled the corpses from the mass graves and threw them into the ravine to burn them. When the fires burned down, Leon and his brigade collected whatever bones were left. They had built a patio out of gravestones from a Jewish cemetery and on this they pounded the bones to dust so as to leave no trace of the mass murders. They also sifted the ashes of the dead so that they could pick out any gold from fillings or jewelry and give it to the guards. Their group became known as the Ash Brigade. They were well fed and were kept away from the rest of the inmates of the camp because, above all, the Germans wanted to keep this operation secret. Sometimes they even gave them beer and cakes. Leon had begun to gain weight.

As the brigade burned more and more bodies, they improved their skill at mass cremation. On June 23, 1943, for example, they were able to burn more than 2,000 bodies. On the thirty-first, they opened a grave in which the bodies were so badly decomposed that the men had to use hooks and bare hands to drag out body parts. They counted severed heads. "The work is gruesome," Leon wrote in his diary. "The inmates are up to their knees in puddles of foulness." When all the bodies had been removed, several men got down into the grave and sifted the soil through their hands to pick out any hair or bone. They collected those remains in a bucket and then put them into the fire. Then they sprayed the interior of the grave with chlorine to hold down the smell. They filled the pits with soil, leveled the earth, and then seeded the ground with grass. The effect was seamless. On a sunny day with birds singing, no one who walked by would ever suspect the terrible deeds that had been done there.

ONE DAY at four o'clock as their work ended, the brigade was ordered to get into a bunker that the men had built near the fires. The guards told them there was an air raid coming. They told them not to peek out. As Leon watched through a crack, a group of people arrived from the camp. They were driven forward with whips and police dogs. At the ravine, the people were forced to strip and then marched to the edge five at a time. The SS shot each person in the head and one by one kicked them into the ravine. Leon watched them execute 275 people in half an hour. Then the workers were ordered out of the bunker and told to throw all the bodies onto the growing pyre. Leon reported that as they threw one of the corpses onto the fire, it cried out. "The man was still alive!"

As summer wore on, the effect on Leon was completely numbing. The SS referred to the bodies as "figures" but used that term for the inmates as well. When one of the guards capriciously shot someone dead, he'd call out, "Two figures! Now!" meaning that he wanted two men to carry away the man he had just murdered. Leon, still a teenager, wrote in his diary about the mechanics of his job as if describing any other engineering problem. He noted the times it took the bodies to burn, depending upon whether or not they wore clothes, whether or not they were fresh. "Children and women," he wrote, "burn faster."

In August, the lieutenant in charge of the Death Brigade added another bizarre twist to the musical accompaniment. He had a craftsman fashion hats for the fire chief and his assistant. These were the men who pumped the oil onto the bodies. They received leather helmets bedecked with the horns of devils. Since those men carried long hooks to stir the fire, they now truly resembled the demons of hell. The lieutenant had a machine brought in that was powered by a diesel engine. It had been specially designed to crush bones to dust more effectively than men could do by hand. The workers scattered the fine talc of human bones over nearby farm fields.

As 1943 drew to a close, it became clear to Leon that the entire population of the camp was being exterminated just as fast as possible. On more and more occasions, the workers of the Death Brigade were ordered into their bunker and told not to look, as if they didn't know what was going on. Again and again, they watched through the cracks as people were driven with whips and dogs to the ravine, forced to strip, and shot at point-blank range. The mothers were made to remove their own clothes and then to undress their children. Then the naked mothers had to carry their children to the slaughter. One little girl put up a fuss. A German soldier picked her up by her feet and swung her around, smashing her head against a tree trunk. If a mother cried out, she was tied and suspended upside down from a tree and left that way to die.

Leon Weliczker endured and survived. He stayed socially connected even in his dreams. While still in the concentration camp, he saw his mother from beyond the grave. He saw that she was sad about losing her last child, Leon himself. He resolved to survive for her. He comforted himself in the worst of times by reminiscing about the nights of Seder—the food, the candlelight, the smiles. We must cherish rituals because they create memories that may one day be necessary for our own survival.

But Leon and several others were not merely surviving. They were taking action. In the midst of the madness of singing and dancing after their unspeakable work, the inmates were actively plotting their own escape. There was a thriving black market at

Janowska and in preparation for escape, Leon's group had amassed gold and money equivalent to a small fortune. Much has been made of the puzzling way in which many Jews went to their deaths without protest. Leon's answer was that they were completely broken, and with all their family members already dead, they had nothing to go home to. But Leon had the indomitable will of a true survivor. And on the night of November 19, 1943, he and several others staged a charade. Once again, the German organization carried the seeds of its own destruction.

For months, the prisoners had been stealing some of the gold that they collected from the corpses. At night, they traded it with the guards for food, medicine, liquor. They would also take the guards things they wanted, such as a watch or a new pair of boots that had been taken from the dead. Each night they also carried firewood for the guard houses. So the guards were accustomed to seeing prisoners go in and out of the gate at will.

On this particular night, two groups of prisoners went out carrying wood and a new pair of boots that one of the guards had ordered. They attacked two guards at once, killing them outright and taking their machine guns. As soldiers poured out of the guardhouse firing their weapons, everyone in the camp made a chaotic break for the woods. The members of the orchestra, who had been playing the dance music for the evening, threw down their instruments and made a break for it. Leon took off into pitch blackness. They had chosen a moonless night for the escape. Now stumbling through the woods, he ran into two of his comrades by chance. They made their way to a friend's house and once again went into hiding. They found themselves in an underground chamber that had been excavated beneath a barn. A straw-covered hog pen, generously spread with stinking feces, concealed the trapdoor and discouraged investigation. Sixteen men and five women hid in a hole that measured 10 by 13 feet. It was so crowded that not everyone could sit at the same time. Someone had to sit on the toilet at all times.

As these people hid beneath the hogs, Christmas approached and with it the Russian offensive. Early in the new year, the Russians took the town of Tarnopol, 80 miles from Lvov. News was delivered to Leon and the others along with their daily ration of food.

But in February 1944, the Germans put horses into the barn, and all day long, Leon and his companions had to keep absolutely silent while German boots sounded on the boards above their heads. As spring approached, the Russian front moved into Lvov, yet Leon and his group remained in the hole. The Germans moved out of the stable at last. Then they moved back in. Then they moved back out. And all the while, Leon sat in darkness, reduced to a single meal a day and feeling lucky to have that. Months and months and months passed in immobility and darkness.

When the Russians arrived at last and the Germans fled, Leon and his group slipped out one by one under cover of darkness to protect their host, who feared reprisals from anti-Semitic Poles. Leon wandered in a stupor through Lvov and experienced what so many survivors go through in the immediate aftermath. He was a stranger in his own home. Yet he was rapidly moving from being focused on immediate survival to caring about others. "Today," he wrote, "the anguish for those who had been killed flooded over me." Even so, he faced a monumental effort before he could reenter his life. His emotional system had been ravaged. "I felt as though I were under an anesthetic." He returned to his family's apartment to find someone else living there. They took him in and fed him and gave him a bed.

Leon gradually began going out on the street and meeting other survivors and hearing their stories. He had always been resourceful, and now he teamed up with a fellow survivor. They stole some uniforms and went to the houses of people Leon's family had known, people who were now dead. The two boys acted official and explained to the residents that they had orders to make a record of belongings that were to be returned to the rightful owners. When the astounded residents expressed their shock, Leon and his buddy said that they could make an exception if they were well fed. Soon Leon regained his health and found a job with the railroad, running supplies from Russia back to Lvov. He engaged in a brisk business selling his own black-market goods on the side. He began to come back into his own. "We were adjusting to life," he wrote, "taking slow step after slow step, back to a saner, more normal view of people."

His parents had always wanted him to be educated. He hired a tutor to help him prepare and then took the entrance exams for college. He was admitted to the Polytechnic Institute. He threw himself full time into his studies. He had been annealed in the fires and felt that all the suffering and horror had actually made him stronger. He felt "an indomitable determination to rebuild life," he wrote. "Setbacks and hardships didn't count." He had distilled his experience into the essence of survival in the aftermath, and now that he had lived through hell, he was determined to make a life for himself.

Leon was employing strategies we have seen before. As with Jessica Goodell, he was using higher education. He was keeping busy with something about which he was passionate. And he was seeing the beauty after so many years of seeing what was hideous. He and other students went hiking in the mountains and let the beauty wash over them. After being a savage, an animal, he felt that he was slowly becoming a human being again. He used writing as therapy, publishing a short version of his own story, which he later expanded into a book. He transferred to an engineering school in the American Zone of West Germany. He formed close friendships with other students there. They spent all their time together. They studied relentlessly. He testified at the Nuremberg trials. Because he had kept a diary, his testimony was particularly useful. The prosecutor mentioned him several times. He and a friend even caught a Nazi war criminal single-handedly. A friend of Leon's who had been in the Death Brigade spotted on the street a notorious murderer named Rauch. Rauch was tried and hanged in 1949, the year that Leon earned his PhD in engineering and left for the United States. He was twenty-four years old.

Leon went on to live a rich life. He taught mathematics at New York University and did research for the Office of Naval Research. His work in optics eventually led to the development of the first video cassette recorders. He carried out one of the primary tasks of the survivor: He made himself useful.

William Helmreich is a professor of sociology at City College of New York. In his book *Against All Odds*, he describes the survivors he had interviewed as displaying a "stubborn durability, . . . quiet dignity," and "persistent endurance." He wrote, "Despite the severest deprivation in early childhood. . . . None express the idea that the world owes them a living. . . . On the contrary, most of their lives are marked by an active compassion for others." It is this quality of insisting on living and on giving that sustains the survivor long after the traumatic events have passed.

Even so, the traces remain and always will, whatever your trauma or loss. Some 72 percent of survivors of the genocide said that trivial things—the sight of a uniform, a knock on the door, the barking of a dog, or smoke issuing from a chimney—could set off attacks of anxiety. If the insult is great enough, most people develop some symptoms of post-traumatic stress and, though they are not necessarily debilitating, they may last a lifetime. "I have a terrible reaction to Clorox," said Herbert Kalter, a survivor of Auschwitz-Birkenau and Buna-Monowitz. When the death battalions stacked up the corpses, they poured bleach on them. Many survivors came out with a lifelong compulsion to hoard food. Some could never buy striped clothing again, while others suffered panic attacks when any official document arrived in the mail. Kalter said he panicked in traffic because "if you follow other people, that's the end."

One woman who had been in the concentration camps was compelled to call her daughter every day at three-thirty in the afternoon to make sure her children had come home from school. Once, when they were 20 minutes late, she jumped into a cab in the Bronx and battled rush-hour traffic all the way to Brooklyn to make sure that the children were safe. It turned out that three-thirty was the time of day when she had been snatched from the ghetto in Poland and taken from her home. She had never seen her parents again.

Leon Weliczker, who changed his name to Wells, was married in 1956. His wife, Frieda, told me that in those early days, he often had nightmares of running, running with his brothers, away from the

Nazis. At the end of his life, she said, when he was dying in a hospice, she watched his feet running as he lay in bed. "He yelled out and was agitated." She believed that he was having those dreams again. As he came to complete the arc of his life, the ancient traumatic memories surfaced again from the depths where he'd kept them wrapped in the layers of his life. During all those productive years, Frieda said, "He didn't keep it in. He spoke easily about his experience. He was extremely bright, a scientist. He lost every single person in a large family, and then he went on with his life."

Frieda was attracted to him because he was emotionally whole. "He was against hatred and prejudice," she told me. Leon and Frieda raised three children. "We have a German daughter-in-law, and he accepted her into his heart," she said. "He didn't hate the Germans. He was a humanist. He was not embittered. He considered himself to have had a happy life."

Leon Weliczker Wells appears to have known this secret: that our lives are written in the indelible ink of memory. And only by writing over those memories in bolder script can we ever hope to tame them.

FOURTEEN

THE SCIENCE OF ADAPTATION: THERE'S NO REVENGE LIKE SUCCESS

WILLIAM GRANT WAS born in 1876. By 1936 his W. T. Grant dime stores were earning $100 million a year and he had formed a foundation to give his money away. Arlie Bock and Clark Heath, two physicians in the student health service at Harvard, believed that research in medicine was too preoccupied with illness. Efforts should be made to understand what makes for healthy, happy people. Grant agreed and gave them the money to study this. The so-called Grant Study (eventually renamed The Study of Adult Development) recruited 268 students who seemed healthy and normal. A second group was added a few years later to make a more balanced sample. It included blue-collar men from poor city neighborhoods. Then Lewis Terman at Stanford University added women to the group to make an even more representative population. The doctors tested and interviewed and measured those volunteers, and those who inherited the study continue to do so today. Most of the surviving subjects are now in their eighties or nineties, making this the longest-running research project of its kind.

One of the main conclusions of this study is that no one gets a break. No one is blessed with a magical set of attributes that leads to immunity from trauma, grief, sadness, and pain. If you read through Vaillant's three-volume distillation of this research, you might come away with this conclusion: "Life is tough. And then you die." On the other hand, the research shows that it is possible to lead a healthy, happy life even in the aftermath of trauma. Perhaps more important, happiness is not a matter of avoiding trouble. It's a matter of how you deal with it. Barry Schwartz, a professor at Swarthmore College and author of many books on social theory, said, "Happiness as a goal is a recipe for disaster." And: "Happiness as a by-product of living your life is a great thing."

When you're in the midst of a crisis, it can sometimes seem as if your distress will go on forever. It helps to know when that's true and when it's not true. For most people in most situations, the pain does not go on forever. Pleasure, laughter, even peace and happiness almost surely await you. And you can speed up the process and make it more complete by taking three simple steps: Do something you love. Do something for someone who needs you. And be with people who care about you. Tolstoy bears repeating: "One can live magnificently in this world, if one knows how to work and how to love, to work for the person one loves and to love one's work." And: "Ah, if only you might learn, through suffering, to believe that the only possible happiness—true, eternal, elevated—is achieved through these three things: Work, self-denial, and love." Even Don McCall, whose suffering went on and on, was able to manage his life through this formula.

Vaillant is the man who has spent the most time with the information accumulated over the decades and the people represented in the Study of Adult Development. His conclusion is that, to put it bluntly, everybody's messed up. "Not one of them," he wrote, "has had only clear sailing." But more than "ninety percent have founded stable families." And: "Virtually all have achieved occupational distinction." The point is that trouble comes to us all. Since most people are reacting to some kind of trauma or loss all the time, most people are employing some sort of strategy for adaptation all the time. Most of this behavior is unconscious. As children, we all begin employing unconscious strategies for coping with the various injuries, large or small, that life deals out. But most people simply continue on an unconscious course throughout life without ever stopping to consider whether a different approach might be more effective. When something really bad happens, it presents an opportunity to wake up from our life on autopilot, our state of mental models and behavioral scripts, and deliberately choose a new strategy.

Another surprising conclusion from the Harvard study (including the women in the Terman study at Stanford, who call themselves "the Termites") was that when it comes to how well you'll do overall in your life, the quality of your childhood has less influence than we might think. Vaillant, who compiled all the data, compared the people whose childhood experiences were rated as the worst with those whose childhood experiences were rated as the best. He found only trivial differences. He could not correlate birth order, health, or even the loss of one of the parents with any significant difference by the time the subjects were fifty years old. Orphans were just as happy and healthy as people who'd had ideal childhoods. Moreover, people from dysfunctional families, living on welfare in inner cities, turned out not much different from upper-middle-class kids. This supports the idea, increasingly popular among psychologists, that people are naturally resilient. Or, as Vaillant put it, "What goes right in childhood predicts the future far better than what goes wrong." It seems that if people really are resilient, they are that way from a very early age. But it can still help to know the best strategies for dealing with adversity.

Many of the strategies for shaping and reshaping a life follow the same patterns that emerge in people going through the process of surviving. Vaillant lists five approaches that were associated with good outcomes:

- SUBLIMATION, which means doing something to channel your energy and anxiety. This is represented by activities such as Ann Hood's knitting (Chapters 6 and 7) or Don McCall's golfing (Chapter 12). It could also be something bolder and much more dramatic, such as moving to India to learn Hindi, as Kathy Rich did (Chapter 10).

- ALTRUISM, which means doing something for someone else, such as Lisette Johnson's helping Betty and Ruth, the two girls whose father had shot his family (Chapter 1).
- SUPPRESSION, which simply means not thinking about your trauma and distracting yourself from it. Many veterans of World War II, such as Jim Jarvis and Paul Murphy, employed this strategy (Chapter 12).
- ANTICIPATION, which means seeing the future clearly and preparing for it. This lessens the anxiety associated with trauma. People who routinely use anticipation study excessively for a test, for example, and are more than prepared when it comes. Kathy Rich did this over and over again in keeping ahead of her cancer (Chapter 10).
- HUMOR. As we've seen, being able to laugh at yourself and your misfortune is one of the most healing abilities of all. Leon Weliczker Wells was able to laugh even on the Death Brigade (Chapter 13). Those who do best are those who can keep a sense of humor. You can't be laughing and worrying at the same time. Laugh when you can. Laugh when you must. Most important, laugh when you mustn't.

George A. Bonanno, a psychologist at Columbia University who studies human resilience, points out that people who simply avoid thinking about bad things are less overtly distressed by them. When interviewed, they deny being distressed. But by objective measures (how much they're sweating, how much cortisol is circulating in their bloodstream), it's possible to show that they are under more stress than normal. Suppression alone may help people adjust to extreme trauma. But when it is coupled with positive emotions, and especially with genuine laughter, it can work wonders. For example, in studies of people who have lost a loved one, the ability to have fond and even funny memories about the person, and to laugh at those funny memories, led to shorter and less intense periods of grieving. Other studies showed that people recovered from exposure to the attack on the World Trade Center more quickly if they could continue to experience gratitude, interest, and love during the aftermath.

Vaillant also identified six strategies that are not effective. He called those the immature defenses.

- PROJECTION, which means blaming someone else.
- PASSIVE AGGRESSION, which means responding to your misfortune with anger. But instead of using that anger to help you get going, you turn it against yourself to manipulate and punish others.
- DISSOCIATION, which means being in denial. It sometimes involves feelings of unreality or even of leaving your own body.
- ACTING OUT, which refers to impulsive behavior that can overwhelm the emotional system and temporarily blot out pain, such as drinking, fighting, or gambling compulsively. Sometimes a fine line separates sublimation from acting out, as with workaholics or compulsive runners.
- FANTASY, which involves taking leave of reality in an almost schizoid fashion. In fantasy, we skip over reality into a world of make-believe.
- HYPOCHONDRIASIS, which means imagining that you're sick all the time. This effectively frees you from the burden of dealing with life.

In *Deep Survival*, I listed 12 steps that successful survivors take to improve their chances of success. As I discussed in Chapter 3 on Aron Ralston, the first of those steps is to perceive and believe. In contrast to the immature defenses listed above, you recognize the reality of the situation, accept it, and prepare to deal with it. The next step is to remain calm. Acknowledge fear, rage, sadness, but then use those emotions to move into seeking mode. To achieve that, we need to think, analyze, and plan. Know what you have. Know what you want. That means to engage the frontal lobes in a realistic assessment of your resources and your predicament, and then to set achievable goals: Okay, this bad thing has happened. Now what? This is the sort of anticipation that Vaillant discusses. You are looking into the future, not ruminating on the past. That prepares the brain to move from rage to seeking. Simply put, this leads to the fourth step: acting on your plan. Movement.

This sequence is essentially what Vaillant means when he uses the term *sublimation*. He gives the example of expressing "aggression through pleasurable games, sports, and hobbies." Sublimation will channel emotional responses that can otherwise hinder or hurt you. It redirects their energy outward, especially into something useful. This can take the form of a long-term strategy, such as Michele Weldon's writing books. It can also be something fast and dirty that is directed at seizing the emotional machinery of the brain and snatching it temporarily away from the grip of fear and desperation. Sublimation represents the stage at which you begin to knit, begin to write, begin to walk or learn Hindi, or begin the long series of tasks (building a house, building a garden) that people such as Trevor Janz and Don McCall undertook.

The fifth step for survival is to celebrate your success once you've taken action. Planning and doing engender seeking and safety pathways in the brain and can help prevent the anxiety disorders of the rage pathway from overwhelming you. Celebrating your achievements activates the areas of the brain involved in motivation and reward, which leads to feeling good through dopamine and other neurotransmitters. Gratitude follows, which calms the negative emotions and quiets the amygdala. That is the sixth step: Count your blessings.

The seventh step is to play. Have fun. Fun is part of living a healthy, happy life. As Vaillant put it, "Sublimation lets you express the strongest of passions. . . . if you can but transform it into play. The verb *compete* comes from *competere*, to seek together." Again, the seeking pathway is the centerpiece of this system and work that becomes like play is the best way to activate it. This leads to the eighth step: See the beauty. Seeing what is beautiful in this world binds you to it so that you are motivated to stay alive to enjoy it once again.

One of the most important traits I found in successful survivors was their ability to get outside themselves and do whatever was necessary, not in their own self-interest but for someone else. Vaillant's trait of altruism points to the effectiveness of this. Gratitude leads to altruism. In a situation where your survival is at stake, this often manifests itself as someone saying, "I'm going to get home alive, because I know how terrible it will be for my son (wife, mother, father, even a pet) if I die out here." Leon Weliczker Wells resolved to survive for his mother, even though she was dead. After a traumatic event, altruism often takes the form of doing real work for others, such as Lisette's holding it together for her children and for the traumatized girls she met. It also may take the form of volunteer work, philanthropy, or sometimes even changing careers to work more closely with people.

My friend Jeanne Giles said that when she was recovering from being treated for breast cancer, a friend of hers got sick, and Jeanne cooked for her. Then she began to make food for others as well. Her husband didn't understand. Jeanne told him, "Don't you remember the steady stream of meals that came to our house for months when I was sick? This is a circle. It's a loop. Sometimes you're on the receiving side of the loop and sometimes you're on the giving side, and the only reason that we were on the receiving side was that I had been on the giving side for so long. Now I want to be on the giving side again. Giving lifts you up and out of yourself."

How well people adapt after trauma is also influenced by personality. For example, a growing psychological literature refers to people who are "hardy." That quality, says Bonanno, comes from a commitment to finding what he calls "meaningful purpose." In addition, he says, you have to believe that you can influence what happens in your life. In other words, you have some control and you're not just blown here and there by the winds of chance. You must also be convinced that, whether your experience is good or bad, you can learn from that experience and use it as a platform for growth. Meaningful purpose, of course, means doing something. And it may well be that the meaning comes from doing it for others, not yourself. But either way, it fits in with the template I've been discussing: Admit what's going on, stay calm, assess your resources, make a plan, and carry it out. Likewise, learning and growing from both positive and negative experiences means having the positive mental attitude that good survivors display in even the worst of circumstances. Micki Glenn, having been attacked by a shark, told me, "I get up every morning and just say: I'm going to be happy, no matter what."

The belief that you can influence events is the ninth step of the 12: Believing that you will succeed has to do with a feature of personality that some psychologists call an internal locus of control. Most people have either an internal or an external locus of control. The external types believe that things happen to them, that others cause their misery, and that they are largely helpless to control events. They adopt the posture of a victim. They tend to complain, to brood, to blame others, and to expect rescue. They do not tend to do well in emergencies nor in the aftermath of trauma.

People whose locus of control is internal believe that they make things happen and are active in doing so. When they make mistakes, they resolve to do better. When something bad happens, they try to find a way to turn it into an opportunity or at least a lesson for the future. They don't blame. They don't complain. In the worst of times, they're still able to see the beauty in the world, even while refusing to deny that which can harm them. They believe in themselves. They recognize (and are not bothered by) certain things that they can't control. People like that tend to have more skills because they've spent a lifetime developing them. They are capable because they have practiced being capable. They can do things. So when bad things happen, they are more prepared.

Lawrence Calhoun, a psychologist at the University of North Carolina, confirms that most people don't go nuts after an experience of survival. They go on with their lives without psychiatric disorders. Moreover, they are made stronger and are able to gain understanding and empathy. They grow from the experience. They are more compassionate; they get along with others better. They have a deeper understanding of their own vulnerability, and yet they feel more able to deal with what life throws at them. Having been tested, they are more confident.

One last category of personality tends to do well after trauma. This is a personality type we can call the Egotistical Jerk. Psychologists call this the "self-enhancer." Therapists used to think that successful coping and adaptation required admitting your own shortcomings. It turns out that thinking the world of yourself, even if you're just an E. J., helps your chances of adapting well after trauma or loss. But, as psychologists point out, people continue to regard you as a jerk. So you might lack social support and its valuable contribution to well-being.

The tenth step is to surrender. Once you have prepared yourself as well as you can, once you have a plan and are ready to take action, you let go of your fears and move forward. The eleventh step is: Do whatever is necessary to make that move happen. You are determined. You know that you have the will and the skill. And the twelfth step is simple: Never give up. You're still here. That means you can do something.

FIFTEEN

THE RULES OF LIFE

SOME YEARS AGO, when I was writing *Deep Survival*, I talked with my daughters, Elena and Amelia, about a project that we were calling, somewhat tongue-in-cheek, The Rules of Life. My concern at the time was surviving an emergency, such as being lost in the wilderness or being castaway at sea. Once I began looking into how people went on with their lives after such incidents, I began to see patterns that suggested how we could thrive in the aftermath of survival. Those patterns suggested not so much rules as strategies that we could adopt to take advantage of the natural systems in the brain that I've been discussing. Those strategies may unfold in whole or in part, in a different order and to differing degrees. But the people who successfully negotiate their lives in the aftermath of trauma tend to follow well-worn pathways. Those paths run parallel to the two central ideas I've been developing. The first is: Want it, need it, have it. You have to desire something and engage in some activity to get it. You can't give up. You can't give in. This, of course, means that you get busy and get organized. The second idea is: See one, do one, teach one, which tells us how to go about achieving the first idea. Here, then, are 12 strategies that you can employ to move forward.

1. **WANT IT, NEED IT, HAVE IT.** Devote yourself passionately to an art, a craft, a musical instrument, a language, a horse, or your own education. Build houses for the poor. Counsel people who have suffered as you have. Become a doctor. Become a cleric. Become a stunt pilot. Your pursuit can be anything. At first, you will want it. Then, if you persist, you will grow passionate and will need it, for it will have formed maps in your brain. In time, you will see that you have it, like Kathy Russell Rich (Chapter 10), who woke one day to the realization that she had a new self inside her, a person from India.

In embracing this strategy, you are in effect imagining your ideal self. This might be someone who is in shape or who plays the piano really well. It might be someone who helps run a soup kitchen. Kathy was in the depths of her cancer and working a job that she didn't really care for when she found a little voice in her head saying, "I want to live a more artistic life." It was a simple idea that gradually led her to India and to learning Hindi and to writing her books and completely changing her life.

When Elizabeth Gilbert, author of *Eat, Pray, Love*, was trying to get her life together after a disastrous divorce, she set herself a simple goal: learn to speak Italian. Gilbert recognized that it wasn't very logical or practical. But "learning Italian . . . was the only thing I could imagine bringing me any pleasure." More to the point, she wrote, "I loved it. Every word was a singing sparrow, a magic trick, a truffle for me." Pleasure (the reward system of dopamine) is life's way of telling you that you're doing something right. You have to find a way to get some joy or things will get worse, not better.

This step also helps you develop an internal locus of control, which reinforces the idea that you have some influence over your life. You can look around at your life and decide to change the things that you don't like about it. Challenge yourself, take action, and win. Develop an active, problem-solving way of looking at the world. Be alert for opportunities to do something useful and to succeed at anything. And notice how these things add up, gradually changing you into someone who is more effective in the world in general.

2. BE HERE NOW. This is the strategy of mindfulness. When Lisette Johnson (Chapter 1) saw the pistol in her husband's hand and stood up, she was existing purely in the moment. But we must strive for that level of attention even when there seems to be no emergency. Life is the emergency. Even when Don McCall (Chapter 12) was grieving for his wife, he was paying attention while he walked all over town to quiet his raging mind. His was that open kind of attention that allowed him to see the golf course and the golfers and to wonder if he'd like the game. As knitting did for Ann Hood (Chapters 6 and 7), golf provided decades of comfort for Don. Thus what seems trivial can become monumental.

This strategy also dispels illusions and makes you flexible. When Chris Lawrence (Chapter 5) returned from Iraq, he was struggling to get his shattered legs to work. He was completely focused on his own legs and his vision of his own future, which involved walking on them again. But when he saw guys with no legs doing back-flips with their prosthetics, he thought, *Hey… what's up with that?* He had his right leg amputated and was up and walking within a month. Soon he was helping others who had just come back from war.

The brain has evolved to give us mental models and behavioral scripts that allow us to function on autopilot. And in these times of always-on electronic communication, that tendency is exaggerated. *Be here now* means: Be quiet. Take time every day to tune out all the electronic noise, the chattering voices that clamor for attention, and then listen to your own mind and body. Tune in to The Stream. Putting in this effort to pay attention means that you'll be much more likely to seize opportunities and avoid hazards. You may find an intuition, a gut feeling, a sixth sense that saves your life, as Kathy Rich did when she sensed the presence of her own cancer (Chapter 10).

3. BE PATIENT. Everything takes eight times as long as it's supposed to. It is worth repeating the words of Eugen Herrigel's Zen master: "The more obstinately you try to learn how to shoot the arrow for the sake of hitting the goal, the less you will succeed in

the one and the further the other will recede." In other words, surrender control of the outcome and trust the process. "Do your work,
then step back." That's what Michele Weldon (Chapters 8 and 9)
did in both her writing and the simple things in her life, such as
repainting the rooms of her house.

4. BE TOUGH. Learn to suffer well. Richard Tedeschi, a psychologist who treats post-traumatic stress, said that "to achieve the greatest psychological health, some kind of suffering is *necessary*." And,
indeed, although in the preceding chapters we have seen many
strategies for suffering well, we have seen no strategies for completely avoiding suffering. In a world where some suffering is inevi-
table, the only sensible thing is to learn how to deal with it. One
survivor of the Holocaust said that she still had nightmares every
week in which she was chased by Nazis with dogs. The barking of
a dog outside her window could set her off, because that sound had
become paired with panic in the camp. But her attitude was: Great.
That scene used to be my real life every day. Now I can wake up
from the nightmare. Living well is a kind of revenge. It doesn't
mean that we don't suffer. One of the best ways to deal with suffering is to look around you at the suffering that is not happening to
you. When it does happen to you, expect it and experience it. Say:
This is my suffering. It is my turn to suffer. Use it to prepare for the
next stage in the journey of survival.

Another way to be tough is to exercise, to eat well, and to stay
strong and healthy, while at the same time practicing what is difficult. Consider the brief but remarkable life of Ben Underwood,
who lost his eyes to cancer of the retina at the age of three. To get
around, he learned to click his tongue and read the echoes that
bounced off the objects in his environment. He became so skilled
at it that he could play basketball, rollerblade, and even skateboard.
The cancer killed him at the age of sixteen. But his life serves to
illustrate the practice and science of changing the brain. It also
provides an inspirational road map of strategies for getting beyond
trauma. If Ben could do it, what's my excuse? Or, to use the words
of Chris Lawrence (Chapter 5), "Here's a straw: Suck it up."

5. GET THE SMALL PICTURE. People who suffer do not have to suffer all the time. Even those in Nazi death camps found beauty and inspiration in their days. *The Last Expression: Art and Auschwitz* is a wonderful and chilling book. It is the catalog for an exhibit that appeared in 2003 at the Mary and Leigh Block Museum of Art at Northwestern University. It reproduces the works of art made by people in Auschwitz and other camps, and it is an astonishing testimony to the resilience of the human spirit. Horst Rosenthal, facing imminent death, created an elaborately illustrated and heartbreakingly funny comic book called *Micky in Gurs*, subtitled "published without permission from Walt Disney." Shortly after creating the comic book, Rosenthal was taken from Gurs and killed upon his arrival at Auschwitz. Rosenthal's triumph over evil was his ability to control that part of his life, his inner life and its outward expression. Like Micki Glenn (Chapter 4) with her farm and horses, find one thing each day to possess as your own and to feel good about. Then try finding two.

6. PUT THINGS IN THEIR PLACE. Traumatic memories don't go away. Rituals are one way of controlling when and how you experience them. If the memories are encapsulated in a ritual time and place, they are less able to torment you the rest of the time. You create a new set of retrieval cues for those memories. That puts you in charge, so that the memories occur when and where you want them. That's why traumatized soldiers go to Normandy on D-day. My wife, Debbie, and I decided to get married on the date when she'd had surgery for cervical cancer. That changed the date from one that recalled loss to one that renewed celebration.

When Leon Wells (Chapter 13) spoke to groups about his experience in the Nazi death camp, he was in effect ritualizing what he'd been through. Michele Weldon (Chapters 8 and 9) did this by writing about her experiences. This type of activity also reduces your chances of falling into depression by introducing predictability and controllability into the experience of pain. Sapolsky has identified four things that you can do to keep stress hormones low. You should learn to tell the difference between a hazardous situation and one that is safe. When the hazard is real, do something about it; don't remain passive. Learn to tell whether what you did was effective. When it isn't effective, change your strategy. Last, when things don't go well, find ways to blow off steam.

Putting things in their place also means facing your fears. When Micki Glenn's (Chapter 4) husband put the photograph of a shark on her computer screen, he was allowing her to put the shark in its place: *It's in the ocean, not in the bedroom.* By facing our fears and putting them into a rational context, we regain control of our emotions and introduce predictability about what we feel. We eliminate the element of surprise.

7. WORK, WORK, WORK. As Richard Mollica said, staying busy is the most effective means of adaptation after trauma. Micki Glenn (Chapter 4) and Don McCall (Chapter 12) stay busy every minute of the day. Survivors turn fear into anger and anger into action. As my brother Philip put it: "The best fuel smells the worst. Use the icky stuff in your life to propel you forward." He should know. He has cared for his severely disabled son, Philip Ryan, for more than a decade. (He recently wrote me: "Whereas your subjects are telling you their stories after the fact, I am reporting directly from the lifeboat, that is, lost at sea.") So don't sit around brooding on whatever's eating you.

This step can also be used in the short term and for troubles less serious than major trauma. It's a good everyday coping tactic.

8. SEE ONE, DO ONE, TEACH ONE. I've discussed the idea of seeing one, either literally or in your imagination, when you desire something. I've also talked about doing one: Work, work, work. The third element of this strategy involves altruism: doing for others, not for yourself alone. You receive several benefits from this. The first is that you can practice the posture of being the rescuer, not the victim. Recall how biting on a pencil can make you feel better because it activates the muscles used in smiling. Having a higher purpose in your efforts can take you out of yourself and make you feel more effective, more in control, more powerful. This is what

Leon Weliczker Wells (Chapter 13) was doing when he took care of his brothers.

I have also discussed finding someone who's worse off than you. This helps you feel grateful ("Every moment is a miracle," said Lisette Johnson [Chapter 1]), shows you the positive side of what you're going through, and recruits a sense of purpose. Your focus shifts from you to someone else. I met a woman who had breast cancer and was undergoing chemotherapy. She was depressed and discouraged because the chemicals were sapping her strength, limiting her life, and wrecking her body. She felt that way until she walked into the ward one day and saw an eight-year-old boy with terminal cancer. Bald-headed, serene, he was meeting life with courage and optimism. The woman began working with the children at the hospital and never worried about her own predicament again. Under some circumstances, doing it for someone else is even more powerful, because it involves someone you already love. At the moment of truth, just when Lisette thought she'd fall apart, she held it together by saying, "You have to be all right, because you have to take care of the children."

9. TOUCH SOMEONE. Staying socially connected is one of the most important and effective adaptations. This means staying close to family and friends and making a decision to be with people who have the right attitudes. Abundant research shows that people who are socially connected are healthier and live longer. Micki Glenn (Chapter 4) told me, "I had a tremendous support system, not only my husband, Mike, and my parents and extended family but also the kind of friends who stuck right by my side, not to mention prayers all across the country, and letters, food, and flowers overflowing from people I'd never met. I wasn't alone."

Lisette Johnson (Chapter 1) said nearly the same thing: "I am incredibly blessed, because I had hundreds of people there for me. They'd bring food for ten people. I had six or seven people at dinner every night." Aron Ralston (Chapter 3), at his lowest point in his ordeal, was joined in the slot canyon by his friends. Friends and family can help even when they aren't really there, because we have mapped them permanently in our brains. Viktor Frankl's wife kept him company in Auschwitz, even though she was dead.

Being socially connected also means physical touching. Like our ancestors, we humans thrive on the physical touch of others. At the University of Miami School of Medicine, Tiffany Field showed that premature infants who were touched, stroked, and massaged grew twice as fast and left the hospital a week earlier than those who were not. She has also demonstrated that touching can reduce pain, relieve depression, lower stress hormones, and improve the functioning of the immune system. Many studies have shown that even having a dog or a cat to pet reduces stress. (The University of California at San Diego has a clinic where you can go to pet dogs to reduce your stress.) And skin-to-skin contact reduces pain and produces oxytocin, the hormone of love. There is a good scientific reason that people hug when something bad happens.

10. BE GRATEFUL. Whatever the survival event was, you're here to deal with it. Maybe, as with a crippling injury, there is no end to that event. No matter how crazy your life seems at the moment, being alive is cause for celebration, for only the living can celebrate. And most people can find much more to enjoy than breathing in and breathing out. Above all, avoid self-pity.

At her lowest point, when she contemplated suicide, Kathy Rich (Chapter 10) made a list of things to be grateful for. For example, the cancer wasn't in her liver. She kept the list with her at all times and took it out and read it when she was feeling bad. She added to it as new reasons for gratitude occurred to her. It sustained her. Lisette Johnson (Chapter 1) said, "I plan to celebrate my birthday as never before. To embrace that I am alive. To use as many talents as I have, for as long as I have to use them. I have been given an incredible gift. A chance. A chance to experience everything."

Micki Glenn (Chapter 4) told me that every year she celebrates the day she was attacked by the shark "like a birthday." She continued: "It's a big deal to me. I typically do something fun like riding horses. Later I schedule a two-hour massage and a pedicure. I then soak in a hot bath while listening to classical music or jazz and sipping a nice red. Then I dress up and take myself out to dinner. So yes, it is a special day!" On that day, November 14, she reviews what was happening to her hour by hour. "It's not bad or sad or anything. It's just remembering and feeling so blessed and so alive. Each year I think that by all rights I should have been in the ground since 2002, and how very, very lucky I am to wake up each morning."

11. WALK THE WALK. Act as if you're better. Find small things that you can do that give you a sense of being normal. When Eileen Berlin (Chapter 2) returned to running after being attacked by the crocodile, she was doing this. On January 8, 2004, Anne Hjelle was attacked by a mountain lion while biking through a wilderness in California. She was nearly killed, and her face, as she put it, was "mangled" by 40 bites. She lost an eye and her wounds took more than 200 stitches and staples to close. "Even on days when I lacked self-confidence, I chose to put on a smile. I *acted* strong when I didn't feel strong—and before long, I *was* strong!"

12. LIFE IS DEEP; SHALLOW UP. Humor is essential, quieting the amygdala and reducing stress. Laugh at the world. Laugh at yourself. Having a strong circle of friends and family helps with this. Leon Wells (Chapter 13) reported that even in the Death Brigade, the workers used black humor to sustain themselves. "Don't eat too much," said one prisoner. "The corpse carriers will have a hard job getting you up on the heap." This at a time when the heaps of bodies had grown so tall that the enslaved workers had to use ladders to place the dead on top.

(Reading this, my wife, Debbie, reminds me, "Crying is good, too. You have to be sad sometimes as well." And indeed, she's right.)

So in time, we may find words such as those of Ann Hood (Chapters 6 and 7): "I cannot say how I got from there to here. I cannot even say where 'here' is." By that time, years had passed since the death of her five-year-old daughter, Grace. Ann was back in the world, where she worked and went to parties and did her domestic duties. She was functioning. On a night out, she could make people laugh over dinner. But she knew a dark secret. She'll know it all her life. "Even though I am here, I know that the smallest thing—a song, a sound, a smell—can send me back there. I do not live here. I only visit."

So it is with the rest of us. Once we depart whatever we think of as our "there," we never truly return, because we are never truly that self again. Each of us becomes someone new. A visitor walking around with new maps of the world. We are, all of us, desperately here, desperately trying to be and do here; and if we are not in passionate pursuit of our doing and being, we're missing the entire show.

I WAS going to write about my own trauma and loss as a way to make this book more personal. Everyone suffers something. But as I began to immerse myself in the stories I've been telling, it put all of my suffering into proportion. I have not been blown up. I have not been in a death camp. I have not been attacked by a crocodile, shark, bear (though I was attacked by man on more than one occasion). I have not had to live, as my brother Philip has, caring for a severely disabled child these past 13 years and sometimes going 90 hours without sleep just to keep him alive. Thinking my way through all of this trauma and grief left me wondering: Is there a natural state of being human? Are all of us in a never-ending search for a lost well-being? It sometimes feels that way. But that lost well-being is an elusive state, and like perfect beauty, an imaginary one that we chase in our dreams. When the chase is done, our efforts spent, we call it a life. We can call it that only when the journey's over, for until then, its shape is incomplete, the outcome uncertain. There was no idyllic time in prehistory, no Garden of Eden. That place must be imagined, for our emotional system is set up to pursue it for just as long as we can endure the struggle. Yet we can see tantalizing glimpses of it at times.

I saw it myself recently. It was that last part of summer when the trees were fleshed out in a full dark green. And yet there was a look about those trees, something subtle that suggested this was just as far as they could go. They had begun in spring, the leaves glinting in yellow and lime and reddish orange, and then they exploded with life, surging out and up toward the sun, blazing, it seemed. But now that light had faded, as if night itself had slipped inside them, full as they were and covering the streets in a dense canopy of green. Ours is a town of trees, known for its trees, a boreal rain forest, and as we emerged out onto the shore of Lake Michigan, it looked as if we could see forever. I walked with my son, Jonas, and my wife, Debbie. Jonas, eight years old, ran throwing a ball up into the air and catching it. Out on the water the million points of light trembled and the wind blew and waves shot up through the rocks piled upon the shore. High-colored sails streaked across the horizon. Gulls tilted and cried across the hazy distance and we watched the clouds mass out over the lake.

Debbie is one of the people from whom I learned much that is in this book. Seeing her now, robust and strong, striding along the lake, it's difficult to grasp the adversity she's faced. She survived cancer at the age of twenty-seven, putting an end to her dream of starting a family. She developed Addison's disease at the age of forty-two. It's a rare enough disease that no one could diagnose it at first, and she came within perhaps 48 hours of dying. Addison's is a condition in which the adrenal glands stop making cortisol, that essential hormone of stress. She was saved by a pill that replaces that steroid in her system. She has to take it twice a day or in about a week she'll die. Seeing her now, smiling at the gorgeous day that's assembling itself around her, you'd never know that anything was wrong. She exercises at the gym regularly. She works as a massage therapist. I see her strategies and adaptations in everything she does. She is generous with the world and open to its gifts. In her view, everything is animated. She talks to her car, strokes and encourages it. She imagines that the dishes make friends in the cabinets where they live and coat hangers reproduce prodigiously in the closet. If she hears a flock of sandhill cranes migrating in the fall, she pulls the car over, stops, and gets out to watch as they wheel around toward the south in great luminous arcs. She sees life as bursting from everything and lives to the fullest the portion that has been allotted her. She has grown a garden that explodes in springtime and fills out to encircle the house, and then she walks among the plants, patting their leaves and encouraging them. She is generally busy from morning to night. She knits and has many other activities that work on her emotional system the way knitting does. She draws beautiful lifelike people in pastel pencils on butcher paper. For her, giving a massage is very much like knitting with living muscle. Debbie knows exactly what she's doing; she knows more anatomy than her doctor does. Debbie absorbs trauma and dispenses healing. She was the first one to observe to me how illness can enrich a life with its deep lessons. She has also observed that it can be a real bore and can make you really angry at times and that there's no contradiction in holding those opposing views simultaneously. She accepts the multiplicity of our selves, the human heart in conflict with itself, to quote Faulkner.

As we crossed the park within sight of the beach, a chaotic flock of gulls, prehistoric in their shape, hunted along the water's edge. A brief gust of cool air, scented with rain, came whirling down and was swallowed up by the afternoon heat. Cumulus clouds were building out across the lake. We returned to the car and I drove the summer streets beneath a canopy of trees. Birds were racketing in the branches. Jonas sat in the back, reading a book. Debbie sat beside me, strong, thriving. I felt it then, that tremendous rush of gratitude, that overwhelming sense of the beauty all around us, and I asked her, "How did we get so lucky?"

She looked at me and smiled and said, as if it were the most obvious thing in the world: "We went through all that bad stuff to get here."

AUTHOR'S NOTE

THE STORIES THAT are most easily interpreted are the ones that have ended. It is easy to say that Leon Weliczker Wells was successful in adapting to life after severe trauma because he is now dead and his wife told me that he led a happy, productive life. In other cases, especially those involving younger people who have much of their lives left to live, it is more difficult to say what will happen. When Eileen Berlin told me her story of being attacked by a crocodile and encouraged me to quote from the diaries she had written and mailed to me, she appeared to be doing fine. The note on which I end her story was the one on which our conversation ended. But when I sought to check up on her as this book was about to go to press, she was unwilling to continue the story. She and Scott were divorced and at his request, I changed their names. (Betty and Ruth—the girls Lisette Johnson helped—are also pseudonyms.) This is not so unusual. Many survivors of trauma I talked with have gone through waves of ups and downs and must struggle through the lows to return to the highs.

Debbie Kiley, who struggled mightily after being shipwrecked at sea, also seemed to be doing fine for a long time. She wrote one book about her experience called *The Sinking*. I helped her write another called *No Victims, Only Survivors*. But the last time I spoke with her, she told me that her son John had died while diving from a bridge with friends, for sport. He was only twenty-three. Debbie left her home in Dallas and went to Mexico. The last I heard, she was spending her days riding her horse in the mountains. I haven't heard from her since then. I respect her need and Eileen's to get on with their lives without having to talk about it any more than they already have.

One conclusion that I draw from all this is that our ongoing survival requires relentless attention. If this were a self-help book full of good cheer, I'd tell you that you can all be as happy as little kids after your world has blown up. But innocence is lost. We are always on the raft, always on the mountain, forever in the water with the shark. So as much as I would like to know with certainty, I don't know where Chris Lawrence will be in 10 years. It looks good for him now, and I hope it stays good. I'll even bet on him. But there are no guarantees. I know that Micki and Lisette and Michele are doing well as I write this. Don McCall is doing well but continues to need a buffer between himself and much of the world. He's lucky to have children who help him. Ann Hood is smiling, raising her adopted daughter, writing books, but, she says, even now, she still travels a lot as part of her strategy for surviving survival. As one of the survivors I interviewed said, "It all comes down to one thing. The moment. There's no guarantee of happily ever after. There's happy. But ever after is in doubt."

So I tell these stories the way I received them and to the extent that I know them. Perhaps in another few years I'll bring them up to date and we'll see a different picture. I hope it will be bigger, better, brighter. But until then, we can only do as the *Tao* says: Do your work. Then step back.

As this book was going to press, I received the news that Kathy Russell Rich had died. Her creativity and determination to live well gave her nearly an extra quarter-century of life, which I think can be a model for us all of what true resilience looks like.

NOTES

PROLOGUE: NO WAY HOME

1 Debbie Kiley's story comes from my interviews with her, from her diaries and notes, and from her books *Untamed Seas* and *No Victims, Only Survivors.*

4 The account of the experiences of Dougal and Douglas Robertson is based on the book *Survive the Savage Sea* and on personal communication with Douglas Robertson.

7 Federal Emergency Management Agency spent $155 million: Konigsberg 2011, p. 146.

7 within two years: Tedeschi and Calhoun 1995, p. 27. See also Bonanno 2004.

7 James Pennebaker, a social psychologist at the University of Texas: Pennebaker 2011, p. 123.

1. BE HERE NOW: FROM VICTIM TO RESCUER

13 Lisette stood immediately: I would never have heard Lisette Johnson's story except for the fact that she wrote to me. It was tremendously humbling to receive her first e-mail, which read in part: "Your 'be here now' rule certainly saved my life. For me, taking note that my reality as I knew it had suddenly changed was the difference between sitting in a chair in disbelief, and immediately standing up to run to survival. To which I can only say—thank you!" It turns out that she was re-reading *Deep Survival* the night before her husband

shot her. Her story comes from my interviews with her and from her diaries, which she courageously allowed me to quote.

19 References to the benefits of helping others are based on Tedeschi and Calhoun 1995, Mollica 2006, and Frankl 1984. The subject has also been discussed in Leach 1994 and elsewhere.

2. THE CROCODILE WITHIN: THE BURDEN OF INVISIBLE MEMORY

20 Eileen Berlin's story is based on my interviews with her and on her diaries.

23 Ben Shaw's essay on coming home: Ben Shaw's website, "The Veteran's Experience" at http://byshaw1.blogspot.com.

24 The material on conditioned responses, memory, and emotion is taken from personal communication with Joseph LeDoux as well as from his books and those of Antonio Damasio and Eric R. Kandel (see especially Kandel 2006, pp. 342–45). Additional material came from Lewis et al. 2001, Chapter 6. For another discussion of conditioned responses see LeDoux 1996, pp. 142–48.

25 They fired together, so they were wired together: LeDoux 1996, p. 214. During the creation of an emotional memory, proteins are assembled that connect neurons together, perhaps permanently. Kandel attributes this discovery to one of his postdoctoral students and spoke of this during an interview on the program "Ideas," on CBC Radio, September 21, 2009. For a fascinating discourse on how the brain might make memories permanent, see Kandel 2006, p. 272–73.

27 Kathy Russell Rich: Rich 1999, p. 54.

27 the emotional part of the brain shuts down the frontal lobes: LeDoux 2002, p. 217.

28 "a kludge": Linden 2007, p. 6.

28 *hsin*: Fu 2000, pp. xxiii–xxv.

29 System One: Kahneman 2011, pp. 20–21.

29 Stress dumps special chemicals: Material about stress hormones comes from Sapolsky 2004 and from personal communication with him. See also Berns 2005, p. 143, and Vaillant 1995, p. 260.

30 Many kinds of memory: Poldrack and Packard 2003.

31 in many cases, talking therapy won't work: LeDoux 2002, p. 292.

31 in the early days: Shay 1994, p. 187.

31 This technique of forcing people to talk: Wilson 2011, pp. 4–6.

32   a system in the brain that produces dopamine: Sapolsky 2004, p. 341.
32   George Vaillant, a psychiatrist: Vaillant 1995, 2003, 2008.

3. THE WAY OF SURVIVAL:
RAGE IN THE REALM OF THE SPIRITS

37   The account of Aron Ralston's experience comes from his book *127 Hours Between a Rock and a Hard Place* and from a news conference I attended at which he told his story to reporters.
38   "It was horrible": Lidz 2003.
39   Material on the rage pathway comes from Pinker 2007 and Panksepp 2004.
42   Yossi Ghinsberg, lost and wandering: Ghinsberg 1993, p. 186, and personal communication.
43   Lauren Elder: Elder 1978 and personal communication.
43   Material on Steve Callahan comes from Callahan 1986.
45   The story of David Boomhower is based on his diary, which his family kindly let me see, and from interviews with Corkey Waite.
47   the multiple selves that we normally perceive as cooperating in a unitary self: Ramchandran 2011, p. 151.
47   Unconscious memory is discussed extensively in Damasio 1995, Kandel 2006, LeDoux 1996, McGaugh 2003, and elsewhere.
47   Material on Joe Simpson is from Simpson 1989.
48   Dissociation during trauma: Bremner 2005, pp. 153–54.
48   Quotes by Douglas Robertson are from personal communication with him.
48   A few days after the accident: My interviews with sheriff's police officers in Emery County, Utah.

4. THE GIFT OF ADVERSITY: A SURVIVOR'S
ATTITUDE AND THE PERSONAL SCUM LINE

50   Micki Glenn's story comes from my interviews with her.
55   A number of scientists have discussed the concept of multiple selves and how the unity of our own self is essentially a trick of timing. Among them are Damasio 1995 and 2003; LeDoux 1996 and 2002; Pinker 2007; and Ramachandran 1998 and 2011. See also Pinker 2002, p. 43. Eagleman writes, "The exact levels of dozens of other neurotransmitters—for example, serotonin—are critical for who you believe yourself to be" (2011, p. 206). He refers to "a time-averaged version" of the self. Llinás says, "This temporally coherent

event that binds, in the time domain, the fractured components of external and internal reality into a single construct is what we call the 'self' " (2002, p. 126). Trauma disrupts that time-averaged version of the self. "Think about the brain," Eagleman advises, "as the densest concentration of *you*ness" (2011, see pp. 206–19).

56 One veteran of the Vietnam War returned home: Bremner 2005, p. 194.

57 "When the world is successfully predicted": Eagleman 2011, p. 50.

58 "Give the autoassociative network part of the content": Buzsaki 2006, p. 288.

62 An experiment done at Pitié-Salpêtrière Hospital: Damasio 2003, pp. 67–70.

63 "baloney-generator": Pinker 2002, p. 43.

63 "One of the main jobs of consciousness": LeDoux 1996, p. 33.

63 In a related experiment: Damasio 2003, pp. 74–76.

65 Indeed, research by James Pennebaker: Pennebaker 2011, pp. 122–23.

5. THE TYRANNY OF REASON: BLINDSIGHT, GUT FEELINGS, AND THE SIXTH SENSE

66 Chris Lawrence's story came from my interviews with him.

69 three-scoop ice-cream cone: Linden 2007, p. 22.

69 "blindsight": Linden 2007, p. 14, and Ramachandran 2011, pp. 249–50. See also Pierce and Jastrow 1884, pp. 73–83.

70 Identifying male and female chickens: Eagleman 2011, p. 58.

70 men can tell when a woman is ovulating: Roberts et al. 2004.

70 lap dancers in strip clubs earned: Miller et al. 2007.

74 The story of Jessica Goodell came from her book *Shade It Black*.

76 Importance of faces: Hatfield et al. 1994, p. 53. The text quotes Paul Ekman, a pioneer in the field of nonverbal communication, as saying, "The perception of another face is not just an information transfer but a very literal means by which we *feel* the sensations that the other feels."

76 supersecret microexpressions: Ambady and Rosenthal 1992.

81 cognitive reserve: Eagleman 2011, pp. 128–29.

82 For more on sixth sense, see LeDoux 2002, pp. 208–9 and Lewis et al. 2001, Chapter 5.

6. WANT IT, NEED IT, HAVE IT:
OF PHANTOM LIMBS AND CHILDREN

89 When the baby nuzzles: Gopnik et al. 2001 and Harris 2006. See especially Chapter 2 of Gopnik.

89 Antonio Damasio calls: Damasio 1995, pp. 173–75.

89 Mirror neurons are the biological substrate: Ramachandran 2011, pp. 22–23 and Chapter 4.

90 In one experiment: Gopnik et al. 2001, pp. 33–34.

91 The story of Ann Hood and her daughter Grace comes from her book *Comfort* and from Hood 2011.

92 emotional contagion: Hatfield et al. 1994.

92 For a discussion of babies, mothers, and emotional communication, see Lewis et al. 2001, Chapter 3.

94 For a discussion of laughter, see Ramachandran 2011, p. 39.

94 Laughter quiets the amygdala: Mobbs et al. 2003.

96 The brain has three general pathways: Ramachandran 2011, pp. 62–65 and Ramachandran 1998, pp. 77–84.

97 Concerning phantom limbs: Ramachandran 2011, Chapter 1.

98 "I want to have a gun in my hands": Shay 1994, p. xiv.

100 A certain type of seagull: Eagleman 2011, p. 143.

101 On stress and sleep: Sapolsky 2004, Chapter 11.

101 Impairment of hippocampus: LeDoux 2002, pp. 223–24.

7. SEE ONE, DO ONE, TEACH ONE:
THE SECRET OF SEEKING

103 History of Tourette's: Schwartz and Begley 2002, pp. 237–41.

104 The story of Carl Bennett: Sacks 1995, pp. 77–107.

104 Ann, too, was beset: Hood 2008, 2011.

106 "We know this centralization of prediction": Llinás 2002, p. 127.

106 Apotemnophilia: Ramachandran 2011, pp. 255–58.

108 the seeking pathway or the seeking system: Panksepp 2004, LeDoux 2001.

110 When you first learn a skill: Goldberg 2001, p. 182.

110 The basal ganglia become involved: Graybiel 2005. See also her website at http://web.mit.edu/bcs/graybiel-lab.

110 They constantly initiate: Gazzaniga et al. 2009, pp. 300–307.

110 "somehow escape from the control normally": Goldberg 2001, p. 182. See also Llinás 2002, p. 141: "In the case of people with Tourette's syndrome, where there is diagnosed partial destruction of the basal

ganglia, there is an abnormal, continuous liberation of very particular types of FAPs." By "FAPs" he means "fixed-action patterns" or behavioral scripts.

111 Anxiety and rage represent efforts: Sapolsky 2004, pp. 319–20 and Groopman 2004.

111 Beta blockers: McGaugh 2003, pp. 124–25.

112 "Work, work, work": Mollica 2006, p. 170.

113 Shortly after the attack: LeDoux 2001.

113 Work done by Ann Graybiel: Graybiel 2005.

113 you can train yourself to feel safe: Kandel, pp. 349–51.

114 Gregory Berns: Berns 2005, pp. 7–17.

114 "We harbor mechanical, 'alien' subroutines": Eagleman 2011, pp. 131–32.

118 Mark Vonnegut: Vonnegut 1975.

118 "As for sickness": Chapelle, p. 99.

8. "PLEASE, GOD, LET ME KILL HER": DISMANTLING THE SELF

120 Michele Weldon's story is based on her books, *I Closed My Eyes* and *Writing to Save Your Life*, as well as on personal communications with her.

124 Seven attributes combine: Ramachandran 2011, pp. 250–53.

125 feel sensation in a rubber hand: Ramachandran 1998, pp. 60–62.

126 trick of neurological timing: Damasio 1995, pp. 95–96.

127 "Severe trauma explodes": Shay 1994, p. 188.

127 It has been suggested: Ramachandran 2011, pp. 286–87.

128 "Identity can be thought of": Bremner 2005, p. 121.

128 Time slows down: Klinger 2004, pp. 95–99.

128 "Time dilates": Ralston 2010, p. 23.

9. SEARCHING FOR FRANKENSTEIN: KNITTING WITH WORDS

132 "Writing helped to save my life": Weldon 2011, pp. 8–11.

133 Tilmann Habermas: Habermas and Paha 2001.

133 we rewrite our memories during sleep: McGaugh 2003, pp. 81–82, and Sapolsky 2004, pp. 231–32.

136 "I was sitting writing on my textbook": Andreasen 2005, pp. 45–46.

136 In the "wet, ungenial summer" of 1816: Shelley 2000, p. xxiv.

138 "Fill your bowl to the brim": Mitchell 2006, p. 9.

139 "a much too willful will": Herrigel 1989, p. 31.

139 a very pleasurable dissociative state: Tolstoy 1965, pp. 265–66.

140 Mihaly Csikszentmihalyi: Csikszentmihalyi 1990.

141 "It is a thing that exists simply, like a sapphire": Epstein 2001, p. 137.

141 Peter Ilych Tchaikovsky: Andreasen 2005, pp. 41–42.

141 When Persinger turned on the current: Ramachandran 1998, p. 175, and Hitt 1999.

141 Andrew Newberg: From his website at http://andrewnewberg.com/ research.asp.

142 "temporal lobe storms": Ramachandran 1998, p. 179.

142 In a lecture: Sacks 2009.

142 a condition called hypergraphia: Ramachandran 2011, p. 24.

143 "After a really good writing session": Perry 1999, p. 31.

10. LESSONS FROM ISHMAEL: THE NEUROPHYSIOLOGY OF TRAVEL

145 Kathy Russell Rich's story is based on her books *Red Devil* and *Dreaming in Hindi* and on personal communication with her.

151 "I never had a nightmare": Yossi Ghinsberg, personal communication.

151 The hippocampus also encodes what are known as place cells: Buzsaki 2006, pp. 290–308. Kandel 2006, pp. 282 and 309.

152 "Theta oscillation is also the hallmark": Buzsaki 2006, p. 308.

153 "Episodic and semantic memory": Buzsaki 2006, p. 333.

153 Language is a special form: Llinás 2002, p. 151.

153 zombie systems: Eagleman 2011, pp. 131–32.

154 The novice burns energy like mad: Eagleman 2011, p. 142.

154 The neuromuscular system is a complex system: I posed this idea to Robert Sapolsky, and he responded with, "I think the idea is great. I suppose I'm willing to think of the neuromuscular system as complex—I'm having to overcome my central nervous system snottiness about the 'really' interesting things that neurons do, as opposed to just getting some boring muscles to move" (personal communication).

154 Glenn Gould: Buzsaki 2006, p. 363.

155 "[We] all have a private world": McGaugh 2003, pp. 49–50.

156 A. L. Becker: Rich 2009, p. 114.

157 Lee Osterhout at the University of Washington: Osterhout et al. 2006 and 2008, McLaughlin et al. 2004, and Frenck-Mestre et al. 2008.

158 Many scientists believe: Murray Gell-Mann, personal communication.

158 put off senility by years: Goldberg 2001, p. 207.

11. THE BEAR:
ONE FLEW EAST, ONE FLEW WEST

161 The story of Patricia van Tighem and Trevor Janz is based on her book, *The Bear's Embrace.*

165 For a discussion of stress, depression, and anxiety disorders, see Sapolsky 2004, Chapters 14 and 15.

165 Michael Ferrara had a 30-year career: Sides 2011.

167 "I haven't really slept": Shay 1994, p. xiv.

168 "Of all the coping mechanisms": Vaillant 1995, pp. 119–20.

168 emotional mimicry: Hatfield 1994, Chapter 1, especially pp. 41–47.

168 secret channels of communication: Etcoff 2000, pp. 240–41.

169 People who have had botox treatments: Neal and Chartrand 2011.

169 "With extreme frights": Bremner 2005, p. 107.

169 responses can be extinguished: Bremner 2005, p. 190.

170 unpredictability is stressful: Sapolsky 2004, p. 258.

174 One veteran of the Vietnam War: Shay 1994, p. xv.

175 "Take a sufficiently severe stressor": Sapolsky 2004, p. 308.

175 On December 14, 2005: Hawtree 2006.

12. THE BRICKLAYER: THE LONG WAY HOME

176 Don McCall's story is based on my interviews with him and his daughter, Peggy Campo, as well as on material in Stanton 2002 and USS *Indianapolis* Survivors 2002.

180 "the dun workhorse": Vaillant 1995, p. 119.

13. THE COURAGE TO SUFFER:
IF HE CAN DO IT, YOU CAN, TOO

187 The story of Leon Weliczker Wells is based on his book, *The Death Brigade*, and on personal communication with his wife, Frieda Wells.

190 helping someone else is as important as getting help: Des Pres 1976, pp. 135–36.

191 "accept fate": Frankl 1984, pp. 85–86.

192 "There is only one thing that I dread": Frankl 1984, p. 75.

199 "stubborn durability": Helmreich 1992, p. 228.

199 "reaction to Clorox": Helmreich 1992, p. 235.

14. THE SCIENCE OF ADAPTATION:
THERE'S NO REVENGE LIKE SUCCESS

201 Material on The Study of Adult Development is from Vaillant 1977, 2002, and 2008, along with information from the William T. Grant Foundation.

202 "Happiness as a goal": Gottleib 2011, p. 64.

202 "One can live magnificently in this world": Troyat 1967, p. 152. The quote is from a letter Tolstoy wrote on November 9, 1856, attempting to get Valerya Aresenyev to marry him.

202 "Not one of them": Vaillant 1977, p. 4.

203 He could not correlate birth order: Vaillant 2002, p. 95.

204 people who simply avoid thinking about bad things: Bonanno 2004.

206 "Sublimation lets you": Vaillant 2002, p. 70.

208 The belief that you can influence events: Peterson 1993, pp. 145–46.

208 They do not tend to do well: Tedeschi and Calhoun 1995, p. 18.

208 Lawrence Calhoun: Tedeschi 1995, p. 101.

209 "self-enhancer": Bonanno 2004.

15. THE RULES OF LIFE

211 When Elizabeth Gilbert: Gilbert 2007, p. 23.

213 "some kind of suffering is *necessary*": Tedeschi and Calhoun 1995, p. 12.

213 One survivor of the Holocaust: Helmreich 1992, pp. 233–37.

213 Consider the brief: Tresniowski 2006.

214 wonderful and chilling book: Mickenberg et al. 2003.

214 to keep stress hormones low: Sapolsky 2004, pp. 314–15.

217 also means physical touching: Touch Research Institute website at http://www6.miami.edu/touch-research.

218 Anne Hjelle was attacked: Morales 2007. See also Anne Hjelle's website, http://www.ocfightcenter.com/annehjelle/index.php?option =com_content&view=article&id=46&Itemid=53.

REFERENCES

Ambady, Nalini, and Robert Rosenthal. 1992. "Thin Slices of Expressive Behavior as Predictors of Interpersonal Consequences: A Meta-Analysis." *Psychological Bulletin* 111, no. 2: 256–74.

Andreasen, Nancy C. 2005. *The Creating Brain: The Neuroscience of Genius.* Washington, DC: Dana Press.

Berns, Gregory. 2005. *Satisfaction: The Science of Finding True Fulfillment.* New York, Henry Holt and Company.

Blakeslee, Matthew. 2011. "The Split Personality of Cognition." *SFI Bulletin* 25: 42.

Bonanno, George A. 2004. "Loss, Trauma, and Human Resilience." *American Psychologist* 59, no. 1 (January): 20–28.

Bremner, J. Douglas. 2005. *Does Stress Damage the Brain?* New York: W. W. Norton.

Buzsaki, Gyorgy. 2006. *Rhythms of the Brain.* New York: Oxford University Press.

Callahan, Steven. 1986. *Adrift: Seventy-six Days Lost at Sea.* New York: Ballantine Books.

Chapelle, Daniel. 1993. *Nietzsche and Psychoanalysis.* Albany, NY: State University of New York.

Csikszentmihalyi, Mihaly. 1990. *Flow: The Psychology of Optimal Experience*. New York: Harper.

Damasio, Antonio. 1995. *Descartes' Error: Emotion, Reason, and the Human Brain*. New York: Avon.

———. 1999. *The Feeling of What Happens: Body and Emotion in the Making of Consciousness*. San Diego: Harcourt.

———. 2003. *Looking for Spinoza: Joy, Sorrow, and the Feeling Brain*. New York: Harcourt.

Des Pres, Terrence. 1976. *The Survivor: An Anatomy of Life in the Death Camps*. New York: Oxford University Press.

Eagleman, David. 2011. *Incognito: The Secret Lives of the Brain*. New York: Pantheon Books.

Elder, Lauren. 1978. *And I Alone Survived*. New York: E. P. Dulton.

Epstein, Daniel Mark. 2001. *What Lips My Lips Have Kissed: The Loves and Love Poems of Edna St. Vincent Millay*. New York: Henry Holt & Company.

Etcoff, Nancy. 2000. *Survival of the Prettiest: The Science of Beauty*. New York: Anchor Books.

Frankl, Victor E. 1984. *Man's Search for Meaning: An Introduction to Logotherapy*. New York: Touchstone.

Frenck-Mestre, C., L. Osterhout, J. McLaughlin, and A. Foucalt. 2008. "The Effect of Phonological Realization of Inflectional Morphology on Verbal Agreement in French: Evidence from ERPs. *Acta Psychologica* 128: 528–36.

Fu, Wen. 2000. *The Art of Writing*, trans. Sam Hamill. Minneapolis, MN: Milkweed Editions.

Gazzaniga, Michael S., Richard B. Ivry, and George R. Mangun. 2009. *Cognitive Neuroscience: The Biology of the Mind*. New York: W. W. Norton.

Ghinsberg, Yossi. 1993. *Back from Tuichi: The Harrowing Life-and-Death Story of Survival in the Amazon Rainforest*. New York: Random House.

Gilbert, Elizabeth. 2007. *Eat, Pray, Love: One Woman's Search for Everything Across Italy, India, and Indonesia*. New York: Penguin.

Goldberg, Elkhonon. 2001. *The Executive Brain: Frontal Lobes and the Civilized Mind*. New York: Oxford University Press.

Gonzales, Laurence. 2003a. *Deep Survival: Who Lives, Who Dies, and Why*. New York: W. W. Norton.

————. 2003b. "One Way Out." *National Geographic Adventure Magazine*, August: 38–43 and 90–92.

Goodell, Jess. 2011. *Shade It Black: Death and After in Iraq*. Havertown, PA: Casemate Publishers.

Gopnik, Alison, et al. 2001. *The Scientist in the Crib: What Early Learning Tells Us About the Mind*. New York: Harper Perennial.

Gottleib, Lori. 2011. "How to Land Your Kid in Therapy." *The Atlantic*, July/August.

Graybiel, A. M. 2005. "The Basal Ganglia: Learning New Tricks and Loving It." *Current Opinion in Neurobiology* 15, no. 6: 638–44.

Groopman, Jerome. 2004. "The Grief Industry: How Much Does Crisis Counselling Help—or Hurt?" *The New Yorker*, January 26.

Habermas, T., and C. Paha. 2001. "The Development of Coherence in Adolescents' Life Narratives," *Narrative Inquiry* 11, no. 1: 35–54.

Harris, Judith Rich. 2006. *No Two Alike: Human Nature and Human Individuality*. New York: W. W. Norton.

Hatfield, Elaine, John T. Cacioppo, and Richard L. Rapson. 1994. *Emotional Contagion*. Cambridge: Cambridge University Press.

Hawtree, Christopher. 2006. Obituary, *The Independent*, January 18.

Helmreich, William. 1992. *Against All Odds: Holocaust Survivors and the Successful Lives They Made in America*. New York: Simon & Schuster.

Herrigel, Eugen. 1989. *Zen in the Art of Archery*. New York: Vintage Spiritual Classics.

Hill, Kenneth. 1997. *Lost Person Behavior*. Ottawa: National SAR Secretariat.

Hitt, Jack. 1999. "This Is Your Brain on God." *Wired Magazine*, Issue 7.11 (November).

Hood, Ann. 2008. *Comfort: A Journey Through Grief.* New York: W. W. Norton.

———. 2011. "The Runaway." *More Magazine,* September.

Kahneman, Daniel. 2011. *Thinking, Fast and Slow.* New York: Farrar, Straus and Giroux.

Kandel, Eric R. 2006. *In Search of Memory: The Emergence of a New Science of Mind.* New York: W. W. Norton.

———. 2009. "The Biology of Mind" on CBC Radio. "Ideas," September 21.

Karl, Frederick R. 1989. *William Faulkner: American Writer.* New York: Widenfeld & Nicholson.

Kiley, Deborah Scaling, and Meg Noonan. 1994. *Untamed Seas: One Woman's True Story of Shipwreck and Survival.* New York: Houghton Mifflin.

———. 2006. *No Victims, Only Survivors: Ten Lessons for Survival.* Fort Worth: Novos Publishing.

Klinger, David. 2004. *Into the Kill Zone: A Cop's Eye View of Deadly Force.* Hoboken, NJ: John Wiley & Sons.

Konigsberg, Ruth Davis. 2011. *The Truth about Grief.* New York: Simon and Schuster.

Kraut, R. E., and R. E. Johnston. 1979. "Social and Emotional Messages of Smiling: An Ethological Approach." *Journal of Personality and Social Psychology* 37: 1539–53.

Leach, John. 1994. *Survival Psychology.* New York: New York University Press.

LeDoux, Joseph. 1996. *The Emotional Brain: The Mysterious Underpinnings of Emotional Life.* New York: Simon & Schuster.

———. 2001. "A Call to Action: Overcoming Anxiety Through Active Coping." *American Journal of Psychiatry* 158:12.

———. 2002. *Synaptic Self: How Our Brains Become Who We Are.* New York: Viking.

Lewis, Thomas, Fari Amini, and Richard Lannon. 2001. *A General Theory of Love.* New York: Vintage.

Lidz, Franz. 2003. "A Tale of True Survival." *Sports Illustrated*, May 12.

Linden, David. 2007. *The Accidental Mind*. Cambridge, MA: Harvard University Press.

Llinás, Rodolfo. 2002. *i of the Vortex: From Neurons to Self.* Cambridge, MA: MIT Press.

McDougle, Christopher J., Steven M. Southwick, and Robert M. Rohrbaugh. 1990. "Tourette's Disorder and Associated Complex Behaviors: A Case Report." *The Yale Journal of Biology and Medicine* 63: 209–14.

McGaugh, James L. 2003. *Memory and Emotion: The Making of Lasting Memories*. New York: Columbia University Press.

McLaughlin, J., L. Osterhout, and A. Kim. 2004. Neural Correlates of Second-Language Word Learning: Minimal Instruction Produces Rapid Change. *Nature Neuroscience* 7: 703–4.

Mickenberg, David, Corinne Granof, and Peter Hayes, eds. 2003.*The Last Expression: Art and Auschwitz*. Evanston, IL: Northwestern University Press.

Miller, Geoffrey, Joshua M. Tybur, and Brent D. Jordan. 2007. "Ovulatory Cycle Effects on Tip Earnings by Lap Dancers: Economic Evidence for Human Estrus?" *Evolution and Human Behavior* 28: 375–81.

Mitchell, Stephen (trans.). 2006. *Tao Te Ching*. New York: Harper Perennial Modern Classics.

Mobbs, D., Michael D. Greicius, Eiman Abdel-Azim, Vinod Menon, and Allan. L. Reiss. 2003. "Humor Modulates the Mesolimbic Reward Centers." *Neuron* 40, no. 5: 1041–48.

Mollica, Richard F. 2006. *Healing Invisible Wounds: Paths to Hope and Recovery in a Violent World*. New York: Harcourt.

Morales, Tatiana. 2007. "Mauled by Lion, Woman Recovers." CBS News at CBSnews.com, December 5. http://www.cbsnews.com/stories/2004/05/05/earlyshow/living/main615684.shtml.

Neal, David T., and Tanya L. Chartrand. 2011. "Embodied Emotion Perception: Amplifying and Dampening Facial Feedback Modulates Emotion Perception Accuracy." *Social Psychological and Personality Science* 2, no. 6 (November): pp. 673–78. First published on April 21. doi:10.1177/1948550611406138

Osterhout, Lee, Judith McLaughlin, and Ilona Pitkänen. 2006. "Novice Learners, Longitudinal Designs, and Event-Related Potentials: A Means for Exploring the Neurocognition of Second Language Processing." *Language Learning* 56, no. S1 (July): 199–230.

Osterhout, Lee, Andrew Poliakov, Kayo Inoue, Judith McLaughlin, Geoffrey Valentine, Ilona Pitkänen, Cheryl Frenck-Mestre, and Julia Hirschensohn. 2008. "Second-language learning and changes in the brain." *Journal of Neurolinguistics* 21: 509–21. doi:10.1016/j.jneuroling.2008.01.001

Panksepp, Jaak. 2004."Toward a Neurobiologically Based Unified Theory of Aggression." *Revue Internationale de Psychologie Sociale*, no. 2.

Pennebaker, James W. 2011. *The Secret Life of Pronouns: What Our Words Say About Us*. New York: Bloomsbury Press.

Perry, Susan K. 1999. *Writing in Flow*. New York: Writer's Digest Books.

Peterson, Christopher, et al. 1993. *Learned Helplessness: A Theory for the Age of Personal Control*. New York: Oxford University Press.

Pierce, C. S., and J. Jastrow. 1884. "On Small Differences in Sensation." *Memoirs of the National Academy of Sciences* 3.

Pinker, Steven. 2002. *The Blank Slate: The Modern Denial of Human Nature*. New York: Viking.

———. 2007. *The Stuff of Thought: Language as a Window Into Human Nature*. New York: Viking.

Poldrack, Russell A., and Mark G. Packard. 2003. "Competition Among Multiple Memory Systems: Converging Evidence from Animal and Human Brain Studies." *Neuropsychologia* 1497: 1–7.

Ralston, Aron. 2010. *127 Hours: Between a Rock and a Hard Place*. New York: Atria Paperback.

Ramachandran, V. S. 1998. *Phantoms in the Brain: Probing the Mysteries of the Human Mind*. New York: William Morrow.

———. 2011. *The Tell-Tale Brain: A Neuroscientist's Quest for What Makes Us Human*. New York: W. W. Norton.

Rich, Kathy Russell. 1999. *Red Devil: A Memoir About Beating the Odds*. New York: Crown.

————. 2009. *Dreaming in Hindi: Coming Awake in Another Language*. New York: Houghton Mifflin Harcourt.

Roberts, S.C., et al. 2004. "Female Facial Attractiveness Increases During the Fertile Phase of the Menstrual Cycle." *Proceedings of the Royal Society of London B* 271: S270–72.

Robertson, Dougal. 1994. *Survive the Savage Sea*. Dobbs Ferry, NY: Sheridan House.

Sacks, Oliver. 1995. *An Anthropologist on Mars: Seven Paradoxical Tales*. New York: Alfred A. Knopf.

————. 2009. "What hallucination reveals about our minds" TED, September. http://www.ted.com/talks/oliver_sacks_what_hallucination_reveals_about_our_minds.html.

Sapolsky, Robert. 2004. *Why Zebras Don't Get Ulcers*. New York: Henry Holt and Company.

Schwartz, Jeffrey M., and Sharon Begley. 2002. *The Mind and the Brain: Neuroplasticity and the Power of Mental Force*. New York: Harper Collins.

Shay, Jonathan. 1994. *Achilles in Vietnam: Combat Trauma and the Undoing of Character.* New York: Simon and Schuster.

Shelley, Mary. 2000. *Frankenstein*. New York: Penguin Putnam Signet Classic edition.

Sides, Hampton. 2011. "The Man Who Saw Too Much." *Outside*, January.

Simpson, Joe. 1998. *Touching the Void: The Harrowing First-Person account of One Man's Miraculous Survival*. New York: Harper Perennial.

Stanton, Doug. 2002. *In Harm's Way: The Sinking of the USS* Indianapolis *and the Extraordinary Story of its Survivors*. New York: St. Martins Paperbacks.

Tedeschi, Richard G., and Lawrence G. Calhoun. 1995. *Trauma & Transformation: Growing in the Aftermath of Suffering*. Thousand Oaks, CA: Sage Publications.

Tolstoy, Leo. 1965. *Anna Karenina*. New York: Modern Library.

Tresniowsky, Alex. 2006. "The Boy Who Sees with Sound." *People Magazine*, July 14.

Troyat, Henri. 1967. *Tolstoy.* New York: Doubleday & Company.

USS *Indianapolis* Survivors. 2002. *Only 317 Survived!* Broomfield, CO: The USS Indianapolis Survivors Organization.

Vaillant, George E. 1995. *Adaptation to Life.* Cambridge, MA: Harvard University Press.

———. 2003. *Aging Well.* New York: Little, Brown and Company.

———. 2008. *Spiritual Evolution: How We Are Wired for Faith, Hope, and Love.* New York: Broadway Books.

Van Tighem, Patricia. 2001. *The Bear's Embrace: A Story of Survival.* New York: Pantheon Books.

Vonnegut, Mark. 1975. *The Eden Express: A Personal Account of Schizophrenia.* New York: Praeger.

———. 2010. *Just Like Someone with Mental Illness Only More So: A Memoir.* New York: Delacorte.

Weldon, Michele. 1999. *I Closed My Eyes: Revelations of a Battered Woman.* Center City, MN: Hazelden.

———. 2001. *Writing to Save Your Life: How to Honor Your Story Through Journaling.* Center City, MN: Hazelden.

Weliczker Wells, Leon. 1978. *The Death Brigade.* New York: Holocaust Library.

Wilson, Timothy D. 2011. *Redirect: The Surprising New Science of Psychological Change.* New York: Little, Brown and Company.

Yoffe, Emily. 2009. "Seeking: How the Brain Hard-Wires Us to Love Google, Twitter, and Texting. And Why That's Dangerous." *Slate,* August 12.

ACKNOWLEDGMENTS

I am indebted to the people portrayed in this book, who bravely told their stories. I also want to thank Carolyn Lorence, who helped me with early drafts and showed me what a real survivor looks like. Special thanks to my brother Stephen for all his hard work. Thanks to Joseph LeDoux at New York University, Robert Sapolsky at Stanford, and Chris Wood at the Santa Fe Institute for help with the science in this book. (Any mistakes are mine, not theirs.) Thanks to Patricia Lear. I could not have written this without my wife, Debbie, nor without the inspiration of my children, Elena, Amelia, and Jonas, and my grandson, Emmett.

CREDITS

Agent: Gail Hochman
Assistant: Jody Klein
Editor: Starling Lawrence
Assistant Editor: Melody Conroy
Copy Editors: Arlene Bouras and Carol Rose
Production Manager: Devon Zahn
Publicist: Erin Sinesky Lovett
Readers: Kent Berridge, Alan Bliss, Peggy McCall Campo, Ari Chaet, Constance Conroy, Jonas and Betsy Dovydenas, Marci Enos, Susanne Feigum, Eileen Feldman, Jeanne Giles, Francine Girard, Michelle Glenn, Philip Gonzales, Chrisanne Gordon, Lisette Johnson, Victoria LeFrere, Jody Mack, Nancy Moffett, Alix Pitcher, Kathy Russell Rich, David Standish, Michele Weldon, and Lesley Williams.

INDEX

Page numbers beginning with 225 refer to endnotes.